ROLAND N. STROMBERG

Redemption by War

The Intellectuals and 1914

By war's great sacrifice
The world redeems itself.

—JOHN DAVIDSON

When war is declared we all go mad.

—GEORGE BERNARD SHAW

THE REGENTS PRESS OF KANSAS—*Lawrence*

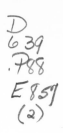

Library of Congress Cataloging in Publication Data
Stromberg, Roland N., 1916-
Redemption by war.
Includes bibliographical references and index.
1. World War, 1914-1918—Public opinion—Europe.
I. Intellectuals—Europe. I. Title.
D639.P88E857   940.3   81-10715
ISBN 0-7006-0220-8   AACR2

Contents

Acknowledgments

I would like especially to thank the Woodrow Wilson Center, at the Smithsonian Institution, Washington, D.C., and the Center for Twentieth Century Studies of the University of Wisconsin at Milwaukee, for fellowships enabling me to devote time to research on the subject of this book. I would also like to thank Martha E. Beier for typing and editorial help.

Chapter 6 of this book appeared in somewhat different form in *Midwest Quarterly* (Vol. 18, No. 3, Spring, 1977), and is used here by permission.

I feel like dedicating this book, if it were not an impertinence, to the tens of thousands of writers, thinkers, poets, artists, students, who, perhaps not knowing what they did, went forth in the 1914–18 war to die with such heroism and gallantry, pursuing an ideal—an example, as Gibbon might have put it, of the vigor and weakness of the human mind, the folly and grandeur of the human spirit—leaving us to wonder why.

R.N.S.

Fox Point, Wisconsin

—1—

The Strangest Crusade

I

The young, rebelling against their parents and the establishment; the artists, the "bohemian" set, the avant-garde; university students and their favorite professors; the most brilliant philosophers, poets, dramatists, novelists, also scientists; clergymen, moralists, and—for good measure—the political activists of the Left, the Socialists, Anarchists, and other radicals: do not all these according to our present conceptions have at least one thing in common, however else they may differ, in that they abjure war and cherish peace, deploring all things military? So almost everyone would think today, surely. It was not so in 1914, when the "pax Europa" broke down, plunging the world into that deadly cycle of armed conflict from which it has scarcely yet recovered, and which cost millions of lives while overturning old regimes and inaugurating revolutionary despotisms. Then, the picture was more nearly the opposite. It is suggested by Romain Rolland's anguished cry at the beginning of the war, in his *Au-dessus de la melée*: "Among the elite of each country, there is not one who does not proclaim and is not convinced that the cause of his people is the cause of God, the cause of liberty, and of human progress."

Watching the growing mountain of tracts and manifestoes in which the intellectual elite of Europe embraced the war not merely as unpleasant necessity (enough to get one branded a renegade, as Shaw discovered) nor even as potential excitement after many dull years, but as spiritual salvation and hope of regeneration, Rolland soon decided that the struggle against it was futile. A roster of all the notable defectors to the side of Mars is impossible, since although Rolland's "not one" was a slight exaggeration, there were very few exceptions. Though his many admirers deny this, it is likely that Rolland's own immunity resulted from his happening to be in Switzerland as the war began and thus insulated from the overpowering wave of feeling that surged through the belligerent countries. Among leading philosophers, Henri Bergson of France and Max Scheler of Germany wrote passionate paeans to war, as "the moral regeneration of Europe." It was not only the idealists who cheered for war; one could add Ernst Haeckel, Frederic Harrison, Sigmund Freud, Émile Durkheim, or the venerable Russian Marxist Georgy Plekhanov. "Idealists and materialists alike preach war and hate," the editor of the *Atlantic Monthly* observed in January, 1915.

With equally rare exceptions the greatest poets and novelists were included: Stefan George, Thomas Mann, Rainer Maria Rilke, Paul Claudel, André Gide, Marcel Proust, Anatole France (who did a hasty retreat to superpatriotism after an initial *faux pas*, offering to shoulder arms at the age of seventy), old Henry James and Thomas Hardy, Arnold Bennett, H. G. Wells, and the Russian poets Mayakovsky, Esenin, Gumilyëv, Blok. A letter written by Ezra Pound in November, 1914, remarked that all the artists and sculptors were volunteering.[1] Expressionist poets joined the always warlike Futurists, whose famous Manifesto in 1909 had announced war to be "the only hygiene of the world," and others of all kinds. "We were all flame and fire," Isadora Duncan recalled.[2] "I adore war," said the young British poet Julian Grenfell.[3] Among European musical composers, Alban Berg agreed with Igor Stravinsky and with Scriabin, who saw the war as sent to "shake the souls of people" and "prepare them for spiritual things."[4] The September 17 patriotic statement signed by fifty-three British luminaries reads like a *Who's Who* of the English literary firmament —Barrie, Galsworthy, Kipling, Haggard, and Doyle were perhaps more predictable than Wells, Chesterton, and Hardy. It was matched in the other belligerent countries.

In such an endless list one can only pick out the more piquant cases: Freud "giving all his libido to Austria-Hungary"; Gandhi, the Tolstoyan, recruiting for the British in India; R. H. Tawney, the radical and socialist English historian, joining other Socialists in seeing the war as needed "to build social democracy in England"; or Albert Mathiez, Socialist historian of the French Revolution and admirer of Robespierre, finding in World War I a reincarnation of the great 1792–94 struggle for revolutionary democracy.[5] Or Alphonse Aulard, proponent of "objective" historical writing, now authoring what a recent study describes as "the basest form of jingoist hysteria."[6] Hewlett Johnson, subsequently the "Red Dean" of Canterbury, was prowar in World War I, as were Peter Kropotkin, the Anarchist, and a large majority of English Quakers.[7] Gabriele D'Annunzio turned from Decadent eroticism to become the least likely of war heroes, in his fifties; the British suffragettes Emmeline and Christabel Pankhurst switched their formidable wrath from native targets to the Huns, and became themselves the most chauvinist of all. In his journal Rolland noted "the complete bankruptcy of the Christian Churches both Protestant and Catholic," embracing everything from young liberal theologians of the Ritschl school and German Mennonites, along with the English Quakers, to cardinals of the Church of Rome; if the Germans, in contrast to 1939–45, then produced no Bonhoeffers, Rolland pointed to the Manifesto of two well-known French Catholics, titled "La guerre redemptive," which made the German Manifesto signed by ninety-three professors "look like a model of moderation."[8]

There was only a tiny handful of conscientious objectors in this war. But we must not suppose that war fever was confined to excitable types like priests and poets. The professors who signed the famous German Manifesto in October included many scientists, among them Röntgen and Max Planck, who as rector of the University of Berlin declared that those who remained behind were overcome with envy at not being able to sacrifice their lives for "the highest of all earthly ideals." Among the more extreme annexationists in Germany were Haeckel and Ostwald, both well-known scientific figures, the former celebrated for his archmaterialistic "monism."[9] The 150 British scholars who penned a defiant counterblast to the German Manifesto (October 21), declaring that "Germany stands revealed as the common enemy of Europe and of all peoples," included Thomson, Haldane, Cavendish, and other eminent scientists. Émile Picard and Pierre Duhem of the French Academy of Science wrote a book proving that German science was degenerate and should be boycotted.[10] Despite the cases of Einstein and Russell, and the German G. F. Nicolai, it is

3

hard to prove that scientists were any more war-resistant than others, and a certain perfervid missionary scientism was often in evidence, more intolerant than any other. (This crusading positivism was much more in evidence then than it is today.)

These attitudes later seemed so strange that today they are often either simply ignored or greeted with total incomprehension. There are many examples of this lack of historical imagination. For example, a student of Frank Wedekind's finds it "impossible to say" why the Munich playwright approved of the war, but opines that it is "unlikely that he actually became convinced of the righteousness of the German cause" because, after all, Lulu's creator belonged "to the liberal left."[11] The author thus passes over the question of why this rebel, satirist, and hater of the bourgeoisie threw himself whole-heartedly into the war, as he obviously did, with speeches and publications extolling the newly found national unity in a just cause and in *Vaterlandstolz*. Heinrich Mann more pertinently observed that Wedekind's writing, viewing life as a battleground, was a part of that literary spirit which anticipated 1914.[12] As for the "liberal Left," it just as enthusiastically backed the 1914 war as did the illiberal Right.

Another version of this historical amnesia is the tendency to exaggerate opposition to the war. Almost all the justly famous few who set themselves to oppose the war spirit did not do so at the beginning, in August, when it counted, but only after some interval of time. This is true of Stefan Zweig; of Bertrand Russell; of Karl Kraus, the Viennese Shaw, whose *Die Fackel* was silent at the start of the war; of Wilfred Owen, Henri Barbusse, and others who at length, but not in the beginning, turned on the war with disgust and loathing, like the great Russian poet Mayakovsky who began by shouting patriotic verses from atop a monument. It is true even of Lenin, who took a few weeks at least to gather his thoughts, as a majority of the Russian Social Democrats, and even of the Bolshevik faction, accepted the need to defend Russia; and of Gramsci, the Italian Marxist who later was a founder of the Italian Communist party.

Such cases can be multiplied many times over; it is hardly an exaggeration to say that almost every biography makes an embarrassed pause at the war and hurries on as hastily as possible: Ken Russell leaving the war out of his movie about Isadora; the faithful Ernest Jones baffled, for once, by Freud's 1914 war statements; and so on. We feel inclined to forgive these naïvetés and even dishonesties when we

4

find that the participants themselves later were mystified by their statements at the time.

We are thus faced with a problem of the inadequacy of interpretation of this phenomenon, the almost manic bellicosity of the European intellectuals, writers, artists, scientists, at the crucial beginning of the terrible war of 1914–18, under the violent shadow of which so much of world history has lain in the twentieth century. (We need only recall that the Communist, Fascist, and Nazi revolutions, and World War II, were its obvious consequences.) One could say, following T. S. Kuhn's suggestion in *The Structure of Scientific Revolutions*, that a paradigm was subsequently built up which did not allow for the phenomena of 1914, and so they were simply ignored, or even falsified (forced into another mold). The paradigm was shaped as a result of the phenomena themselves, which were too embarrassing to face. After the war the whole process was seen in an entirely different light, and was subject to a crude Marxism *cum* pacifism, the result of a revulsion against the war, and of the Russian Revolution that came at the end of it. In this perspective it was simply impossible to conceive that virtually all the intellectuals, including those of the Left (and including the working class, immensely patriotic in 1914), could have approved the war so enthusiastically.

The antiwar spirit was, to be sure, not entirely absent from the years prior to 1914. The war spirit of 1914 was in good part an anomaly, departing from typical intellectual attitudes both before and after. Through the nineteenth century strong antiwar currents had buffeted the European intelligentsia. The Enlightenment perpetual-peace utopias of Kant and Bentham, not to mention the Abbé St. Pierre, led on to the great bourgeois ideologies of Comte and the Manchester School, each of which argued that in various ways war had become irrational and obsolete—the sport of outmoded aristocracies or the illusion of prescientific mentalities. The new order of a progressive Europe would render war impossible, Saint-Simon's socialist program agreed. A humanitarian age abhorred bloodshed, a commercial one valued the arts of peace above those of war. It is true that Proudhon saw war as "an integral part of human life," destined to endure as long as humanity; certainly the thrust of Darwinian thought was in this direction. The upward strivings of a dynamic society could hardly be without struggle; and to Tennyson's "Better fifty years of Europe than a cycle of Cathay," Karl Marx, his ideological

5

opposite in so many ways, agreed heartily. Tennyson burst forth with militant archaisms during the Crimean War, rejoicing, in a way that predicts 1914, that a miserable commercial outlook had been swept aside for heroes, while Marx and Engels welcomed the Franco-Prussian War and looked forward to other such midwives of history. So the rich legacy of nineteenth-century social thought was at best ambiguous. Still, the foremost sage and prophet of its latter days was Leo Tolstoy, who thundered mighty jeremiads against the swordbearers from Yassnaya Polyana. The British Labour party in its pre-1914 programs pronounced that "under socialism there would be no cause of quarrel between nations." A significant minority among British liberals opposed the Boer War in the first years of the 1900's,* and there were protests against European force applied to "lesser breeds" as the epoch of Imperialism began in confidence but ended in concern about brutal injustice, as for example in the Belgian Congo. In an age that spawned secular eschatologies, few could doubt that in the end the plowshare or the pen would overcome the sword. Though we are too much inclined to see the war spirit of 1914 as a total apostasy because we have imposed on it a later (post-1918) paradigm of interpretation (the pre-1914 Peace Movement was a feeble enough thing, though it existed), yet this spirit was a startling rejection of many prominent strains of thought regnant up to the very moment of war's outbreak in August, 1914. The received doctrine, indeed, was that war had already ceased to be a possibility—so said Norman Angell, in *The Great Illusion*, and a host of others.

Because embarrassing, then, as well as inexplicable, the phenomenon has been much under-studied, and explanations occasionally proffered for it are weak and unconvincing. It was called an attack of inexplicable insanity, involved with mass hysteria: when war is declared we all go mad. But even the most superficial examination of the war's reception in European thought reveals some serious intellectual themes. The more obvious motifs, superficial at first glance, lead us to some profound prewar ideas. At least they seemed profound then, being the stock of outstanding philosophers, sociologists, and literary sages.

Thus, perhaps the most noticeable ingredient in the "August

---

* Throughout my book, I have used "1900's" to refer to the first decade of the twentieth century.

geoisie with war (this seems to be a grave error, but two generations of simplistic Marxism have planted it deeply), whereas in 1914 the bourgeoisie meant peace. The war "stripped away the façade of lies of the Wilhelmine, 'bürgerlich' epoch," Friedrich Gundolf wrote.[18]

A long list of bored and restless writers (André Gide with his pet bird, D'Annunzio with his dogs, Arnold Bennett with his yacht, come to mind as examples of leading European writers wearying of trivial toys), all of whom turned eagerly to the excitement of war, drives home the simple point that an event so vast and so stunningly real had to command their attention. "But the thing was in full blast!" John Cowper Powys said, explaining what overcame all his cerebral objections to the war; intellectually he assented to Rolland and Russell, but his heart responded to this "great burning fiery furnace."[19] Bennett and Freud found life suddenly interesting again, as did other sideline observers like Henry James and Marcel Proust, who soon became completely absorbed in the unfolding drama of the first few weeks.[20] This attraction of the bustle and stir has to be set against both the dullness of peacetime life and the neurasthenia of the intellectual-artist, easily bored and ever on the search for new *frissons*. Many used war as an excuse for breaking off some intolerable personal situation, like Kokoschka's affair with Anna Mahler; it was "a release from social bonds" (Quentin Bell), a new "challenge of life" (Herbert Read), a chance for sexual adventure. Given the erotic revolution just then occurring, this motive can hardly be overlooked. No one will ever know how many joined to escape their families, Shaw quipped. Herman Hesse wrote *Rosshalde* in 1914, a novel in which the artist-hero, plagued by a disastrous marriage, finally makes the break by going to India, where he hopes to find a "new atmosphere." The Western Front, or some sort of war service, supplied a closer and less lonely refuge.[21]

These motives just discussed, war as restoration of community and as escape from a trashy and trivial way of life, odd as they may seem today, are probably more understandable than war as salvation. Yet the commonest images aroused by the shock of August were the cleansing fire or flood, or "the blacksmith that will pound the world into new shapes" (Ernst Jünger). Maurice Barrès was sublimely sure that "this war will bring about a resurrection." The noted French poet and playwright Paul Claudel spoke of the "regeneration" of France.[22] In England the young Jewish poet Isaac Rosenberg wrote

11

("On Receiving News of the War") that the "ancient crimson curse" would "Give back the universe/Its pristine bloom." In Italy D'Annunzio's rhetoric played constantly on themes of renewal and salvation.[23] The angry god of battles reaping a human harvest, a god when no other exists, appeared in Rilke's five poems inspired by the coming of the war. The avant-garde French poet Apollinaire was awed at the hungry earth demanding its blood sacrifice—a theme that had been celebrated just before 1914 in Charles Péguy's remarkable poem "Éve."[24] These Old Testament archetypes, sacrificial and redemptive, joined humbler metaphors of housecleaning or winnowing. That the old house was rotten through and through and deserved to burn was always implied.

The assumption that from the ashes something new and better would arise probably cannot be grasped without reference to the prevailing "historicism," at once optimistic and irrational. The Hegelian vision of the spirit producing ever-new forms had combined with Bergson's creative evolution to produce a willingness to welcome the new and surprising as necessarily valuable. A popular German representative of the fashionable "Life Philosophy," Rudolf Eucken, hailed the war in 1914 as "a mighty spiritual movement," maintaining that "Life is too rich and colored, too mobile and variable, to be reduced to the forms and formulae of Thought. The stream of life breaks through the dam which was meant to enclose it, and flows out of its limited enclosure into the open and the boundless."[25] As Pasternak's Dr. Zhivago said, "Life itself is a constantly self-renewing, self-transforming category. It is constantly refashioning and realizing itself and it is far above our boneheaded theories." "Our age," wrote Anna Tumarkin in 1912, commenting on Wilhelm Dilthey, "needs an orientation which leaves unconfined the manifold of individual forms and the wealth of life which, in its totality, remains forever incommensurable." "We see everything in the river of Becoming," Ernst Troeltsch declared in his *Die Krisis des Historismus*, to which the great Italian philosopher Benedetto Croce assented; his "religion of liberty" endowed history (that is, whatever happens) with value. Many currents of thought at this time shared this tendency to regard the ongoing current of life, expressed in spontaneously evolving cultural forms, as self-justifying, not to be judged by any external yardstick, "incommensurable." During the war, Carl Nielsen paid tribute to this life-force of creative evolution in his Inextinguishable Symphony. Life constantly renews itself, even in death, and charges on again to a prodigal abundance. Thus, whatever mysterious movement the Spirit made had to be accepted and was bound to be creative, i.e., good. And the war came in an uncanny way, out of the blue, bearing with it even in its terribleness an apparent quality of spiritual renewal. A mixture of religious archetypes and scientific concepts had prepared the most advanced European minds to accept as good whatever powerful and violent storm descended upon human affairs.

And in fact the rationale for war that accompanied the outbreak of war in 1914 was substantially a new concoction. Pacifists in the pre-1914 years were acquainted with, and sought to refute, certain venerable apologists for war, usually highly vulnerable: moralists who insisted that peace erodes character, Darwinian biologists for whom progress demanded conflict, gloomy religious purveyors of original sin, etc.[26] There were some echoes of traditional apologetics in the 1914 ideas, to be sure. The brotherhood of battle, war's adventure, honor above material things, and other ingredients in the August brew had been around for ages. Still, the peculiar mixture of them that erupted so violently at the beginning of the First World War was unique. It had never been found before exactly like that, and would not be repeated again. It was wrung from the European consciousness at a certain stage of its evolution. After the war some of those who had not cast off its spell were largely responsible for the Fascist/Nazi revolutions. The majority of Western intellectuals reacted violently against it in that rash of pacifist plays and novels which fed the "peace at any price" mentality of the 1930's, and almost delivered the Continent to Hitler. World War II precipitated no such mystique.[27] That the same or similar impulses which played on the mind and spirit of an educated elite in 1914 survive, having percolated down to broader circles, is, however, strongly suggested by the recent outbursts of violence among young people at the universities and elsewhere. And that fact makes the study of this strange chapter in modern intellectual and social history all the more interesting.

—2—

Some Prewar Moods and Movements of the Intellectuals

I

In Wilhelmine times life was devoted so exclusively to economic ends, Rudolf Eucken ruminated after the war, that "a common human purpose was lacking, an inner exaltation was lacking, a clear confrontation with the problems and dilemmas of modern life failed to take place; the leading feature of the times was increasingly an unconditional affirmation of life, striving became more and more an end in itself."[1] People of the land of thinkers and poets (he meant Germany) no longer cared for philosophy or art or religion, he added. In these halting phrases the old philosopher, a characteristic and very popular pre-1914 figure, attempted to put a Teutonic finger on the unsatisfactory state of the spirit just before the war. Certainly most "intellectuals" would have agreed with the judgment passed on an age of materialism, of philistinism, of widespread popular neglect of things of the mind, against which bustling, burgeoning bourgeois society a small band of increasingly alienated artists and thinkers defiantly made art or energy or revolution an end in itself.

The epoch was far too complicated to describe as simply as this, but that an estrangement of the intellectuals was one significant feature seems clear. For one thing, the very notion of an "intellectual" as a person different from others, a special breed of humanity set aside and marked off from the masses, seems to have originated in these years. The definition might be fuzzy, but the concept did arise. Students have tended to agree in tracing use of the word, as a pejorative noun, to the Dreyfus case in France, that is, around 1898.[2] But it was not entirely a rightist epithet pinned on the Dreyfusards (and accepted by them), for no one contributed more to the defamation of "intellectuals" than the radical social theorist Georges Sorel, while it became rather characteristic of many "intellectuals" themselves (i.e., serious writers and artists and thinkers) to disparage "intellectualism." "I mistrust intellectual people because they are too negative and are incapable of the warmth of love," young Stefan Zweig declared, finding Verhaeren, the Belgian Symbolist poet and playwright, admirable because "not in any way intellectual."[3] Nietzsche had inveighed against an excess of the conceptualizing reason divorced from the energizing will; a whole bevy of his followers took their stand in quite an extreme way with Ludwig Klages in making the intellect (mind) and the soul or spirit mortal enemies, and in taking their stand on the side of the latter.[4] (The intellectual who hates intellectuals appears almost as soon as the type is born!)[5]

This "revolt against reason" or against the intellect, discussed in a later chapter, pervaded the prewar years and becomes of immense significance, obviously, in connection with the war. Nevertheless, if we use the term "intellectual" in a special but quite recognizable sense, one perhaps conveyed by Leonard Woolf when he remarked that he was "a born intellectual,"[6] we picture not simply "people who have more contact with ideas than with experience,"[7] but people who are separated sharply from the common herd by an unusual sensitivity and (a certain sort of) intelligence; who cannot long endure to stay inside a society which appears to them unspeakably crude, boring, stupid, and silly in its conversation, its style, its taste. The feeling that modern life is ignoble oppressed European (and American) "sensitives," from the mid-nineteenth century on, in mounting intensity. It grows apace as we pass from Stendhal and Balzac (to take French literature as our context) to Flaubert and Baudelaire, pioneers of the absolutely disgusted. ("Shit keeps coming into my mouth," Flaubert wrote. "I want to make a paste of it and daub it over the nineteenth century.") If the "unhappy consciousness" was a familiar Romantic phenomenon, it meant nothing like that total abhorrence of "a hideous society" which drove Huysmans' Des Esseintes (in the celebrated Decadent novel *À Rebours*) to cut all his ties with it and cultivate a religion of art, or Mallarmé to write incomprehensible poetry the better to infuriate the "vile bourgeoisie," or Gauguin to flee to the South Pacific—to mention but a few of the better-known gestures of the *fin de siècle*.

Such "intellectuals" were a peculiarly de-classed group. Normally themselves members of the affluent bourgeoisie (though a few like Wells, Bennett, and Shaw fought their way up from humble origins), they could not abide the manners and values of this class. We must distinguish the true intellectual from the academics, dull scholars with comfortable posts, though clearly there are marginal cases (literary dons like Walter Pater, or writers who grew inordinately respectable with success): the intellectual was outside the educational Establishment, typically, and fought it with secessionist salons (such as the famous Viennese salon of Klimt, Schiele, and others in 1899), with "little magazines" and experimental reviews, with the scorn which a Sorel or a LeBon visited upon the *universitaires*. (Nietzsche had been emblematic in fleeing from an academic career.) The Futurists' cry "Burn down the museums!" was a facet of this hatred of the embalmed and the traditional over which public officials kept custody. At the same time, intellectuals usually mistrusted what remained of the old aristocracy, of which they seldom had any great knowledge and which seemed decadent, impotent, and out of tune with the times. (Compare the attitude of Huysmans' Des Esseintes, himself of noble descent.) The leisured classes as they appear in the works of Chekhov and Proust or in Shaw's *Heartbreak House* not only do not understand forces such as the new mass democracy but they have lost faith in their own class and its traditional religion; they sit talking futilely while the world crumbles. The modern intellectual has wanted to be much more "with it" than that; he has been a child of the cities, despite his bucolic fantasies conceived in hatred of the industrial society, and an occasional sneaking admiration for old aristocratic values.[8]

Toward the "proletariat" or the peasantry, intellectuals occasionally felt the kind of naïve attraction to an idealized demos so notably displayed by the Russian university students in the 1870's, but any real contact normally terminated this love affair and sent them scurrying back to study or café. (Even Karl Marx, confronted with actual German workingmen, called them "stupid asses."). Hatred of the possessing classes joined with a powerful ego-drive in the typical intellectual, finally to create, in Lenin, a mind deliberately toughened

17

and purged of all feeling, to fit it for the realm of power; but Lenin, needless to say, was a most exceptional case. Between 1889 and 1914 the Social Democratic party in Germany attracted many educated people who were deeply loyal to their vision of a future ideal society, but the true intellectuals among them never were happy as or with party functionaries.

A restless, alienated group on the whole, their creations were as perverse as they were brilliant, from the viewpoint of the general public. It was in the 1890's and the 1900's that artists began to break drastically with tradition, proclaiming wholly noxious a nineteenth-century past that included Beethoven and Liszt, Hugo and George Eliot, realistic painters and sculptors. The breach between the culture of the bourgeoisie and the culture of an intellectual avant-garde occurs at this time; the real world and the world of thought break apart. It is "a world where action is not the sister of the dream" (Baudelaire). In his remarkable study of nine generations of Hamburgers, the historian Percy Schramm documented the steady dropping behind of a serious bourgeoisie which tried to "keep up" with art and literature.[9] At the beginning of the nineteenth century it could do so, but the gap widened with each generation until at the end there was a veritable chasm across which angry, frustrated burghers glared at mocking, irreverent artists and thinkers, closer to bohemia or the black flag of anarchy than to the drawing room or concert hall.

The struggles of artistic temperaments with a hostile environment emerge in novels of adolescent revolt and unhappiness, hardly a new theme but presented with startling intensity in the 1900's: for example, Hermann Hesse's *Beneath the Wheel*, Robert Musil's *Young Törless*, Frank Wedekind's *Spring's Awakening*, Heinrich Mann's *Stormy Morning*. "All over Europe the younger generation felt the urge to break with the bourgeois world, to revitalize a culture which seemed to have lost its vitality."[10] Reaction against this culture was frequently marked by a morbid sensitivity, as in Maeterlinck's Melisande who cannot bear to be touched or addressed (the play *Pelléas and Mélisande* inspired four great composers to set it to music between 1898 and 1905); or in Gustav Mahler's almost frighteningly poignant musical subjectivity. From all sides came testimony to a profound malaise, expressed in terms of profound foreboding. "A cold wave of cynicism and brutality has blown over the world," Croce cried.[11] "Dunkel ist das Leben," Mahler's *Song of the Earth* intoned; "this Stygian hell of pointless and abnormal existence," cried Dostoyevsky. In England, Graham Wallas expressed "fear . . . lest the civilization which we have adopted so rapidly and with so little forethought may prove unable to secure either a harmonious life for its members or even its own stability."[12]

Oscar Kokoschka says that about 1910 (a singularly crucial year) he knew "suddenly, intuitively" that "the whole of humanity was smitten with an incurable disease."[13] A sense of real horror in a dismal world filled with meaningless, pathetic lives—wholly at odds with one's inner world—afflicted young T. S. Eliot.[14] In that same year Stefan George's Spiritual Movement began, announcing that the threat to modern man comes not from war, class conflict, or oppression, but from dehumanization of the individual through commercialization, standardization, democratization—Americanization. (See the introduction to the 1912 *Jahrbuch für die geistigen Bewegung*.) The Futurist Manifesto having launched its violent, revolutionary-esthetic message in 1909, the same year brought to birth Expressionism, with its frequent images of the sinister, the violent, of death, decay, blood. At this same time Robert Musil started his long and curiously significant (unfinished) novel, *The Man without Qualities*—a search for ways to make the human personality at home in a scientific, rationalized, and specialized society. And Franz Kafka began his battles with the chains of a bureaucratic world.

Kafka is emblematic in his agonizing sense of the split between inner world and outer, private and social realities. Branded "unfit for life" by his father, aware that he was, and (like T. S. Eliot's Prufrock in the poem written just before the war) rather ashamed of it, Kafka was horrified by the social reality of his times and utterly unable to adapt to it, yet yearned deeply for some sort of integration into the group, *in den menschlichen Kreis*.[15] He felt as did the English poet A. E. Housman:

> Oh grant me the ease that is granted so free,
> The birthright of multitudes, give it to me,
> That relish their victuals and rest in their bed
> With flint in the bosom and guts in the head.[16]

But for the civilized consciousness, in this "age of consciousness" ("the time of human consciousness," Anatole France called it),[17] there could be no community with the flint-bosomed and gut-headed urban mass-man or bourgeoisie, and so the outcast "sensitive" was condemned to distill art from his anguish and hope that somehow the illusion became reality. If we think that this was entirely new, we of course remember the Brontës and other tortured illusionists of preceding generations; and yet there is no doubt that this alienation was a peculiar nineteenth-century phenomenon which grew steadily more acute.

When we remember that the psychoanalytical movement of Freud and Jung was just getting organized in 1909–10, the evidence for a severe identity crisis, a widening of the breach between public and private life, seems overwhelming. Nietzscheanism made its way through Europe, forming the basis for a "new culture" of radical individualism and the supremacy of art.[18] André Gide's novel *The Immoralist* had already raised the issue of artistic egoism, and Max Stirner, who reduced everything to this subjective element, was now more widely read than Karl Marx.[19] The young British novelists D. H. Lawrence and James Joyce produced their first significant works at this time, 1910–13, causing such older writers as Joseph Conrad and H. G. Wells to sense a deep crisis in literature, at stake being subjectivity versus objectivity, art for art's sake versus a utilitarian esthetic. "The last years have been years of demolition," Lawrence wrote in 1912.[20] The eagerness (ironical, in view of the subsequent wartime hysteria against him) with which British writers absorbed Nietzsche's influence at this time; the discovery of Dostoyevsky; exhibitions of "post-Impressionist" art, to the great scandal of respectability—these, and more, testified to the work of demolition.

A series of personal crises among European cognoscenti around 1910 tantalizes us with evidence of a general crisis in the relation between society and the intellectual consciousness. In that year Gustav Mahler sought a conference with Sigmund Freud, the greatest of twentieth-century composers feeling a "shattering insecurity" which he traced to "the liberal order"—that is, an impersonal, urban, irreligious society lacking community. The Expressionist pioneer Edvard Munch also sought psychoanalytical aid. Likewise, in 1910 Joseph Conrad experienced a mental breakdown, evidently connected with his confronting the new subjectivity; rejecting it, he recovered but was not thereafter the great writer he had been.[21] One might compare Jan Sibelius' retreat from the awesome depths of his Fourth Symphony, written 1910–11, never again to regain his high genius. Max Weber, the giant among sociologists, suffered from a debilitating psychic malady on and off in the 1900's.

The critical factor was the stress between two exceedingly complex and wholly different worlds, the interior consciousness and the exterior society. In the former area, the expansion and enrichment of consciousness had been going on throughout the nineteenth century accompanied by ever-diminishing social inhibitions against frank expression of ego urges and personal fantasies: Romanticism had opened the way to a subjectivity from which there was no turning back. The relentless criticism of traditional faiths and values, including above all Christianity itself, eroded secure standards and a hundred prophets rushed in to offer a replacement: Hegel, Marx, Schopenhauer, Nietzsche, the Darwinists, the Positivists, Anarchists, the Monists, the idealists, naturalists, realists, believers in art for art's sake, and in occultism (in which the *fin de siècle* intelligentsia were heavily involved), and many more. The Marxists would split into factions,[22] likewise the idealists, while some would attempt a sophisticated return to Christianity, treating it as myth: a splendid error, the naturalistic idealist Santayana affirmed. Europe had poured forth a profusion of literary and musical riches throughout the century. The Romantic generation of Chopin, Liszt, Keats, and Heine gave way to the earthier Victorians, George Eliot, Browning, Meredith, Hardy; French Parnassians and Symbolists from Baudelaire and Flaubert to Verlaine and Mallarmé offered fascinating, diabolical wares; the great Dostoyevsky headed an imposing Russian cast.

In 1910 Leo Tolstoy died, amid the confusion of visitors from all over Russia and indeed the world, seeking advice or giving it to one who had become an institution and an oracle. A quarter century earlier Richard Wagner had died after similarly becoming a national monument, as well as an international beacon for the bewildered. The age did not lack geniuses and messages. That, on the one side, was its problem: a spiritual anarchy.[23]

"The age is intensely introspective, and the younger generation is beginning to protest that supreme interest in one's self is not sin or self-conscious weakness or to be overcome, but is the essence of progress," as a British girl, Vera Brittain, put it a bit primly at this time.[24] The inward turn was of the essence: Nietzschean "become what thou art," poetic private worlds, Expressionism. The name given to one of England's most prominent new avant-garde journals was *The Egoist*, the title of George Meredith's best novel. Ludwig Marcuse said that Nietzsche had taught him above all that "the heart of the world is not a Good God, a Good Nature, nor a Good Reason, but rather a Being-There who is enclosed in less than two meters and a few pounds of flesh, blood and bone, and some heavy Spirit."[25] In 1910 T. S. Eliot began "The Love Song of J. Alfred Prufrock," and Joyce started his explorations of the stream of consciousness. Edmund Husserl had already started his attempt to isolate and chart the pure subjective consciousness. The goal of Symbolist poetry, as Edmund Wilson described it, was, by a complex literary technique, to "communicate unique personal feeling"; the ineffable mood structures which expository prose cannot get at. Kandinsky, whose first abstract painting belongs to 1910, aimed at depicting "something completely other from the appearances of the actual world." "Objects hinder my meaning." "The spirit is everything; I can do without Nature," Ludwig Meidner declared on behalf of all the Expressionists. "Away from the Thing, away from Matter, back to Spirit" (Julius Maier Graefe).[26]

This intense introspection was closely related to a feature of the new art that contributed to its bad public repute, its eroticism. Lou Andreas-Salomé's *Die Erotik* belongs also to 1910, a year in which H. G. Wells shocked British respectability by both his open defense of "free love" (*Ann Veronica*) and his behavior; and in which Freud joined lesser lights such as Havelock Ellis in the candid discussion of forbidden topics. It was a year in which both Lenin and Max Weber turned to extramarital affairs. Arthur Schnitzler, Freud's fellow Viennese physician, conveyed his psychology in the play *Reigen* (*La Ronde*), which saw sexual gratification as a desperate expression of alienated, isolated souls driven inward on themselves—the only means of communication left in a dying society. ("The only god capable of breaking down the barriers of his [modern man's] individualist isolation," Erich Heller wrote in *The Disinherited Mind*. "Something in which one can drown oneself and all one's fears of the monotony of the days," Musil's *Törless* observes.) Sociologist-philosopher Georg Simmel, in a 1911 essay, found erotic adventure an escape from bourgeois conventionality, a kind of daring almost equivalent to war as antibureaucratic behavior. Max Weber agreed that eroticism is a means of escaping the banality of everyday routine.[27] Naturally, many socialist and liberal discussions of the "new woman" and "sexual emancipation" presented a less gloomy view of the erotic movement. But to a great degree cultivation of purely personal values was an alarmed retreat from the reigning social modes.

Arnold Schoenberg expressed an "awareness of chaos and disintegration both within the psyche and the external world."[28] Religious and political ideals were in decay, Chesterton declared: "man's two great inspirations had failed him altogether." At the turn of the century a feeling of decadence and degeneration was in the air, among the intellectual minority, while the unthinking public continued to revel in shallow notions of unlimited progress guaranteed by technology and science. The frightening chaos sensed in the realm of social relations stemmed less from the wave of strikes that swept through Europe beginning in 1910 and from other overt disturbances than from the massive march toward bigness, urbanism, impersonal forms, mass phenomena. Nineteen ten was also the year which hailed the first crowd of a hundred thousand at Wembley football stadium in London, in which the underground rail system (started about 1870, as was the Football Association) was extended to the suburbs, and in which (as Henri Lefebvre stresses) the reign of electricity really began.[29] The 1910 election campaign in Britain was the first one to shock patrician tradition by its "ballyhoo" methods. Even though Futurists hailed these surging city crowds and mechanized factories, their bravado rings a little false.

In 1910 Max Weber was occupied with that comprehensive sociology of the modern state which he never finished but of which the most fascinating fragments are those dealing with "bureaucratic" and "rationalization" phenomena. The impersonal apparatus of technologically oriented society converts the human person into an automaton or at best a small specialized cog in an infinitely vast social machine. The mass institution, even if it be ideologically democratic (the mass political party) or socialist,[30] must be governed bureaucratically—that is, written rules rather than human understandings. Such propositions are the clichés of today; they were new before 1914.

Popular culture, mass society, democratic politics, all combined to thicken that crust of vulgarity Baudelaire had noticed forming half a century earlier, and which drove him to his persona of disreputable dandyism. Dandyism made an appearance in the D'Annunzio–Huysmans–Oscar Wilde–Aubrey Beardsley 1890's, accompanied by Decadence, misty Symbolist plays and poems, a cult of beauty tinged with hints of a darker voluptuousness: the Romantic Agony, as Mario Praz called it. Since the philistine, a calculating "objective man," never knows any high ideals, middle-class intellectuals were frequently attracted by the dream of a higher, heroic life. Yeats in the 1890's celebrated heroes of Irish mythology who defied the odds, faced death and even welcomed it. The heroic ideal was a counter to the bourgeois ethic. The Expressionist dramatist Georg Kaiser, looking for anything to stimulate men to pursue the ideal, wrote a successful play in 1914 based on the siege of Calais in the Hundred Years' War.

II

Thus one of the responses to a bourgeois style of life was the aristocratic heroism of battle. Dandies might turn into warriors, as happened in the case of D'Annunzio. Sensitive esthetes might become partisans of integral nationalism, following the example of Maurice Barrès. Flight into fantasy, dreams of primeval innocence, the pure subjectivity of a Paul Klee, represented one way of escape from an unbearable present reality.[31] But images of violence seemed to be more frequent on the eve of 1914. Among the artists, Franz Marc called his *Destiny of the Beasts* (1913) a premonition of war.[32] Ludwig Meidner's *Apocalyptic Landscapes* (1912–13) and the sculptor Wilhelm Lehmbruck's *Grieving Woman* (1913) and *Rape* (a painting) join other Expressionist works, notably the famous *Cry* of Edvard Munch, in a preoccupation with grief and violence. Such images litter the work of the brilliant Expressionist poet (and physician) Gottfried Benn (see his 1912 poem significantly titled "Morgue") and also the work of Georg Heym, who died in an accident in 1912 at the age of twenty-four, after having written of sickness, death, and war ("Der Krieg," "Nach der Schlacht"). "If only there were a war, even an unjust one," he wrote. "This peace is so rotten."[33] Kokoschka made his *Murder the Hope of Women* into an Expressionist play linking love and bloodlust (which caused a commotion upon its performance in Munich in 1908). "I am not a peace-loving man," the athletic Kokoschka conceded, and he went off to war eagerly in 1914, though later he had difficulty in reconstructing his motives. His friend Frank Wedekind also wrote exciting modernist plays featuring the revelation of brutal, instinctive urges. Lulu, his most extraordinary dramatic

24

creation, is an *Erdgeist*, an amoral and archetypal female, a Dionysian maenad rioting against civilization. A famous literary figure of this age was the manic Swedish genius, August Strindberg, whose preoccupation with sin, crime, and the black depths of the soul may be seen in his famous preface to the play *Miss Julie* (1888); in the 1900's his more experimental, Symbolist-Expressionist plays such as *The Ghost Sonata* (1907) are no less overhung with dark despair tempered by religious mysticism.

The vision of a vaguely violent Armageddon had been persistent for a number of years among Europe's poets, a fact suggested by Yeats, writing in 1896 that he envisaged "revolution after an impending European war, like us all."[34] "In being apocalyptic, Scriabin is simply a man of his time absorbing the pollen of ideas already in the air," Faubion Bowers writes of the celebrated Russian musician-mystic whose life he has chronicled. "Everyone was talking of doomsday."[35] Russia was a particularly fertile soil for a feverish religious messianism, promulgated by theologians like the brilliant Vladimir Solovyëv (who did battle against the Tolstoyan pacifists) but eagerly taken up by a variety of intellectuals. Dmitri Merezhkovsky, a powerful writer who passed from Nietzschean to Christian versions of the apocalypse, sang of "children of darkness" on the edge of the abyss, awaiting the sun in whose rays they would die.[36] Vyacheslav Ivanov preached the mystical union of Christ and Dionysus, "ecstasy for ecstasy's sake," while the magicians Gurdiyev, Ouspensky, and Blavatsky emerged from this Russian Orthodox world to reach as far west as Frank Lloyd Wright's circle on the American prairie. The fact that Russian thinkers were cut off from the normal expression of political opinions and of political activity had something to do with creating "this tense and nervous atmosphere," in which "every kind of new religion and superstition proliferated."[37] (These were the Rasputin years.) Maxim Gorky tried to marry religion to Marxian revolution, becoming a "god-builder" and a "people worshiper." Merezhkovsky's revolutionary Christian anarchism was not so different, though the poet was to reject Lenin's revolution decisively. Gorky's book *The Destruction of Personality* (German translation, 1909) presented a potent vision of the masses functioning as the instrument of a bloody *eschaton* which would trample a dying culture under the boots of a "new barbarism" able to restore values and vitality.

Russia was indeed a caldron seething with esthetic, philosophic, and theological heresies, feeding on the frustrations of politics in the ancient despotism. Ever since the Populist days a small minority of educated, Westernized intellectuals had yearned to be reunited with the dark masses. Russian Symbolism was both more mystical and more activist, it would seem, than its European counterparts. Seer and prophet, the artist penetrates arcane mysteries of life not available to scientific reason; at the same time, according to the "mystical anarchism" of Ivanov, he should somehow use this wisdom to transform life and build a new world.[38] The message of the great Dostoyevsky —back to the peasant life, contact with the soil and the Slavic soul— could not be forgotten, the more so as Leo Tolstoy had underscored it.

A Russian proponent of the virile life was the "Acmeist" poet N. S. Gumilyëv, whose poetry reflected the reaction against Symbolist ethereality that marked the years just before the war. He enlisted early in the war. After a season of being wan dandies and pale lost lilies during the esthetic 1890's, it was refreshing to become, at least in imagination, wolves and warriors, ready to drink blood and wage war. The "Leonardists" in Italy preceded the Futurists in advertising this mood, in which German Expressionism participated.[39] All the artistic and literary movements of the 1900's were sharper, bolder, tougher, than those that appeared in the first generation of Modernism during the 1880's and 1890's. The mood then was misty and effeminate; superesthetical young men wore lilies and cultivated a blasé world-weariness. The violent, aggressive spirit of Futurism and much of Expressionism was a reaction.

Expressionism is a vaguer term than Futurism, bestowed by classifiers on a variety of artistic phenomena of the 1908-14 years, and somewhat beyond, particularly in Germany. It embraced painters as different as Edvard Munch, Vasily Kandinsky, Paul Klee, Oskar Kokoschka; writers such as Gottfried Benn, Georg Kaiser, Frank Wedekind. The composers Alban Berg and Arnold Schoenberg are sometimes placed within this *tendance*. The tendency was international; Expressionism interacted with the simultaneous schools of Fauvism and Cubism in France, Futurism in Italy and Russia, Vorticism in England (which Wyndham Lewis and Ezra Pound regarded as the London equivalent of Parisian Cubism and Berlin Expressionism). The European *episteme* was a single breed with local variations. Influences on the German school came from Baudelaire and Rimbaud, from Dostoyevsky, Nietzsche, and Ibsen. In their urgent desire to regain contact with a primitive *a priori* of the consciousness and express this immediately, the Expressionists touched closely on the irrationalist thought of the Swiss colleague of Freud, Carl Jung, but also on the Parisian master (actually of Polish-Jewish and English parentage) Henri Bergson and the Italian philosopher of art and history Benedetto Croce. Expressionism owed a debt to the *Fauves,* Matisse, Dufy, the Belgian Vlaminck, as well as to the Norwegian Munch. Kandinsky, chief theorist as well as practitioner of German Expressionist painting, was a Russian. The leading Expressionist organ, *Der Sturm,* gave its place of publication from 1913 to August, 1914, as Berlin/Paris. The years just before 1914 seemed to belong above all to the poets and artists. Stefan Zweig said that this era's "fanaticism for art" was such as could hardly be reconstructed, even when he wrote this in 1922, in his *Autobiographical Sketch.* The world was to be saved by Art, the Scriabins, Georges, and Marinettis proclaimed. Journals called *The Storm, Action, Blast, The Torch,* and painters called Wild Beasts or Blue Riders made known by their very names the revolutionary intent of this painting, poetry, music, and sculpture. The movement was everywhere, from Ireland to Russia, creating a kind of international of art-intoxicated activists who seldom failed to achieve their intent of shocking the respectable public. Into this game the Futurists entered most exuberantly.

Of Italian provenance, Futurism found adherents all over Europe, the Russian branch claiming to be of independent origin. The celebrated 1909 Manifesto of Futurism, which first appeared in the Paris paper *Figaro* (February 20), was indicative of Futurism's close links to France, where it blended with Fauvism and Cubism, as in Germany it could not easily be distinguished from Expressionism. Futurist exhibitions were held from Naples and Moscow to London and San Francisco. Marked by scuffles and affrays, their deliberately provocative enterprises, stemming from an "orgiastic world view," brought the Futurists forcefully to Europe's attention in the five years before the war. "Boisterously chauvinistic" from the beginning, the Manifesto glorified war *(sola igiene del mondo)* and Marinetti rushed to view and admire, if not to fight in, the Tripoli War of 1911 and the Balkan War of 1912. In Futurist painting, no less than in Expressionist, themes of physical brutality abounded—boxers, football players, "action, heroism, life." Luigi Russolo painted *Revolution.* The destructive impulses of Futurism took special aim at "tradition": the classics were to be murdered along with Romantic sentiment ("Let's murder the moonlight" was one of Marinetti's pieces of gaily nihilistic prose); among the detested objects were museums, "immortal masterpieces," the whole nineteenth-century style. The Futurists claimed to find delight in the clang of streetcars, factory whistles, the noise of motors and automobiles, crowds in city streets. ("We will sing of great crowds agitated by work, pleasure and riot; we will sing the multicolored, polyphonic tides of revolution in the modern capitals.") This symbolic acceptance of the modern age included a Fascist-like bravado; many Futurists later joined the Fascists, who learned much from them. But then the still later New Left borrowed Futurist "happenings," Living Theater, black humor. In Russia, the Futurists, led by Mayakovsky, eagerly embraced the Bolshevik Revolution of 1917. Despising the past, the Futurists adopted a historicism which embraced whatever happens next as necessarily best.

"There is no beauty except in strife," was a Futurist slogan; "without violence nothing would ever have been created." Christ was violent, Caesar was violent, so also the Reformation, the French Revolution, everything worthwhile.[40] After the war started, Futurists agitated for Italian entry, sponsoring meetings, tearing up Austrian flags, converting their organ *Lacerba* into an anti-Austrian political journal. With Gabriele D'Annunzio, they flung themselves into battle with real courage and celebrated the marriage of art and war, not only in war poems and paintings but in such attempts as Fedale Azari's to choreograph an aerial dance of aviators!

Futurism was a part of the revolt against Romanticism which may be found pervading avant-garde circles of the 1900's, affecting T. E. Hulme and T. S. Eliot in England, Paul Valéry as well as Charles Maurras in France, and others. Hardness, discipline, and elegance were favored over sentimentality, sloppiness, and the "moonshine" which Marinetti was out to knife. Even love was suspect. "Nauseated by erotic books," doubtless including those effeminate *fin de siècle* productions of the Beardsleys and Lotis, Marinetti's "man of today" is inoculated against *amore*, "learns to destroy in himself all the sorrows of the heart," diverts his energies from women to machines—or war. (He can look after his bodily needs by "swift, casual encounters with women,"[41] but Marinetti was delighted to find homosexuality in young Englishmen and elsewhere; the George circle in Germany preferred it,

28

and there was to be a cult of it among intellectual warriors such as Ernst Jünger.)

The basis for an objective music which Schoenberg and Berg found in a mathematical device (twelve-tone scale serialism) rested on a feeling that Mahler and Rachmaninoff, in different ways, had carried Romantic subjectivity as far as it could possibly go (listening to Mahler's late work, who could doubt it?), and was the counterpart of Barrès and D'Annunzio reacting against the *culte de moi* by swinging to an extreme nationalistic communalism.

Artists of the first Modernist generation, itself only a few years old, were of course still around, and sometimes changed in accordance with the fashions. But art, so fascinating a toy, could also be boring, illusory as its world was. Awarded the Nobel Prize in 1911, almost mobbed when he visited New York, the Belgian Maurice Maeterlinck was one of the world's most popular writers in the 1900's; like D'Annunzio a remnant of the Decadent and Symbolist 1890's, he suddenly gave up literature in 1913, victim of that restless malaise found in so many writers on the eve of the explosion. Like Gide and D'Annunzio, he interested himself in pets, wondered about the meaning of life, cultivated his eccentricities. He was to welcome the war and later applaud Mussolini's Fascism. So also, of course, did the other famous Decadent, the Italian D'Annunzio. In the years just before 1914, the "archangel Gabriele's" conversion from Decadence to Futurism was significant. There had been, to be sure, a great deal of disease, death, sin, and sadism in the Decadent D'Annunzio. Like Wilde's *Salome*, which Richard Strauss turned into a great opera (an indignant public prevented Strauss from collaborating with D'Annunzio on a day in the life of a prostitute), the D'Annunzio-Debussy *St. Sebastian* found in lascivious religious martyrdom a perfect subject. Recalling Flaubert's *Temptation of St. Anthony*, Symbolist painters loved to display gorgeous female flesh flashing before the tortured saint's disordered imagination.

D'Annunzio's fabulous virtuosity in literature and love made him a living legend in the two decades before 1914, though his great fellow Italian Croce called his a greatness *manqué*, lacking any coherent or sustained vision or faith—"a dilettante of sensations." No one had consumed more sensations; these had tended to be esthetic and erotic. In the 1900's, Philippe Jullian writes in his biography of the great Decadent, "d'Annunzian ladies roamed across Europe leaving a trail of scandals and tuberoses in their wake, loving pleasure even to the point of being prepared to perish in its pursuit." "Living dangerously" to the Nietzschean-D'Annunzians meant unrestrained and illicit sex carried on amidst exotic surroundings (often Petronian in their extravagance). But by 1914 D'Annunzio was "a syphilitic, debt-ridden Don Juan" (Jullian), a bit passé, issuing increasingly mediocre poems and novels, a figure no longer taken seriously by the authenic literary world, even if still madly sought by American women. War was a last source of *frissons* for the used-up Decadent-Romantic. The war transformed him, and he became a genuine hero. More at home in France than Italy, D'Annunzio experienced the first days of the war in Paris and returned to lead the war faction in his native land, which succeeded some months later. In 1913 he had told Maurice Barrès' receptive ears that "a great national war is France's last chance of salvation" from a democratic degeneration, a plebeian inundation of her high culture.[42]

III

A kind of literary adventurism and a thirst for violence were present in European literature on the eve. Péguy, Ernest Psichari, and Romain Rolland were men of the hour in France where "national revival" stressing discipline, heroism, and national genius was the watchword.[43] Paul Acker's *Le soldat Bernard* (1910) and Paul Adam's *La Ville inconnue* (1911) joined Psichari's *L'Appel des armes* (1913) among books which frankly appealed to the taste for war. Psichari preached a "mysticism of violence," writing of "the great harvest of force, toward which a sort of inexpressible grace hurls us and ravishes us." Ironically enough, in view of his wartime role, Rolland's *Jean Christophe* (winner of the Grand Prix), which had a sensational vogue in 1913, rather fitted the mood of war and chauvinism that was in the air, in its stress on heroism of soul, disdain for bourgeois pettiness. Daniel Halévy's *Quelques nouveaux Maîtres* (1913) placed Rolland alongside Péguy, Maurras, and Claudel among masters of the spirit. In 1897 Rolland had said a noble war was better than a dull peace.

The search for escape from bourgeois values could lead to the "savage" world. In his *Terres de soleil et de sommeil* (1908), Psichari sought refreshment in the dark depths of Africa, where he imagines "life's inexorable law" of strength prevailing: "la force, n'est-elle la beauté?" In John Buchan's novel *Prester John* (1910), to the accusation of wanting to "wipe out the civilization of a thousand years and turn us into savages," a character replies, "It is because I have sucked civilization dry that I know the bitterness of the fruit. I want a simpler and a better world." Before the age of the movie star, or sports hero, late Victorian mass minds ate up the adventures of Africa-explorers, Zulu-fighters and other Haggard- or Kipling-inspired imperial supermen. (The popular press "reeked of blood and reverberated with thunder," Esmé Wingfield-Stratford wrote in his *Victorian Aftermath*, noting fantasies in which the British fought all the armies of Europe combined and defeated them.)[44] Sophisticated intellects, in flight from a Europe that "bored" them (Gide's term), feeling their civilization sucked dry, shared this taste for the primitive: "a basic belief of the age everywhere among the leading artists," Ernst Nolde thought.

In his well-known inquest into French university youth of 1913, co-authored with Alfred de Tarde, Henri Massis (*Young People of Today*) found Péguy to be the leading influence together with Maurras and Barrès. Péguy's conversion came in 1905 during the first Moroccan crisis. (See especially *Notre Patrie*.) He saw France threatened, and identified France with "civilization" against "barbarism." He changed from a pacifist and internationalist to an ardent and uncritical patriot, moved by the vision of tragic France, menaced and divided, vanquished but exalted, chief guardian of what liberty and civilization remained in a sinking world. Germany, the enemy, was a land of "underlings and submitters" ruled by barbarians, signifying simply brute power. But in 1913 (in *Notre jeunesse; L'Argent*) Péguy presented war as of value almost for its own sake, because it brings regeneration. The vision of France redeemed, resurgent through a war that would be for the justest of causes, received perhaps its most eloquent expression before the war from this leading French intellectual light, who drew near to his old adversaries of the Right, Barrès and Maurras, at this time. What annoyed him most was the presentation of peace as republicanism and democracy. The Republic must be defended; pacifism means its extinction, by placing a value above it. If one wishes to be pacifist, very well, but let us be clear about it—it means surrendering everything:

It is a scale of values in which honor is less dear than life. . . . It is madness to want to associate pacifism with the Republic and the Revolution and the Rights of Man. . . . The Republic of pacifism is the Republic dismembered. It is the Republic divided and disunited.[45]

Patriotism, which today almost always disgusts "high-brow" minds, to whom it is pablum for the general, was in 1914 not only a reputable but modish idea. It ranked not as something ignoble but as an ideal capable of stirring men out of their selfishness; thus it was the enemy not the accomplice of commerce, capitalism, the bourgeoisie—the last too cowardly and self-interested to fight for the general welfare. To many, patriotism offered the possibility of a viable myth or faith for those who had lost the capacity to believe and act—the central problem for modern man. "Futurism is fanatical love of Italy and of the greatness of Italy," Papini declared on behalf of the Futurists, to which group he came from an earlier (1906) "New Nationalism" movement. "Better the dreams of nationalism than the miserable disputes of shabby interests between parliamentary groups." For Rupert Brooke, "The actual earth of England held a quality which . . . if he'd ever been sentimental enough to use the word he'd have called 'holiness.' "[46] Literary pose or sincere emotion? It would perhaps be difficult to say. In some ways nationalism was a substitute religion, involving a quasi-religious veneration for the symbolized figure of the Nation, sometimes visualized as the very soil or earth. "She is all we know and live by," Edward Thomas cried:

> But with the best and meanest Englishmen
> I am one in crying, God Save England . . . .

Thomas Hardy's "Men Who March Away" saw well what they were doing: they could not leave England in the lurch. "Cambridge," writes Quentin Bell, "like the great majority of the nation, had been converted to the religion of nationalism; it was a powerful, a terrible, at times a very beautiful magic."[47] Nationalism exerted its magic on the most sophisticated and educated in 1914, a fact that later generations, to whom the least common denominator of any intellectual worth his salt was a contempt for the idols of the tribe, found hard to grasp—but a fact nevertheless. The prewar years had seen the rise of

32

the cult of nationalism among important writers and thinkers in all European countries.

National languages held a special appeal for writers. "A beloved and priceless treasure of our past," Ludwig Klages called his tongue; Wilfred Owen gave as his reason for enlisting, to defend "the language in which Keats and the rest of them wrote."[48] Nationalism coincided with the search for membership in a community, the pervasive theme of 1914 (see further below, chapter 5). The theme of many of Joseph Conrad's novels, so important and successful in the 1900's, prior to his 1910 collapse, is the rootless man who saves himself by identifying with some sort of human community, often a primitive or a violent one, the fellowship of a ship crew or a savage tribe, conquering his turbulent ego. "I am not a peace man, not a democrat," Conrad said. He himself was one of the uprooted.

Nationalism also could be an idealism. Though Nietzsche had expressed scorn for the *Reichsdeutsch,* less attention was paid to this, even by his disciples, than to Wagner's nationalism,[49] while in France the great voice of Péguy—virtual re-creator of the Joan of Arc cult—made French nationalism seem little short of sublime. Georges Sorel himself swung around from the myth of the general strike to the myth of the national people, as an energizing and heroicizing force. "Tout un monde litteraire," Julien Benda later wrote scornfully, "ne voulut plus savoir que l'âme 'française,' les verités 'françaises.' "[50] The mood was summed up in the title of Étienne Rey's book *The Renaissance of French Pride* (1913).

The impossible dream, in the last analysis, took precedence; nationalism, patriotism, and battle were only its expected instruments. The classic story of 1914 for the French was that of Henri Alban Fournier, better known to readers as Alain-Fournier, author of *Le Grand Meaulnes* (1912), translated into English as *The Wanderer.* It is the story of a quest by a young student. For what? The quest leads to a half-ruined manor where peasants eat and drink according to ancient customs; a bygone age of heroism, love, and romance, the oldest of archetypes. Here Meaulnes sees a beautiful girl, but he loses his way, falls asleep, and cannot find his way back to the chateau. For the rest of his life he hunts for her, as Fournier himself supposedly hunted for a girl he once met in the park. The evocative, musical language conveying hints of nameless mysteries under the surface of things is characteristic of Symbolist writing and a key to most of the best literature of this era. (Stefan Zweig: "Human life has currents running deeper than the external events. . . . A deep magic of life, perceptible only to the feelings and not to the senses, rules our fate.") Clearly, Fournier's lost chateau, like Kafka's castle, is a symbol, his story both fantasy and allegory.

Because he went serenely off to a war he knew he would not return from, and because he died on the Marne with Péguy, Fournier became a legend. But there were other such writings in the few years before 1914. For example, the novels of Émile Clermont, *Amour promis* (1910) and *Laure* (1913), reveal the same quest for an impossible love, mystic passions leading to tragic suffering, and sacrifice —quite romantic subjects in themselves, raised to the level of literature by the Symbolist imparting of grace in the details. A profound yearning for some cause great enough to redeem life and satisfy its ineffable desires is what one chiefly carries away from a reading of these books *avant le deluge:*

> To turn, as swimmers into cleanness leaping,
> Glad from a world grown old and cold and weary,
> Leave the sick hearts that honour could not move,
> And half-men, and their dirty songs and dreary,
> And all the little emptiness of love!

[Rupert Brooke]

In 1913 and 1914 Franz Kafka was at work on that enigmatic masterpiece *The Trial.* It seems to tell of a gulf between "real" life, such as unreflecting peasants live, and the artificial life of K., a bank clerk (like T. S. Eliot's "young man carbuncular") who lives mechanically; or between an ideal world of spontaneity, imagination, poetry, life as it should be, and the actual daily routine that deadens us to all beauty. How to connect the two realms is a motif running through Kafka's other writings of these years, including *Amerika.* He told Gustav Janouch that people were about to be replaced by machines in today's society.[51] "The chains that bind tormented mankind are made out of red tape." The civilized consciousness of Europe's bearers of culture glimpsed images of a deep, rich, spiritually satisfying life which they contrasted with the contemptible society of machine-appendages seen around them in the real world. The tension became unbearable.

IV

Reactions to this uncomfortable gulf between self and society, inner and outer realities, could take various forms. One could simply withdraw to the inner world, a strategy that might lead to the asylum but in the case of a great artist produced masterworks dredged up from the imagination. (Carl Jung diagnosed Van Gogh as a clear case of schizophrenia, and artistic insanity occurred in the case of the Swedish painters Carl Hill and Ernst Josephson.) Paul Klee, "as though new born," evidently painted the pictures he saw within, strange but archetypal visions to which his viewers responded. That deep within the unspoiled unconscious lie "archetypes," which may be visual images or narrative themes, was the myth which Carl Jung erected into an imposing scientific theory. The Nietzschean advice to "become what thou art," ignoring the idiotic masses, seemed prepared to overlook all of what Sigmund Freud called "the reality principle." Such advice was obviously not easy to follow. But many artists, from Rimbaud on, seceded from society to become outcasts, damned souls, grotesques. Some, like Alfred Jarry, Ernest Dowson, and Francis Thompson, made a cult of this splendid defiance, dying of drink and self-neglect.

Drug addiction was of course an old strategy. One might flee Europe altogether, like Gauguin; or intermittently, like Gide, Oscar Wilde, Richard Burton, and other exoticists of this era, many of whom admired African and Japanese art, Chinese poetry, Indian religion and philosophy. (It remained for Lorca to discover the gypsies, Lawrence the Aztecs and Etruscans.) Musil's couple try a Mediterranean island, which does not work. Marcel Proust fled to his sealed room to re-create and embalm the whole society in a work of art.

Retreat or withdrawal from a hideous society, in whatever way, has as its opposite an angry attack on the offending reality, the attacker hoping to change it drastically or, in the last resort, to destroy it. One could dream an ideal society, and then seek somehow to impose the dream on reality, by force or guile. The myth of revolution fascinated intellectuals far more than anyone else.[52] Their tendency to be "outsiders," natural Ishmaelites, together with their extreme sensitivity, engendered deep feelings of resentment and alienation. They sensed hostility to all that they held dear from the dominant class of philistines or "hearties." Dependence on this class for their welfare scarcely

35

lessened the dislike. The intellectual revolutionary makes his appearance at least as early as 1848, year of "the revolution of the intellectuals." But extreme disenchantment followed every venture into political waters; and a precipitous retreat into ivory towers of art or pure science, accompanied by Schopenhauerian gloom, marked the aftermath of the 1848 failure, as it did the extraordinary "to-the-people" trek in Russia in 1874, and to some extent the Dreyfus crusade of the late 1890's in France. There was a stir of excitement through much of intellectual Europe over the Russian Revolution of 1905 (Mahler marched in a socialist parade), but again the sequel was disappointing.

The rapid growth of trade unionism, bringing numerous, often violent strikes, encouraged a Syndicalist theory that from this spontaneous process the better society of tomorrow was being engendered; but by 1910 it was clear that a "trade union consciousness" was neither socialist nor revolutionary. The great lesson of the hour was that Marx's proletariat rejected Marxism, rejected socialism; Marxian socialism was an ideology of the alienated bourgeoisie, or of the intellectual class. The Polish revolutionary Machaisky held that Marxism was the ideology of "mental workers," or even "capitalists of the brain," while the French Syndicalist Edouard Berth thought that Marxian Social Democracy was a "half bourgeois" philosophy appealing to intellectuals, not workers. It was all too evident not only that the workers didn't read Marx, but that their leaders didn't: one of them, a French unionist, made the classic reply, "I read Dumas." The revisionist Social Democrat Eduard Bernstein saw this as clearly as did Lenin or Georges Sorel.

In the years just before the war, others of Europe's more advanced thinkers appear to have been in retreat from the socialist impulse widely felt in the 1890's and the early 1900's. The withdrawal of Péguy and Sorel from orthodox socialism, together with the popularity of Maurras's rightist *Action Française* among university youth, is one case in point; in England, Fabianism lost some of the appeal it had had in intellectual circles a few years earlier. Beatrice Webb thought French Syndicalism more popular in left-wing coteries than German Social Democracy. Guild Socialists, led by G. D. H. Cole, sowed dissension within the Fabian Society. Beatrice found university youth often rude and hostile.[53] Art was more interesting than politics. The very success of socialism as a mass movement in Germany and France decreased its attraction for the intellectuals.

Lenin's secession to the idea of an elite party, culled from a few indomitable wills and prepared to exercise a ruthless terrorist dictatorship, seemed in these years to be a counsel of despair, which the great majority of Socialists rejected as un-Marxian. But the split within the great German Social Democratic party reflected a similar unease about the methods of securing socialism's triumph. The orthodox determinist version of Marxism assured the faithful that the kingdom of perfect freedom comes to those who wait, as the mills of the gods of history grind slowly away. To criticize this historical inevitability as naïve or superstitious was to incur charges of heresy and undermine the whole foundation of a large and growing mass movement, based on uncritical acceptance of the Marxian economic analysis. Such revisionism led either to a collapse into mere reformism, *ad hoc* and "opportunist," or it led into wild adventurism. Eduard Bernstein and Antonio Labriola, on the Right, were in this sense not so far from Georges Sorel and Arturo Labriola and Lenin, on the Left; for both queried the automatic processes of "mechanical" Marxism.

The hope of revolution had gotten bogged down in such confusions during the 1900's. Of the attraction of revolution for the intellectuals, there could be no doubt. "The really new and potentially revolutionary class in society will consist of the intellectuals," Hannah Arendt wrote more recently, in *On Violence*. It already has, for a century. The difficulty is that intellectuals, while attracted to the idea, are unsuited for its execution, and thus pass from sloganizing to sullen disenchantment, as each grandly hopeful mystique decays into *politique*, losing its way in the baffling complexities of the real world. In great movements such as socialism the intellectuals were always the most radical and the least helpful, incurring the mistrust of "practical men" whom they in turn despised as opportunists. The path which led to the Chinese drama of recent years, during which Maoist revolutionary romanticism waged warfare on "pragmatism" within the inner council of the Chinese Communist party, began long ago with the first intellectual in politics.

A sudden event which would end the impasse by providentially burning the whole wasteland—Vico's thunderclap signaling the end of one epoch and the birth of another—was more than welcome as a resolution of these revolutionary dilemmas. The war would be hailed in 1914 as a revolution. "A war against capitalism!" Max Scheler cried.[54] Another 1789. Relief from "the crimes of England," according to

G. K. Chesterton. The famous Roman Catholic's book by that name, published in 1915, depicts a class-ridden country, dominated by a selfish, privileged oligarchy, which the war came to revolutionize and democratize. "Simple men with simple motives came out of their dreary tenements and their tidy shops, their fields and their suburbs and their factories and their rookeries, and asked for the arms of men."

In 1910 Rupert Brooke described the intellectual tastes of his generation: "Nietzsche is our Bible, Van Gogh our idol. We drink the lessons of Meredith and Ibsen and Swinburne and Tolstoy."[55] It was of some such mixture of ideas that the war spirit of August, 1914, was concocted. For young André Breton, future Surrealist poet, 1913 was the year of Proust, Apollinaire, and Gide. For other French intellectuals, it was the time of Barrès, Péguy, and Rolland. Whatever the names, Europe's climate of opinion was restless, turbulent, intense, exciting, abnormal—ready fuel for the spark of war. "Rolland and Jaurès spoke to us of the heroic life, Barrès and Gide of the tragic life, Nietzsche of the dangerous life," Jean Guehenno recalled—it was all the same to him and his friends.[56] Only war combined the heroic, the tragic, and the dangerous.

—3—

Greeting the War: The Reactions of Some European Writers

I

The liberal German historian Friedrich Meinecke recalled the first days of the war as "for all who lived through them one of the most precious and unforgettable memories of the highest sort."[1] The Socialist pedagogue Konrad Haenisch was proud that his party had made possible "the great August experience of the German people." Stefan Zweig, the Austrian Jewish novelist who soon cooled off on the war, recalled in his memoir *(Welt von Gestern)* that "each individual experienced an exaltation of his ego." Exaltation was indeed a much-used word: Karl Vossler, writing to Benedetto Croce, spoke of "the magnificent drama of the exaltation of a nation of 70 million people."[2] English Socialist H. N. Brailsford recalled in 1917 that his nation had lived in a state of "moral exaltation" the first year of the war,[3] a judgment corroborated in Robert Graves' "Recalling War":

> Never was such antiqueness of romance
> Such tasty honey oozing from the heart.

"This war is fine and great and just," French novelist Alain-Fournier wrote from training camp on August 4.[4] Making his way homeward from Germany amid taunts and insults (stimulated by his dressing his year-old son in the tricolor!), Paul Claudel arrived back in Paris to find the city "deserted, silent, and purified."[5] There was a similar welcoming of war in Russia by the major writers and intellectual leaders, "for having freed Russia of narrowness and pettiness and for opening new perspectives on greatness. Some viewed war as a spiritual awakening . . . ."[6] A friend wrote to Hugo Hofmannsthal that in Austria "the whole people is transformed, poured into a new mold. To have experienced this will probably be the greatest event of our lives."[7]

The suddenness with which the storm of war feeling broke should be stressed. There were antiwar demonstrations and meetings in France and Germany July 27–29. On August 1 *The Nation* declared that any British minister who led the country into war would be responsible for as unpopular a war as any in all history. In his autobiography Bertrand Russell recalled that he had no trouble collecting signatures on an antiwar manifesto on August 3; the next day all the signers changed their minds. "No one here wants war and cursed be those who have conjured up this horrible evil," the conservative *Kölnische Zeitung* could write a few days before the war began. Konrad Haenisch recalled that antiwar rallies took place "in every German district" (see his *Die Deutsche Sozialdemokratie in und nach dem Weltkrieg*, Berlin, 1916). Almost magically, the conventional antiwar rhetoric was replaced overnight by an entirely different one.

Thus the August madness descended. Examples of its vocabulary could be multiplied dozens of times over, so often in almost the same words that one might suspect occult forces. Exaltation, spiritual awakening, transformation, salvation from narrowness and pettiness, above all the surge of unity reuniting people of all kinds, not least plain people with intellectuals: these were the commonest watchwords. Perhaps the least understandable to people today, to whom this admiration for war is most "unseemly" (as a recent discussion of Hofmannsthal puts it), is the association, then quite natural, between war and revolt. Young Alec Waugh had just written a precocious attack on his public school (*The Loom of Life*),[8] and this adolescent rebellion carried over into his rush to enlist; the war would wash away all that dreary past, Europe's restless youth felt. It is hardly surprising that war should be seen as a destructive force; what startles us is the accompanying assumption that destroying a contemptible society would open the way to a better one: slaughter as a purifying or cleansing fire, the image so often found among the "ideas of August."

A frequent reaction among creative writers was a kind of breathless fascination with the mighty drama, not untinged with admiration, marked by wide-eyed astonishment but essentially neither approval or disapproval, just total absorption. This may relate to the historicism previously mentioned: one did not, after all, quarrel with whatever wonders the creative evolution of man and nature brought forth, one accepted and marveled. But to this was added the natural tendency for the novelist to be charmed by evidences of human action and energy, without moralizing about them. He had, after all, ever since Flaubert and then the Naturalists, learned not to be didactic, which was naïve and *outré*. Edmund Gosse described Henry James as one who "ate and drank, talked and walked, slept and worked and lived and breathed only the war." In Paris another great writer forced to sit on the sidelines, Marcel Proust, "lived in the war," absorbed in it and fascinated by it.[9] That the war had made life infinitely more interesting for observers of the human scene was manifest on all sides. The journal of André Gide is a study in the sudden breathless excitement that takes over beginning August 1 (replacing a concern over the loss of a pet bird on July 31!) and carries through September, climaxing with the Marne victory. "The idea of the war lies between my two eyes as a monstrous barrier upon which all my thoughts stumble" is the initial reaction; "the air is full of an abominable anguish" on August 2. Then admiration, as the war begins, for "the skill, the order, the calm and the resolution of all spirits."[10] (Many Frenchmen were heartened by the difference from 1870; old Count Albert de Mun assured them that "nothing that we see today recalls it": then disorganization, defeatism, anxiety as the war began; today the complete opposite.)[11] While a momentary scepticism about "everybody being afraid of seeming to be less a 'good Frenchman' than the others" intrudes, Gide is soon caught up in the war, working for the Red Cross and Belgian relief organizations, questing endlessly for news from the front, and finding Jean Cocteau's frivolous chatter now suddenly rather obscene. (But Cocteau himself was soon driving an ambulance to the front.)

Leon Edel notes that James' letters at this time are "among the most eloquent of all his utterances"; the war energized writers.[12] The tragic sense was not altogether missing—"the plunge of civilization into this abyss of blood and darkness." "What an affliction! How will Europe look, inwardly and outwardly, when it is all over?" Thomas Mann wondered (August 7). But on reflection he was sure that "the

41

German soul will emerge stronger, prouder, freer, happier from it."
Thank God, the soldiers had come to put an end to the rotten old
world, with which we were fed up! "On that never to be forgotten
first day . . . a wave of deep moral feeling overwhelmed us."[13]

Tragedy was tempered by the abundant assurances from sages and
savants that the war would bring about a resurrection, a purification,
a liberation. Such was the faith, and there were few doubters. An
Adolf Hitler, down and out in Munich, would naturally entertain the
hope that "the war would overturn all relationships, all starting
points."[14] Socialists had never forgotten that "war is the midwife of
history," and would in one way or another assuredly hasten the birth
of the revolution. But such nearly rational views do not typify the
mysticism of violence and renewal that flickered behind the August
guns.

A philosopher like George Santayana, whose naturalism had led
him to a quiet despair ("There is eternal war in nature, a war in
which every cause is ultimately lost and every nation destroyed"[15])
and who therefore was neither very surprised nor very aroused by the
war, could still succumb to admiration for the courage of the volunteers, "really wonderful in their disillusioned courage and humble
gallantry."[16] British historian E. L. Woodward noticed this same
simplicity of sacrifice, going to war without "hurrah-patriotism" yet
taking it for granted that one served one's country, while Socialist
editor Robert Blatchford commented on "the absence of bitterness or
anger" among young people going to war.[17] Frenchmen of all political
colors rallied to defend the *Patrie en danger* in 1914. Alain (Émile
Chartier), a Radical and Dreyfusard who had opposed the three-year
service bill, later a critic of war's stupidity (*Mars*), volunteered in 1914
and was happy at the front, serving as a private and rejecting pro-
motion. Among others who made this same gesture of refusing to
fight otherwise than as a common soldier was that most sophisticated,
fastidious, and warlike of British writers H. H. Munro ("Saki") who
volunteered at age forty-four. (He was killed in 1916, a corporal.)

The chiefs of French literary culture included, in addition to
Charles Péguy, Charles Maurras, and Georges Sorel, the leading novel-
ist-statesman Maurice Barrès. Almost unique in combining careers as
writer and member of the Chamber, Barrès at the beginning of the
war through his pieces in *Echo de Paris* brought the atmosphere of
sacred union in the Chamber directly home to the public (August 4):

Fair and good day, perfect in every point, summit of parliamentary perfection! We will never do better; we have only to adjourn until the hour when we will reunite around France victorious.... This day, I will not call it a historic one—every day is that in this era when a new world begins—but I will name it with M. Viviani, with Viviani our adversary of yesterday, today our chief of all and our friend, a sacred day.

The mysticism of sacred union was the most extraordinary aspect of the August spirit, and deserves a careful examination in the light of all that had happened to Europe and the "intellectuals" in the past two decades. That the Right would welcome such "class collaboration" seems more explicable than that the Left would. But Socialists felt it as much as anyone. There were emotional scenes in the French Chamber where Communards and anti-Communards who had not spoken to each other for forty years clasped hands and embraced. "Our petty social divisions and barriers have all been swept away," Kipling exulted in an address of September 8 at Brighton. In celebration of this unity a flow of manifestoes, addresses, pronouncements, open letters—signed by multitudes of writers, scientists, intellectual leaders, professors, teachers—began to appear in pamphlets, in newspapers, in books: the bibliography of such manifestoes is alone matter for a book.[18]

While the Germans were most noted for the ecstasy with which they greeted the recovery of community, this theme was in actuality hardly less evident in England and France: "One beautiful result of the war is the union of hearts," Edmund Gosse reflected in London. Gilbert Murray, the famed classical scholar, whose excess of bellicosity drove Bertrand Russell to distraction, admired "the quickened pulse, the new strength and courage, the sense of brotherhood, the spirit of discipline and self-sacrifice," which doubtless reminded him of the Attic virtues.[19] Disunity—labor, feminist, Irish—there had been in abundance in Britain on the eve to which the war brought welcome surcease. Some noted with satisfaction the "rally of the Empire" as the Dominions, drifting away in recent years, were pulled back toward the center—"a triumphant vindication of the principles which animate the world-amalgam gathered under the British Crown."[20] In Russia, it was equally a commonplace that the war's blessing was its healing of the many divisions within the country, between conservatives and progressives, old and young, intelligentsia and peasantry.

There is a large amount of evidence suggesting that the war was welcomed for reasons other than patriotism, however. Compton Mackenzie was among many who put it simply in terms of excitement:

> Do not suppose that this longing [to get into the war] was inspired by any lofty sentiments of patriotism or even by sympathy with "plucky little Belgium." No, no, it was inspired by the realization that this was the greatest moment in the history of my time and that somehow I must be sharing in the excitement of it.

Mackenzie was one of many who feared the war would be over by February and rushed to avoid getting left out of the fun.[21] "Having grown up in an age of security we longed for dangerous risks, for the extraordinary, for mighty and fearful experiences," Ernst Jünger explained.[22] Peace was the "Establishment," the bourgeois norm to be escaped, the creed of the nodding fathers. If most young people hoped for war, as Alec Waugh reports, it was in the spirit of a great adventure and crusade, expressed in Rupert Brooke's "Now God be thanked who has matched us with this hour." The young German *Wandervögel* were not very patriotic; the *Jugendbewegung* had been fiercely anti-Establishment. The mood of revolutionary ecstasy, aiming to purify a corrupt world by a great consuming fire, was there, but along with it simpler and more personal motives were often the more real. Like Graham Greene, they would rather have blood on their hands than Pilate's water.

Richard Aldington's recruit in *Death of a Hero* says, "I don't care a damn what your cause is—it's almost certainly a foully rotten one. But I do know you're the first real men I've looked upon." Alain-Fournier went eagerly to a war in which he knew he would die because of "a thirst for violent adventure."[23] "I don't want to die for my king and country," Herbert Read wrote from the trenches. "If I do die, it's for the salvation of my own soul."[24] The ultimate expression of this attitude was Yeats' Irish airman, who had no interest in the war at all, did not love those he guarded nor hate those he fought, but was driven to seek his fate somewhere in the clouds by "a lonely impulse of delight" which he balanced against the waste of the years behind and ahead.[25]

Unquestionably, among nonintellectual folk tens of thousands welcomed a chance to break out of their "clipped and limited lives," of which a writer such as H. G. Wells (who had escaped via literature from their dismal ranks) was so painfully aware. Barrès spoke of "their grey monotonous lives," redeemed now, he felt, by their heroism. It was an aspect of the reconciliation of masses and meditators which colored the pathos of "restored community." But the intellectuals too escaped from the boredom of inactive life, joyously rejoining the world of reality in a cause they could accept as both ennobling and healing. Often the war provided an opportunity to escape from some unhappy personal situation, make a break with the past, reach for new horizons of freedom and adventure. It meant, Herbert Read recalled, "a decision: a crystallization of vague projects: an immediate acceptance of the challenge of life. I did not hesitate."[26] Malcolm Muggeridge comments on a point we previously noted, the sense of sexual emancipation that accompanied the war: heroes who "found comfort and recompense in the arms of lovely women."[27] To be sure, there were the reverse cases. Muriel Ciolkowska in *The Egoist*, September 15, 1914, reported the case of a Frenchman near her who killed his child, wounded his wife, and killed himself at the prospect of having to leave them to go to the front; also the suicide of a German about to be expelled, who was married to a Frenchwoman and had lived long in Paris; and the case of a poor German woman in Paris (August 5). (Mistreatment of Germans in France and England was common.)

Arnold Bennett—to take the case of that popular and successful British writer who was to respond eagerly to the war—faced a crisis, as Margaret Drabble describes it in her biography, marked by depression, restlessness, an increasingly unhappy marriage, and a feeling of the triviality of life. He amused himself with his yacht (as D'Annunzio did with his dogs, and Maeterlinck his bees) while his wife joined a golf club. At forty-seven he felt on the decline, his best work behind him; his novel *These Twain* (1913) suggests as much. Not approving of the war at first, by September he was saying, "I haven't been so interested in life since I was born as I am now." He was soon launched on a career as war propagandist.[28] H. G. Wells, too, perennially restless, had quarreled with his Fabian friends, attacked Henry James for his estheticism; he needed, it would seem, some fresh crusade to feed his overflowing energy, and found it in the war he so resolutely championed.

45

II

Possibly more revealing than the enthusiasm of most intellectuals was the silence of those from whom one might have expected resistance, some of whom *later* did criticize the war or the war spirit. Max Brod cites the example of *Die Fackel*, Karl Kraus' widely read journal which was known for its scorching criticism of "bourgeois" hypocrisy, Kraus himself being of course a scion of the wealthy bourgeoisie. A hero of the prewar Viennese intelligentsia, Kraus had specialized since 1900 in exposing corruption, attacking and being attacked by almost everybody, stepping gleefully on every sizable toe in sight. *The Torch's* special foe was the respectable *Neue Freie Presse*, but it spared few sacred cows, major or minor, showing little respect for Herzl's Zionism, Feminists, Freudians, esthetes, anyone with a reputation. But this perennial gadfly, the Viennese Shaw, who had often denounced ultra-nationalism, war, and diplomacy, was silent at the beginning of the war. The satirical thrusts at the war mentality, for which he became famous, did not begin until 1915.

Elsewhere in the German-speaking world, among the avant-garde, the illustrious Berlin Expressionist organ *Der Sturm*, which had an international clientele, said nothing about the war. This was the case also with *The Egoist*, across the North Sea, which after an initial outburst by Miss Weaver against "all this glorification of the fifteen-penny hired cut-throat" (October 1) paid little attention to the war and was absorbed in efforts to get the rest of Joyce's *Portrait of the Artist* through from Trieste (and finding a printer who would print it).[29] The left-of-center *Neue Merkur*, founded just a few months before the war, also shrank from resisting the war spirit.[30]

The well-known writer Herman Hesse, sometimes known as a foe of the war, volunteered (he was rejected) for German military service at the beginning, though he was living then in Switzerland. He apparently did not experience any disillusionment until November, when, much like Shaw and Russell, he objected not so much to the war as to the strident accents in which it was glorified: "O Freunde, nicht diese Töne!"[31] He was careful to affirm his patriotism, and approve of the "moral values of the war," while rebuking his fellow intellectuals for piling inflammatory words on the fire of international hate when they should be trying to dampen it down. The piece drew on his head German denunciations similar to Shaw's in England.

Hesse thereupon lapsed into silence until 1917. Similarly, the potentially disaffected Kurt Tucholsky (alienated, satirical, later the scourge of the Weimar bourgeoisie) did not respond to the 1914 mystique but did not oppose the war during its first year; he simply fell silent.[32]

Those who failed to show enough enthusiasm received the treatment reserved for heretics. Shaw, who held that Great Britain was quite justified in going to war against Germany, and who wrote a (not very good) play (*The Inca of Perusalem*) making fun of the Kaiser and the Junkers, was expelled from clubs and made the target of a parliamentary inquiry simply because he could not shed his customary levity, which at bottom, as usual with Shaw, was a serious point frivolously put: "The War is a Balance of Power war and nothing else." This did not mean it did not have to be fought, but it should be fought without moralizing and even without hate, as Shaw had already argued in a great play, *Caesar and Cleopatra*. That the world is a place where the devil's business must be done without illusions was a viewpoint perhaps far more tragic and certainly more sophisticated than that of those who hastened to greet the final battle of good and evil, in the guise of British democracy versus "Prussian militarism." But the Shavian "cynicism" aroused the same disgust in a solemn hour as Cocteau elicited from Gide. His *Common Sense about the War* (November, 1914) struck almost everyone as wildly uncommonsensical, despite its many concessions to Hun-hating.

The French counterpart to Shaw's case was that of Anatole France, a writer quite as famous and with a similarly Voltairean temperament. France underwent a harrowing experience ending in his total abdication and abject penitence. Long a rhetorical radical who flayed the army and the bourgeoisie, this celebrated literary figure seemed to offer promise of withstanding the war fever. But after an initial *faux pas*, for which he received a storm of censure, France, who presumably could not endure leaving the limelight, capitulated and became as fervent a patriot as any, pouring forth what a biographer calls "a stream of treacly propaganda."[33] In joining a protest against the German bombardment of Reims cathedral—which Shaw, incidentally, refused to sign—France had suggested that his country would never stoop to retaliate but would treat the Germans with gallantry after defeating them. It was this which brought the storm down on his head! France replied to his critics by volunteering to serve at the front (he was seventy). After the war he was to turn leftward again, in the direction of the Communists.

Almost all those who in later years were to claim credit for having resisted the contagion did not do so in August, when it counted. Like Shaw, they disliked the form more than the substance. They were uncomfortable in the presence of such portentous emotionalism, but they did not question the need to fight. This was even true to some extent of Romain Rolland, who from Switzerland attempted to rally the intellectual forces of Europe for peace, the most notable case of war resistance near the beginning of the war. (The famous *Au-dessus de la melée* did not appear until the fall of 1914.) Rolland could not really live up to his appeal to stay "above the battle" (see further below, pp. 153–56). In Germany Professor F. W. Foerster and W. Schücking, later known for their pacifism, "in the first weeks of the war were still thoroughly convinced of the blamelessness of Germany, which so it appeared, was engaged only in a struggle for 'self-preservation' (Schücking) against the 'conspiracy' of her enemies (Foerster)."[34]

Bertrand Russell has earned a reputation as an unremitting foe of the war, on the whole deservedly. Nevertheless, as his biographer Ronald Clark notes, Russell was scarcely a militant opposer in the first few weeks; writing to his mistress, Lady Ottoline Morrell, he expressed a hope that her husband, an MP, would not say anything in Parliament "damaging to our success in the war." By September he was reacting strongly, like Shaw, not so much against the war (a grim necessity) as against the hysterical tide of war propaganda, especially the extreme unfairness to Germany, which shocked his sense of justice. There were others whose acceptance of the war was "sorrowful," like the English social philosopher L. T. Hobhouse, lamenting that "all the great work of social organization that constitutes the progress of 100 years has gone to make the states of Europe more determined adversaries in a more deadly struggle," but who nevertheless saw no option save national defense against attack.[35] Rather different was the course pursued by Keir Hardie, the colorful but erratic labor leader and Socialist MP, something of a working-class hero, whose small Independent Labour party attempted to oppose the war. Shouted down in his own Welsh mining constituency on August 6, subjected to further savage heckling in the ensuing days, Hardie retreated to the extent of agreeing that German troops must be ejected from France and Belgium before peace was possible.[36] (This considerable qualification was adopted also by the "antiwar" Union of Democratic Control to which various discontented spirits, including Russell and Ramsay MacDonald, soon gravitated.) Hardie soon took sick and died, partly perhaps because of this shattering defeat. Much more representative of British working-class opinion was Ben Tillett, who declared that capitalism with all its evils was better than enslavement to Kaiserism.[37]

And indeed the voices of socialist opposition to the war at its beginning were not only few but feeble. This memorable collapse is discussed in a later chapter.

Maxim Gorky signed an appeal from Russian intellectuals accusing the Germans of atrocities and blaming them for starting a war against European civilization. Later he moved to Finland and associated himself with Romain Rolland's position against the war, but not at first. Gorky's countryman Lenin was, of course, in one sense not an enemy of war: welcoming it with glee because it promised to bring revolution in its wake, he advocated not its termination but its conversion into civil war within each country, and quarreled with the Rolland pacifists on this point, as well as with the patriotic "defensists." Rosa Luxemburg suffered a nervous collapse.

Stefan Zweig, the Austrian novelist, was to be known too for his later disenchantment with the war, but he was caught up in the initial excitement. "In spite of my hatred and aversion for war, I should not like to have missed the memory of those first days."[38] Returning to Vienna from a holiday in Belgium, Zweig felt that "although I am not a soldier of the first line I do not want to be missing in these days." "Most of our poets, from Hofmannsthal on, are already in national service. May God protect Germany." Unable to qualify for service in the field, this most international of persons took up information work, defended the German bombardment of Reims, and did not turn against the war until the spring of 1915. He explained that he felt no qualms about the chastisement of his beloved France, since it would do her good, and broke cleanly with his longtime friend the distinguished Belgian writer Émile Verhaeren.

Robert Graves, in his classic memoir *Goodbye to All That*, notes that Siegfried Sassoon did not oppose the war in the beginning, as is the case also with that great poet who, before being killed, ironically, just hours before the 1918 Armistice, wrote of the war's pity and horror: Wilfred Owen. England's poets marched away gladly though they might seek, as did Edward Thomas, editor of the anthology *This*

49

England (1915), to distinguish their private, poetic patriotism from the public kind of the "fat patriots" (see his memoir, *The Last Sheaf*).

III

Approbation for the war extended broadly throughout the range of writers, artists, scholars, scientists; Left, Right, and Center, the tough and the tender-minded alike, outcasts and public figures. The war made a special appeal to poetic temperaments. It was in fact to be "a poet's war." (The war brought "a tremendous consumption of new poetry," Frank Swinnerton observes.) With Rupert Brooke leading the way in England, Péguy and Alain-Fournier in France, Richard Dehmel and Ernst Lotz in Germany, the writers marched off to war in an extraordinary manifestation of the death wish. Brooke, Péguy, Alain-Fournier, and Lotz died early in the war, becoming its most famous literary martyrs. Dehmel won fame for insisting on front-line service at the age of fifty-one (and fighting bravely). (Mahler and Richard Strauss had set this popular poet's songs to music; he tried to become the poet laureate of the war.) Brooke's "Come and die, it will be such fun" was the echo of an appealing literary tradition. Charles Sorley, killed in 1915, wrote

> Pour your gladness on earth's head
> So be merry, so be dead.

This was an echo of that passionate ode to death, Péguy's "Éve," with its incantatory "Happy are they who die" (happy as the ripe corn and the harvested grain, if they die in a just war).

It was from observations during the war that Freud got his seemingly curious conception of a death wish, Thanatos to pair against Eros. For a young poet in 1914, death and love were much the same thing. Alain-Fournier wrote of being in love with life because he knew he would die. Ernst Jünger, who became a hopeless addict to the mysticism of battle (and thus contributed something to the later Nazification of Germany), used a vocabulary of religiosity tinged with both sexual and apocalyptic tones: the war as a red storm, a soaring flight toward Eros, a hammer blow smashing the old world and heralding the dawn of a new one in ecstasy. Julian Grenfell declared that "one loves one's fellow man so much more when one is bent on killing him"; and Apollinaire "turns no-man's land into a vast erogenous zone," the author of a book about the French avant-garde poet remarks.[39]

Among other European artists, Stefan George's disciples saw the war as the fulfillment of the master's prophecies, especially in *Stern des Bundes* (1913): "Tens of thousands must perish in the holy war" to cure the soul's sickness. Friedrich Gundolf wrote on October 10 of "the dream of evolution of the German spirit and the spiritual evolution of the German nation" being fulfilled through the war. August 4 seemed a *Schicksalwende*, the end of one era and the start of another.[40]

Previously mentioned were the enthusiasms of Scriabin, Berg, and Stravinsky, who welcomed the war as "necessary for human progress."[41] Among other musicians, Erik Satie as a corporal must have been a match for Berg, who suffered a nervous breakdown soon after joining the Austrian army. Saint-Saens saw a chance to attack Wagner. Claude Debussy said he'd offer his face to be bashed in if it was necessary for victory. Burlyuk, the Russian Futurist, given to bizarre dress and ornamentation (such as a bird painted on his cheek), now organized lectures on war and art, while Kandinsky and Kokoschka almost stopped painting, the former returning to Russia from Germany as a passionate patriot, the latter entering the Austrian army. So it went in all the warring countries. Somerset Maugham joined the Red Cross ambulance service, later worked in espionage, found his long-time homosexual lover on the Flanders front.[42] The frivolous Edwardian novelist Reggie Turner sought Home Guard service at the age of forty-four.[43] The sober *Manchester Guardian* editor, C. E. Montague, enlisted at forty-seven after dyeing his gray hair.

If poets, novelists, musicians, and artists proved surprisingly war-like, they were scarcely more so than their more pedagogical brethren. Albert Einstein was reported by Rolland as claiming that "the mathematicians, doctors and the exact sciences are tolerant; the historians and the arts faculties stir up nationalistic passions."[44] The first clause is questionable, but it is certainly true that historians and sociologists were among the more aggressively belligerent. Practically all the high priests of German professorship responded with immense enthusiasm to the war and supported it with their pens, gladly turning from scholarship to propaganda. Erich Marks' *Wo Stehen Wir?* (1914) set the tone: "We have never felt with such intensity and power the holiness of the great-power grounds of our existence." Karl Lamprecht

51

spoke of "this marvelous upsurge of our national soul"; "happy are those who have lived in a time such as this."[45] Friedrich Meinecke, Hans Delbrück, and Max Weber led a small group among German historians and political scientists who during the war urged moderation in the name of realism on such issues as annexation and U-boat warfare; the large majority of their fellow savants remained true to the "ideas of 1914" in opposing any loss of nerve or weakening of will, thus supporting annexationism, war to the utmost, refusal of peace terms, and internally, refusal of democratizing tendencies. The moderates were by no means opposed to the war, and indeed they responded as enthusiastically as any in the initial stages. "No matter what the outcome will be, this war is great and wonderful," Max Weber thought; evidently it was a cure for the psychological malady that had plagued the great social scientist. "The war seemed to him a worthwhile experience because it evoked the supremely noble qualities of which men are capable when caught in a crisis situation, revealed in patriotism, in battle, in the spirit of fellowship, and in unity at home."[46] Though previously an Anglophile, Friedrich Tönnies was enthusiastically prowar; like others, including Henri Bergson, he succeeded in relating the issues of the war to his own key concepts: Germany represented *Gemeinschaft*, England *Gesellschaft*.[47] (Durkheim reversed this equation in France, finding anomie in scientific-technological Germany.)

British historians were equally patriotic. Six Oxford modern historians collaborated early in the war to argue their country's case in *Why We Are at War*, and historians continued to participate in war propaganda. Lowes Dickinson thought the defection of the historians the most disillusioning part of the whole affair, E. M. Forster reported in his biography of Dickinson. R. H. Tawney, radical and socialist as he was, "thought a war against oligarchic, militarist Germany clarified and sharpened the challenge to build social democracy in England."[48] A sergeant in the war, he was wounded at the Somme; he wrote many war pieces, mostly to urge democratic and socialist war aims. In a *mea culpa* passage of his *Experiences* (1969), Arnold J. Toynbee, who elsewhere records that he felt his civilized world "shattered by a thunderbolt" in August, 1914, recalls that

> In the First World War, almost all of us, in both camps, were not only whole-heartedly belligerent; we were also naively sure that

our cause—whichever of the two it happened to be—was one hundred per cent righteous . . . .

Toynbee was responsible for several volumes of "atrocity propaganda," which he later regretted. He eventually embarked upon his massive study of the causes of the decline of civilizations partly because, incapacitated for war service by an illness, he felt impelled to atone for thus being spared a death that met many of his schoolmates and colleagues. A similar motive operated in the case of Harold Laski, the Socialist historian and political theorist.

Among French historians, Marc Bloch rose to the rank of captain and received the Legion of Honor, anticipating his courage and martyrdom in World War II. Charles Seignobos and Ernest Lavisse stayed home to write much tendentious commentary. Albert Mathiez, Socialist historian of the French Revolution, volunteered but was physically disqualified, then wrote material on the war marked by an extreme anti-Germanism, shared by another Socialist scholar Charles Andler. Mathiez "attacked not only the Imperial Government, which had plotted the war, but the Germans as a people."[49] Born for slavery, they respect only force. Famous for his sympathetic study of Robespierre, Mathiez held up the 1792–94 "nation in arms" under the "Terror" as a model for wartime France. Along with Lavisse, a tireless propagandist who assailed the Rollandists in *La Revue de Paris* and insulted Germans at the Peace Conference in 1919, the most ardent producer of war propaganda among French historians was Alphonse Aulard. Prior to 1914 Aulard was viewed as a model of "objective" historical writing, an epitome and leader of the academic experts who spurned dilettantes and ideologists, directed austere doctoral dissertations by the score, and claimed history was at last becoming truly scientific.

Émile Durkheim, *doyen* of French sociologists and one of the world's most eminent intellectual figures, thought the war would accomplish his cherished goal of "reviving the sense of community."[50] Shattered by the loss of his son, Durkheim died during the war but had not lost his faith in it. Younger than the veteran Durkheim, a noted Italian historian and sociologist of the future, Carlo Antoni, volunteered and was wounded in the war. It is interesting to imagine a wartime symposium, if such had been thinkable, in which Durkheim and Antoni, say, debated Max Weber and Friedrich Tönnies, or

Richard Tawney and Albert Mathiez did verbal battle with Karl Lamprecht and Friedrich Meinecke. The tragedy was that the war severed virtually all such contacts.

It almost goes without saying that the clergy followed suit in enthusiastic war spirit. The whole atmosphere of perfervid idealism mixed with images of apocalypse and self-righteousness invited religious rhetoric, which was forthcoming in copious quantities. The Church, too, was bored and avid for some exciting role. Bishop John Percival's recognition of the Allies as "the preordained instruments to save the Christian civilization of Europe from being overcome by a brutal and ruthless paganism" was a representative British utterance.[51] There were eschatological visions: "We felt astir with the pressure and the heat of those tremendous forces by which the energy of God is always driving our human story forward toward its great culmination." The favorite theme of national unity stirred clerical responses: bickering brethren miraculously reunited, women and men, Ireland and England, employers and employees, were pleasing to contemplate. Physical force, pastors were at pains to make clear, when "charged with moral energy" is "transfigured," becoming paradoxically a little like love (a parallel here to the poets' love and death).[52] The Regius Professor of Divinity at Oxford explained that Prussianism was in fact the Devil. British clergymen were appalled at the *Appeal to Evangelical Churches Abroad* issued by eighty German theologians in September, 1914, bearing such well-known names as Harnack and Eucken, which pictured Germany as defending Christian civilization against Russian barbarism; the Anglican reply, *To the Christian Scholars of Europe and America*, enlisted a battery of divines headed by the Archbishop of Canterbury to retort that Louvain proved who the barbarians were (Reims was then yet to come).

Albert Marrin, author of a monograph on the Church of England in the war, cannot identify a single pacifist then in this congregation, though many were to become known for it later. A few among the dissenters, especially the Quakers, certainly were, George Lansbury being one; the tiny handful of conscientious objectors were drawn from Adventists, Jehovah's Witnesses, Plymouth Brethren, Christadelphians, along with some Quakers, a majority of whom supported the war. The Church Militant, scouring the ungodly, defending the weak and helpless, putting down the overmighty, was well-entrenched within Biblical Christianity. And Fundamentalists were quick to note that the subversive "higher criticism" of the Bible had long had its center in Germany. British ministers were among the leaders in uncovering the heinous ideological crimes of that famous unholy trinity so incessantly cited during the war as proof of German guilt: Nietzsche, Treitschke, and Bernhardi. Shaw recalled "ferociously bellicose clergymen" recruiting in Trafalgar Square. And, according to Maurice Bowra, the Principal of Cheltenham School preached powerful sermons on the Christian duty to fight, arguing that "though our Lord might not have wished to be a combatant, he would at least have joined the RAMC [Medical Corps]." Arthur Marwick records a minister invoking the "terrible wrath" of Christ against iniquity—"the wrath of the Lamb." An American, James Stevens, later recalled army chaplains who exhorted soldiers to "sweep the hellishness of the Huns from God's beautiful earth."[53]

Claudel saw France awaiting the Day of Resurrection during the great battles of the first few months.[54] Ernst Troeltsch treated belief in the high value of *Deutschtum* as equivalent to belief in God's divine order.[55] Religion flourished during the war, under the influence of what is widely reported as a generally more serious mood, marked by more reading and attention to cultural events as well as church-going. There were many conversions, such as Max Scheler's to Catholicism (which he repudiated after the war). The Chestertons, Gilbert and Cecil, depicted a deeply pious, Catholic French peasantry assaulted by Prussian paganism; Shaw noted how "absurdly fictitious" this was while admiring the prose in which it was presented. In Protestant Germany, of course, the reversed image revealed Lutheran piety confronted with godless, cynical Frenchmen. "The theologians unanimously pronounced Germany innocent of having plotted the war," declaring England to be the villain. In this and in other themes they developed, German theologians seemed to repeat and parallel the arguments of other, secular writers; thus, they stressed German heroes versus low-minded British tradesmen (*Helden und Haendler*), and debated annexationism, a liberal group headed by Troeltsch and Harnack opposing the extreme annexationists.[56] There were few strictly clerical ideas; religion, or at any rate morality, had grown secular. The 1914 ideas were holistic, cutting across boundaries of thought to unite all manner of people—evidence of their role as communitarian healers of a divided society desperately seeking to regain wholeness. That religious moods and words found their way into lay prophecy is evident in the case of D'Annunzio, among others—images of salvation, of Italy as the suffering mother; consecration, holiness, martyrdom. This quasi-Christian language of sacrifice and redemption became common political coinage throughout the war (and suffered a considerable debasement).

Even those who opposed the war, it is interesting to note, were drawn in a religious direction. Bertrand Russell, who reported that his call to resist the spirit of war came "as if I heard the voice of God," described his attraction to religion in *Principles of Social Reconstruction*, written during the war: "By contact with what is eternal, by devoting our life to bringing something of the Divine into this troubled world, we can make our lives creative . . . ." The war brought out a religious feeling even in the normally antireligious. H. G. Wells at this time departed from his socialism and positivism to venture in search of *God the Invisible King*: Mr. Britling undergoes such a conversion in *Mr. Britling Sees It Through*, another of Wells' wartime books. During the war, Arthur Conan Doyle became a convert to Spiritualism, convinced that death was "a most glorious improvement upon life."

There was profound religious meditation at the front in cases such as Fr. Teilhard de Chardin, whose war journal is filled with it, or Jacques Rivière, while prisoner of war (see his *Carnets 1914–1917*). A German Jesuit who later became a notable foe of the Nazis lost a leg in World War I and never regretted his patriotism.[57]

In Germany the first surge of feeling for solidarity drew Jews closer to the national community and diminished anti-Semitism.[58] Jews were among the most passionately patriotic; the author of the wildly popular "Hate Song against England" was a Jewish poet, Ernst Lissauer, and among signers of the German Manifesto were Paul Ehrlich, Max Reinhardt, Fritz Haber, and a number of other Jewish cultural figures. The well-known lawyer Max Bodenheimer and the sociologist Franz Oppenheimer headed a German committee for the liberation of the Russian Jews, which young Martin Buber joined. "All Jewish groups issued patriotic declarations" and many prominent Jewish leaders in pledging total support for the war expressed the hope that, in Walther Rathenau's words, "a purer peace of inner sincerity will be reached and a new life, strong, charitable and united" will be founded. It is doubtful if Germany could have stayed in the war as long as she did without the brilliant services of Rathenau and other Jews. In the end the results were disappointing to the Jews, for hyperpatriotism unleashed some anti-Semitism, but in the beginning at least the fatherland front or sacred union embraced Jew as well as Christian—this was also the case in France. French Jews rallied enthusiastically to the defense of the country, as the formerly anti-Semitic Maurice Barrès welcomed them into the sacred union and Leon Bloy was converted to philo-Semitism (*Jeanne d'Arc et l'Allemagne*, 1915). Of 190,000 Jews in France and Algeria, 46,000 were mobilized, of whom 14,000 were volunteers; 6,500 were killed. This compares with 85,000 German Jews mobilized and 10,000 killed. Among the most enthusiastic greeters of the war was young Martin Buber, to whom it seemed a "wonderful" moment.[59] And it is well known how ardently scientist Chaim Weizmann served the Allied cause, forming that friendship with the British Foreign Secretary which eventuated in the fateful Balfour Declaration supporting a Palestine homeland for the Jews.

Karl Barth, who was then a Christian Socialist, accepted the war as the inscrutable justice of God. Doubtless the Church at Rome did too; but it could not offer support to either side of a war in which its members were in both camps. It did not oppose the war as such, but adopted neutrality; it did oppose Italian entrance, for which it was vigorously denounced in Italy.

Needless to repeat that the war as apocalypse ran through everyone's mind. Visions of destruction abounded in the years before the war; at least, it is striking to read Georg Heym's *Der Krieg* or Stefan George's *Der Stern des Bundes*, or Leon Bloy, or the Russians, from Solovyëv to Merezhkovsky and Blok, predicting red war, pale rider, doom and destruction, the coming of the Cossacks and the Holy Ghost. These prophecies seem almost uncanny at times: consider Solovyëv's little man with a black mustache who will come to pick up the pieces. Oswald Spengler began his *Untergang des Abendlandes* three years *before* the war. This image of apocalyptic decline and fall, prelude perhaps to a total renewal, was an almost archetypal image for Westerners; secularized by Vico, Gibbon, Marx, and Nietzsche, it was still basically religious.

Scientific objectivity broke down at the beginning of the war. Fellows of the Royal Society in England demanded removal of all Germans and Austrians from its list. Arthur Koestler cites a British naturalist who said "I have bound myself to ignore everything published in Germany after July 14, 1914." Émile Picard of the French

Academy of Science declared that none of the great scientific discoveries had been made by Germans, all had come from Latins or Anglo-Saxons; the zoologist Delage called the Germans a physically inferior race.[60]

Mathiez, the French historian, was one who stressed that the total intellectual resources of the community must be mobilized for the war.[61] Scientists in the warring countries responded by devoting themselves to military-related research, including poison gas. In his memoirs (*Experiences*), Arnold J. Toynbee meditates on the paradox of his benevolent uncle, Percy Frankland, devoting his scientific talents to this end, Frankland being especially noted for his fervent belief that science would be the salvation of humanity. It was a common belief in this era of missionary scientism, and perhaps for this very reason scientists proved among the most uncritical crusaders in the 1914 war. The recent biography of H. G. J. Moseley, who died at Gallipoli, records the not unusual case of a scientist who "rushed headlong into the firing line with an overwhelming sense of duty that will itself no doubt soon require a footnote of explanation."[62] No explanation was needed in 1914. An American who tried to promote international scientific cooperation during the war found it impossible; French scientists refused to sit at the same table with German scientists. The breach was not healed until well after the war.[63] So much for the vaunted internationalism and objectivity of the hard sciences.

IV

This sundering of international intellectual communication took place all along the line. The war ruptured friendships, of course, or interrupted them, breaking those many threads which bound together the thinking community of Europe. "The civilized world is to be regarded as now being, for intellectual and spiritual purposes, one great confederation, bound to a joint action and working to a common result," Matthew Arnold had written in 1865. Europe's intellectual and spiritual movements were all profoundly transnational: not only science but socialism, philosophy, literature, and art had their common problems, trends, and themes which draw people together. Symbolist poets or Futurist artists spoke the same esthetic if not the same tribal language, from Dublin to Moscow. And of course educated Europeans normally knew more than one language. Max Weber worked up Russian so he could understand that absorbing event the 1905 revolution, adding it to his numerous other languages. At the other extreme, Hendrik de Man later noted as one of the limits of socialist internationalism that in all his many years of attending international meetings he had only once heard a workingman speaking in a language other than his own. Whatever the average of linguistic versatility, there were certainly many close international friendships.

Stefan Zweig, who just before the war was working on a study of Dickens, Balzac, and Dostoyevsky (*Three Masters* across the European board), was a close friend of Émile Verhaeren's, the Belgian Symbolist whom he had visited, and whose work he had translated. The intellectual world in which Zweig in common with other writers of his generation had grown up was dominated by Nietzsche, Rilke, George; by his fellow Viennese of this golden age, Mahler; by Hofmannsthal, Schnitzler; and also by the French poets Baudelaire, Mallarmé, Valéry, whose word had gone all over the Continent; by the Scandinavians Strindberg and Ibsen; by Dostoyevsky the Russian.[64] To Zweig, who almost constantly traveled, European culture did not quite include England (he was at home in Paris but not London) but extended over the whole Continent.

The Belgian historian Henri Pirenne, soon imprisoned by the Germans (he was able to write his *History of Europe* in confinement, the lack of notes to consult proving an advantage to synthesis!), broke relations with historian friends Karl Lamprecht, Fritz Arnheim, and others; he refused to answer M. R. Hoeniger's knock.[65] "Of all the people in the war the one I care for much the most is an enemy," Bertrand Russell remarked, with Ludwig Wittgenstein in mind. The man who was to become the greatest of twentieth-century philosophers came to England from Vienna to study engineering before the war, was drawn to Russell, and with his encouragement turned to philosophy; years later he would return to Oxford and Cambridge. Given the attitudes of most other British philosophers, including Whitehead and McTaggart, and of the Cambridge which deprived Russell of his fellowship during the war, it is more than doubtful if Wittgenstein would have been welcome there between 1914 and 1919 even had he been able to escape the Austrian army. (The war evidently left its mark on Wittgenstein, contributing to his career as a Tolstoyan for several years after the war when he became a simple village school-teacher and thought about joining a monastery.)

There were those to whom the war came easily in terms of their international intellectual predilections. Arnold Bennett, married to a Frenchwoman, had always been a Francophile, frequently visiting Paris where Gide and Ravel were his intimates, and introducing French writers to the British public. This posture was fashionable in Edward's era when *entente cordiale* feeling accompanied a growing estrangement from Germany. Yet there were many analogues to the Russell-Wittgenstein friendship; married to a German, D. H. Lawrence was to suffer agonies of ambivalence during the war. On August 3 Bernard Shaw had telegraphed Siegfried Trebitsch in Vienna appealing for a common front against the Russian menace.[66] Nietzsche and Wagner were as popular in France as Baudelaire and Mallarmé were in Austria; the world of culture was nonnational. During the war Maurice Ravel had to resist a call to boycott all German music, while pointing out that there was really only one living German composer who counted for much (Richard Strauss); to have proposed such a ban before 1914, needless to say, would have shocked and astonished. In 1914 the powerful pull of national loyalties—wild animals drawing together in time of danger—tore apart the ties that had bound Europe's men of thought together around common programs and common interests. And in the great majority of instances they accepted this erasure of personal attachments without murmur, in the interests of their national community.

—4—

The Revolt against Intellect

I

Movements in philosophical thought roughly matched the sensational developments in the arts during the two decades prior to 1914. To a lesser degree only than Nietzsche, Henri Bergson shaped the *Zeitgeist* and moved the writers to whose quest for the deeper mysteries via art-as-magic his thought bore a near relationship. To his contemporaries Bergson appeared as a liberator from the shackles of a grim scientific materialism and determinism, promising freedom, openness, creativity. "Bergson's teaching . . . supplied his hearers with the possibility of metaphysical work and unmasked the sophisms on which the mechanistic and materialistic theories of the day were founded.... Bergson brought us poetry and mystic intuition, vindicated freedom and idealism, freed the stream of consciousness . . . freeing the mind from matter and insisting on its creative powers."[1] Thus the British literary scholar Enid Starkie, who studied at the Sorbonne around the turn of the century, remembered it. Charles Péguy wrote that "the Bergsonian revolution is installed at the heart and secret of the present," bursting through the barriers of mechanism and of materialism; "it alone has freed us . . . from all our servitudes."[2] Similar tributes to Bergson as liberator into spirituality appear in the memoirs of Étienne Gilson and Jacques Maritain. Though less harsh, less shocking than those other "irrationalists" Nietzsche and Freud, Bergson with his unpredictable "life force" electrified people accustomed to the reign of positivism and the demise of religion. Indeed, Georges Guy-Grand detected in the disciples of Bergson a sort of lyrical insanity, celebrating the chaos of things in "orgies of subjectivism" (he mentioned Albert Bazailles and Alphonse Chide).[3]

Colin Wilson observes that George Bernard Shaw's plays "are all about the same theme: the obscure creative drive of the 'Life Force,' and the way it makes people do things they find difficult to understand in terms of everyday logic." Intelligence, the least interesting portion of the human mind, is turned toward inert matter; it is useful, but superficial; it cannot reach the inwardness of life. Instinct is turned toward life, and through intuition—"instinct that has become disinterested, self-conscious, capable of reflecting on its object and of enlarging it indefinitely"—we may be led to "the very inwardness of life," which is fluid motion, undissected will, the source of the artist's inspiration: the *élan vital*.

The Germans called it the *Lebensphilosophie*. But this surrender of the mere calculating reason to the pulsating force of life as a great throbbing development which cannot be predicted or controlled, but only appreciated and responded to, was nothing peculiarly German. It was an integral part of the *Zeitgeist*. Probably its ultimate sources were Schopenhaur and Nietzsche more than any other individuals, but these sages, after all, were international in their appeal, as well known in France or Russia as in Germany. A rage for Wagner swept France in the late 1880's and early 1890's, leading to a *Revue wagnerienne* and a strong musical influence even on the young Debussy. Maurice Barrès was Wagnerian in 1886–87. Nietzsche attracted many French disciples.[4] Shaw championed both German worthies in England, while the young Yeats felt the fire of Zarathustra as keenly in Ireland as Gide did in France, or Franz Kafka in Prague. A veritable Nietzsche rage swept England from 1904 to 1914, a few years later than in Russia.[5]

Though Nietzsche and Bergson might claim priority, the revolution was too big to belong to any one person or school. Of Nietzsche's corrosive aphorisms a great French writer said, "The influence of Nietzsche preceded for us the appearance of his work, which fell on ground already prepared . . . it did not surprise but confirm." This remark of André Gide's may be compared with D'Annunzio's, that he was without knowing it Nietzschean before he read Nietzsche, and with many other remarks of this sort. Nietzsche was a prophet precisely because he said so well what was lying inarticulate in countless minds. As Chesterton put it irreverently, "He had a remarkable power of saying things that master the reason for a moment by their gigantic unreasonableness"—a real tribute from the master of paradox who seldom agreed with anyone. "Nobody is more representative of the spirit of the age."[6]

"Our intellect—what a very small thing on the surface of ourselves!" Maurice Barrès' exclamation reflected the spirit of the age. Perhaps inadvertently, the very nineteenth century against which the new age announced its revolt had prepared the way for this irrationalism. Schopenhauer had simply substituted Will for Hegel's Reason as the universal potency. Marx had explained that "false consciousness" traps most thinkers in error, their alleged truths of reason being only more or less disguised apologies for oppression. Darwin had shown that the struggle for existence, imposing its iron rule on everything, makes ideas, makes reason itself, into tools with adaptive value—at least, this pragmatist conclusion seemed inescapable on Darwinian premises. Sigmund Freud was revealing the obscure infantile scandals that shape the conscious mind, beneath which lies buried an immense and uncontrollable mass of unconscious determinants. Vilfredo Pareto went Marx one better by refusing to exempt the Marxists, identifying *all* political thought as nonrational. The Italian tried to save science and engineering for "logic"; but the strange events in physics stemming from the Michelson-Morley experiment and radiation phenomena in the Einstein-Planck era (which began as early as the 1890's and was reaching the general public by 1905) cast doubt on pillars of certainty once thought unassailable.

Beginning a little before 1890 in some places, a rebellion against scientific positivism and "naturalism" occurred as a kind of generation reaction, the result of the defects of these once potent Victorian gods. There were many landmarks. One was the rich if confusing impulses arising from Richard Wagner, whose *Bayreuther Blätter* began in 1880 to proclaim the vital connections between religion and art. Wagner's poet-priest was a strange creature, vegetarian, part Indian mystic, part socialist but a great deal nationalist, Christian yet fond of pagan gods and heroes; a tribute to the eclecticism of the spiritual urges that Europe began to feel at this time. (Gustav Mahler and George Bernard Shaw were among those who joined Wagner in expecting salvation through vegetable consumption.) Before long Yeats, whose father was antireligious, was celebrating ancient Irish heroes in verse and would soon join the Hermetic Society; the French Symbolist poets would launch their manifesto at the school of Zola (1885), which they accused of making man into a cog in a blindly functioning world machine. Nicholas Berdyaev with reference to "forerunners of the era of the spirit" mentioned the Russians Tolstoy and Dostoyevsky along with Solovyëv and two Frenchmen, Péguy and Leon Bloy. Martin Buber added the Dane Kierkegaard to Dostoyevsky and Nietzsche as "pathfinders of a new culture."

It was perhaps Nietzsche's most significant contribution that he infused this vegetarian-Christian-mystical mixture (which included much abnegating Orientalism, such as Annie Besant's Theosophy) with a sterner spirit. "Be hard" was an injunction all bona fide Nietzscheans took to heart, as they scorned milk-and-water religion, the slave morality of weaklings. Max Zerbst testified in 1892 to his desire for a new god, "but not one who sits enthroned in the stars, rather a fresh happy Earth God, a Siegfried of the spiritual kingdom, a powerful exuberant dragon-slayer."[7] He found it, he adds, in Friedrich Nietzsche. Horrifying to some, the call to a new barbarism electrified free spirits of the younger generation from about 1890 to 1910. Nietzsche succeeded in making idealism exciting by tying it not to meekness and mildness (or to ethereal Symbolist bluebirds) but to the opposite, a tough-minded spiritual rebellion that battered down the conventional virtues—a true "transvaluation of values." "Nietzsche is for spirited mountain climbers and daredevils."[8] Timid intellectuals took heart and began to think of themselves as toreadors of the soul.

Though Wagner was a pacifist and Nietzsche an internationalist, many of those deeply moved by both seem to have extracted nationalism from Wagner and militarism from Nietzsche. Wagner was not an advocate of war, which he attacked in a debate with the crown prince of war himself, von Moltke. But the young Wagnerians and Nietzscheans were by no means in agreement on this point. "Yes, Moltke is right," one of them declared. "War is a source of the most noble power. Civilization does not make it dispensable, it makes it necessary."[9] *Sagengesellschäfte* sought to re-create the life of ancient gods and heroes as embodied in myths. In England, old John Ruskin tried to found an order based on medieval chivalry. The heroic life might be one of peaceful service to humanity. But Nietzsche broke with Wagner (confusingly enough) on the issues of nationalism and pacifism, the younger man rejecting both: to be *Reichsdeutsch* was simply too gross, but to be a Christian and a vegetarian was also hopelessly bourgeois—life must be more daring, more radical, more disabused than this.

Many young people who responded to both these electrifying intellectual personalities did not apparently pay much attention to their quarrel, but embraced both in a spirit of vague excitement and rebellion, looking for targets to strike, great deeds to do, noble impulses to fulfill. They performed a marriage between Wagnerian nationalism and Nietzschean violence, taking what a latter era would regard as the worst in both (as Lenin has been said to have married the worst parts of Populism and Marxism).

In Nietzschean imagery the energizing force is of course Dionysus, emblem of violent, antisocial primitive energy emanating from the will-to-power, which to be sure must unite with Apollonian reason to bring forth the greatest art. But the power in each of us is a radiant selfishness which realizes our potential in throwing off the shackles of conformity and timidity. And since there is no God or purpose in the universe, we must manufacture our own meanings. Scorning the herd mind along with all the means whereby cattle become masters, such as the popular press and parliamentary government, Nietzsche equally hated a "bovine nationalism," which uses the state, enemy of free spirits, as its instrument. Yet the stress on heroic struggle and hardness opened the way among disciples, almost inevitably lesser people than the master, for martial crusades.

In any case, they rejected thought which is cerebral, objective, and uncommitted, its "cold prying tentacles" draining the lifeblood out of Western civilization. There is another kind of thought, which Carl Jung in 1910 distinguished from logical, i.e., verbal thinking; he called it "analogical" thinking, which is "archaic, unconscious, not put into words and hardly formulable in words."[10] (Yeats' rooted aristocratic families, dignified by inbred values, "high, solitary and most stern," are almost inarticulate.)

"I have always considered myself a voice of what I believe to be a greater renaissance—the revolt of the soul against the intellect—now beginning in the world," Yeats wrote in 1892.[11] The warfare of soul and intellect—"The mind as the soul's enemy"—was the watchword of Ludwig Klages and the Stefan George circle, in prewar Germany. Graf Christian von Krackow named the George circle along with the

Youth Movement and the *Lebensphilosophie* as three prongs of "the struggle against bourgeois society" manifested before 1914.[12] But in truth these three things were blended into one. The *Lebensphilosophie* was a general term vaguely encompassing Nietzsche, Bergson, and Dilthey, joined in the 1900's by the Dilthey-Nietzsche disciple Max Scheler, who had perhaps learned from Husserl the phenomenologist philosopher; it could include William James and the American pragmatists. The common denominator was an impulse to cut through the crust of intellectual concepts to make contact directly with being, a goal also, we know, of most of the modernist artists of the era.

For many, a closely related theme was the reproach against the bourgeoisie, or something representing present-day rationalized and mechanized society. Its crime was inducing the "false consciousness" of abstractness (the impersonality of the market, alienation, reification). A popular German representative of this fashionable Life Philosophy, Rudolf Eucken, who predictably hailed the war in 1914 as "a mighty spiritual movement," was then internationally known, his works translated into English by the dozen; he visited and lectured in Great Britain and the United States (there was an Eucken club in the U.S.).[13] No one was better equipped to present the intellectual fashions of the hour. From Eucken, Max Scheler learned that the spiritual level is autonomous, must be grasped on its own terms and not reduced to some physical or biological source. Among other fountainheads of *Lebensphilosophie*, Wilhelm Dilthey, who died in 1911, was a historian of ideas, a student of life, an impassioned controversialist from whose vast corpus of writings (much fragmentary and unpublished) emerged the idea that life is too vast and deep for our puny thoughts. In historical thought he was the leading figure in the "revolt against positivism" which attempted to reclaim the human studies from those who would distort them into the mold of the physical sciences. The rules for *Geisteswissenschaften* cannot be the same as those of the *Naturwissenschaften*; not general laws of external behavior but intuitive knowledge of unique internal states is the former's goal.[14] (It is true that Dilthey later moved somewhat away from the stress on *Erlebnis* or reenactment of the subjective experience as the only true form of historical knowledge, as did Max Weber, to seek more objective canons.) This *Methodenstreit* filled a large place in German intellectual history at the end of the nineteenth century; but in general the result was a feeling for "the relativity of every his-

66

torical form of life," and of all ideas, none of which can claim absolute validity, each being a peculiar, unrepeatable product of its time and place. With Croce and Gentile, with Bergson, with the British philosopher Samuel Alexander, one conceived reality as an unending dialectical process, perhaps a progress in the sense of developing ever richer and fuller forms of human consciousness. Reality is inexhaustible, everything is related to everything else in infinite ways, as F. H. Bradley pointed out. Empirical reality is indeed "incommensurable," immense beyond counting.

The historian, as Vico had declared, being a man, can understand what man has created; he is not left in subjective chaos. But as a creature himself of the process he is trying to describe, he can never hope to present more than one perspective, condemned soon to obsolescence; there is no absolute observation point. The meanings of the past, chameleonlike, shift and change with each passing hour and each differing observer, who looks partly into a mirror which gives him back his own image. What we can do, giving up any simple-minded search for a single pattern or meaning in history, is to admire all this richness and wait to see what miracles it will conjure up next for our admiration.

To these historicist and creative evolutionary strains, the philosophical school of phenomenology was somewhat related. Edmund Husserl's *Logische Untersuchungen* (1900–1901) contained in its second volume a polemic against psychologism. The *données*, as Bergson would call them, of our intuition are far richer than, and may not be reduced to, classifiable and logically ordered patterns of behavior. (But even psychology in this era, headed by the once celebrated, now largely forgotten Wilhelm Wundt, was far more introspective than it has since become under the sway of American and Russian behaviorists. So too was German sociology.) The study of philosophy is "spirit," which cannot be reduced to biology. It is true that Husserl initially wished to escape from the trap of historical relativism by discovering the structure of the pure consciousness divorced from all specific content. He thought one might, by a heroic purging of the mind, make a kind of exact science of these *données* which may be the same for all consciousness—an enterprise which may be compared with Carl Jung's search for the archetypes of the collective unconscious, or with Kant's quest for the *a priori* element in thought—raised, however, beyond the level of formal, rational logic to a kind of grammar of motives. The enterprise failed, and phenomenology subsequently took on irrational-ist and existentialist interests in the concrete "life worlds" of specific individuals and situations.

A phenomenologist for the hour, interesting to us especially be-cause of his impassioned paean to war in 1914, was Max Scheler, a student of Dilthey's, the sociologist Georg Simmel (at Berlin), and Eucken (at Jena). Scheler's 1897 doctorate argued that ethics, the moral life, cannot be reduced to logic: the true and the good are sepa-rate realms. Scheler's life matched his philosophy: it was a restless one marked by defiance of authority. He was fired at Munich in 1910 as the result of a personal life regarded as scandalous by the elders of the tribe, and held no academic post for nine years, during which time he communed with Husserl at Göttingen and Walther Rathenau and Werner Sombart at Berlin. His philosophical writings are subtle and "modernist" in their aversion to systems, their thirst for phenomenal reality underneath abstract ideas and desiccated words. His reputation has remained high as a pioneer of the present phenomenological school, along with Husserl. He studied human states of mind: sym-pathy, shame, love, resentment. These fundamental qualities of our emotional life, because they cannot be objectified in knowledge, slip away from us as philosophers and psychologists unless somehow we can grasp the whole of that life "as a meaningful sign language."[15]

Looking at Western man from this point of view, Scheler noted that for the first time he does not know what he is. He had been a child of God; a Platonic spirit housed in the dark prison of the body; a Baconian conqueror of nature; Marx's worker-producer. But all of these roles had petered out. Nietzsche saw modern man as a lost soul looking for something—anything—to believe in (a view echoed in William James' essay on "The Will to Believe"). It was evidently this desperate plight that caused Scheler to pen his passionate paean to war. Of all such writings produced by the 1914 hysteria, it would be hard to match *The Genius of War (Der Genius des Krieges und der Deutsch Krieg*, 1915) for sheer bellimania. It hailed the war chiefly for renewing human contacts, breaking down the isolation of individ-uals from their fellows, and inducing a renaissance of belief. Scheler managed to make war mean life against death, surely a singular tri-umph of dialectic, by arguing that war destroys the mechanical-bureaucratic; it is the free act rather than the determined one, the creative spirit over against the calculating reason. Irrationalism joined with communitarianism to produce this outpouring of joy at the triumph of Mars, from one of the era's best minds.

The mind as the soul's enemy: the imagination, the feeling, fantasizing part, free and open, undirected from outside, stands over against the directing, *Mittelrational*, logical intellect. This was reminiscent of Plato's two horses, threatening to pull the driver-self apart; or the Will and Intellect of the medieval philosophers. Goethe and Nietzsche agreed on man's double nature; Nietzsche had visualized a man with a double brain, for science and for poetry. The "two cultures" of scientists and humanists had as such trouble relating to each other in Matthew Arnold's day as in Charles Snow's. Ludwig Klages held that the sensual world, the rich *real* world of feeling, desiring, experiencing, is completely unconceptualizable; concepts, the intellect's instruments, are dehumanizing and sterile. The artist Kokoschka agreed, declaring that logic is the enemy of freedom and the individual, "behind logic stands the police"—theories enslave, only art is free.[16] To rescue the modern soul from its intellectualized sickness, Klages (in 1910) offered "Das Wunder, die Liebe und das Vorbild"— gods, poets, and heroes, not ideas to imitate, but real examples. *Sachsforschung*, factual research, should be replaced by *Sinnforschung*, inquiry into meaning. Dilthey and R. G. Collingwood would call it the historical imagination, which converts a meaningless assemblage of historical facts into a significant narrative.

In 1911 Georg Lukacs published, as his first significant work, *The Soul and Its Forms (Die Seele und die Formen)*, the beginning of his discovery of a "reified" world of human relations which has escaped human control to appear as an external force, determining our lives as if an alien force. He noted the gap between *das LEBEN*, the everyday life of sensations and experiences, and *DAS leben*, the memory of an ideal and memorable life as it should be, touching universal themes. At this time, Lukacs saw art as the only possible means of bridging the gulf. It was the same vision that led Marcel Proust to embark upon his mammoth novel between 1900 and 1913, annihilating the unsatisfactory transience and triviality of real life by transforming it into a coherent structure on the pages of a book: the triumph of art over life.

In explaining why discovery of the people as a living community was one of the war's most important effects, Ernst Troeltsch wrote of that unfortunate separation of abstract-rationalistic and subjectivist society (*Gesellschaft*) from the great community (*Gemeinschaft*) uniting blood and instinct, custom and symbol. This gulf was deeper with us [Germans] and had worked itself out in esthetic, artistic and intellectual questions in quite startling ways.[17]

In this passage Troeltsch was leading up to that miracle of organic unity the war brought, which is discussed in the next chapter. He suggests the close connection between this quest for community and the "irrationalism" of the era. *Gemeinschaft* meant rootedness in an instinctual order, in what D. H. Lawrence called "the belief in the blood, the flesh, as being wiser than the intellect" (which he called "my great religion"). Values in the organic past—*in illud tempore*—were naturally understood, they were not theorized about. In his sociology Émile Durkheim had called attention to the dependence of values on society; social solidarity is the purpose of religion, which exists to solemnize the individual's obligation to obey the rules of the tribe.[18] Fragmentation and loss of social solidarity had their counterpart if not their cause in an excess of intellectualizing and analyzing, which leads to scepticism and paralysis of will. The word, as more recent commentators might say, lost its felt identity with reality, became separated from the object, was seen to be an abstraction totally divorced from the world.[19] The good, the true, the beautiful were once manifest; now they are all "problems," and as such, subject to infinite confusion and disagreement. If we must think out for ourselves all our choices and obligations and preferences, we are thrown into uncertainty and into endless disagreement with our fellows. Intellectualism as the basis for all society, not just the game of a few, is a disaster. A surviving primitivist irrationalism is the only means of keeping society together.

II

The Latin world was equally drawn toward irrationalism. We have already mentioned the role of Henri Bergson, the most popular and the most adored of philosophers, lecturing to large audiences in Paris and writing widely read books in a brilliant style; *Creative Evolution* (1907) was his best known. Evolution and historical change as unpredictables was an idea so pervasive that it affected even Marxist scientific determinism. In Italy Arturo Labriola converted the doctrine of historical materialism into a flux without *telos*, "The unpredictable result of the conscious effort of men to change their social conditions." Antonio Gramsci, who was soon to call *Das Kapital* a bourgeois book, thought mechanical determinism obsolete.[20] Simple Marxian positivism, stressing economic determinism and inevitable "stages" of history in a straight-line ascent in obedience to the "laws" of history and society, was popular with the socialist masses; expounded by such as Achille Loria in Italy, Jules Guesde in France (aided by Marx's son-in-law Paul Lafargue), and Georgy Plekhanov in Russia, it came under fire even within Marxist ranks.[21] As Marx's interpreters wrestled with such questions as how can one square science, which is a practical method, with the smuggled-in religious faith of final causes and popular uprisings, one result was a separation of Marxian science from Marxian socialism, the latter a popular faith.

The Italian Benedetto Croce and the Frenchman Georges Sorel were leaders in this enterprise. Both had been drawn to Marxism in the 1890's; both came to (a) reject "vulgar" Marxism as a science and (b) see that as a popular movement it rested on "notions of finality and providential design" (Croce) which are essentially "myth" (Sorel) and not scientific reason. If Marxism is to be a tenable method of inquiry, it cannot pretend to know final ends and ultimate constituents of reality ("materialism"); it deals with phenomena only, tentatively exploring human relationships in a social and historical setting; critical and dialectical, it is open-minded and nondogmatic. As such, it becomes a rather unexciting branch of the social sciences, doing useful scholarly work but promising no dramatic results. It fell into the hands of the professors (e.g., Antonio Labriola in Italy, or the Russian "legal Marxists" and philosophic "empirio-critics" who goaded Lenin into a rash attempt to defend pure materialism). This academic fare was far too unheroic to serve as the basis for mass rallies and millennial hopes. Popular Marxism obviously did rely on an allegedly scientific determinism, actually a mystique or myth. Not reason but faith promised the apocalyptic ending of history in an ideal classless society repairing all imperfections, after a last great struggle with the forces of evil. Not reason but faith assured the proletariat that it is the instrument of salvation, the suffering servant fated to redeem mankind.

Sorel hated "intellectuals," perhaps because, like Gustave LeBon, he was outside the professorial Establishment. An upstart autodidact who spent most of his life as a bureaucrat (naturally developing a lively hatred of the bureaucracy), he thought that the "intellectuals" were conducting civilization to its ruin, by drying up the springs of spontaneity on which life depends. Violence—proletarian violence, the violence of the general strike—can save civilization by restoring belief, Sorel argued in *Reflections on Violence* (1907). Sorel obviously did not escape the intellectualism he scorned, for he too dealt in words, ideas, abstractions. But he had decided that Marxist bureaucrats were spoiling the spontaneity of working-class action, as their timid parliamentarianism was eroding its revolutionary élan. The Anarchists and Syndicalists within the working-class movement were fond of ridiculing Marxist intellectualism. The trade unionist Griffuelhes wrote in 1908 of "violent opposition" to bourgeois intellectuals among union activists. The French Syndicalist Edouard Berth thought that Marxian Social Democracy was "a half-bourgeois philosophy" appealing to intellectuals, not workers.[22]

It seems clear that, as we have noted, the "intellectual" part of Marxism was an integral part of its emotional appeal. For the workers to recognize that they are deliberately making up a myth seems to require a greater intellectual sophistication than the simple, unreflecting acceptance of vulgar Marxism at face value as "science" (meaning a truth guaranteed by facts). So Sorel's point was scarcely a practical one. As an *aperçu*, however, it was cogent enough. Upon careful analysis it becomes apparent that the allegedly scientific part of popular Marxism is disguised myth. In fact, Sorel, like others, wanted to escape from a depressing determinism and affirm the freedom of man and history, an exciting idea to intellectuals if not workers. His thought was to play a considerable role in postwar Fascism.

To Charles Péguy, who owed much to both Bergson and Sorel, overintellectualization was equally the besetting sin. The basic mistake of socialism was to translate a mystique into an ideology. The hardening of the socialist mystique into a dogma administered by a bureaucracy oppressed Péguy, as it did Robert Michels. Disgusted by "the devouring, abstract collectivism of Marxist doctrine," Péguy left the party, refused all parties and (though he became a devout Christian) all churches, striving to preserve his spontaneity, to avoid being an "intellectual" while also avoiding the trap of vulgarity. Left and Right, he thought, Jaurès as well as Maurras, were alike in being too much the offspring of positivism. He hated above all what he called "the parti intellectuel," among whom he numbered Marxians, Actionists, churchly Scholastics, and—since he too was an outsider—the *universitaires*, professors at the Sorbonne. In his wilder flights this by no means tame personality (he had in fact a positive genius for losing friends) accused the Durkheimian *sociologues*, too, of plotting a dictatorship of the social scientists (dreams by no means lacking, indeed, among these modern priests of learning).

Péguy's very life was an affront to conventional rationality: a man of the people, republican, revolutionary socialist, yet devout Christian (attacking the organized Church, however—a Catholic Kierkegaard), creator of the cult of Joan of Arc through his impassioned writings about the Maid; Christian foe of the Church, Socialist foe of the Marxists, patriotic foe of the Nationalists, Péguy's feverish career was a study in contradictions. "He lives in a world of illusions," Sorel said of his sometime friend.[23] Yet the writings he poured in a stream from his journal, the *Cahiers de la quinzaine*, livest organ of thinking France in the 1900's, had an impulsive genius and a total independence which earned him a place as, in Romain Rolland's words, "la force la plus veridique et la plus geniale de la litterature Européenne." Péguy's failure to win the Academy's grand prize in the controversial 1911 election, while it fed the flames of his paranoia, scarcely diminished his standing among the young men of France, whom the "Agathon" inquest of 1913 (*Les jeunes gens d'aujourd'hui*) found so Péguyist.

It was here that his love-hate relationship with Romain Rolland, friend and collaborator, began its crisis, for Rolland was also a candidate, and at this time Péguy grew warlike. "Wars are the great temporal tests of peoples," he wrote in *Notre Jeunesse* (1910), which Rolland in his perceptive biography of Péguy called a "hymn to sacred unreason." "A whole generation marched to the front joyously, and at their head Péguy marked time . . . ."[24] At the same time, no one more than Péguy established the image of France defending Latin civilization against the German "barbarians." The French carried on the tradition of the Greeks at Marathon, the Romans civilizing barbarian Europe, and, somehow, the medieval Crusaders also, as they summoned their energies to turn back these modern descendants of Goth and Vandal. If this was in some sense a defense of "reason"—and Péguy admired the French classical tradition as well as the romantic one typified by Victor Hugo—it was scarcely rational: to identify the land of philosophers, musicians, and the best university system in Europe with fifth-century savagery required a considerable capacity for fantasizing.

Though Sorel had lost some of his audience by 1910, he too was one of the heroes of prewar French thought. Sorel exerted influence beyond France, reaching to England as well as Italy. In 1910 Péguy and Sorel moved at the same time toward a passionate patriotism that culminated in the former's death on the Marne in 1914. Both, as well as the Rhenish German Italophile Robert Michels, had close connections to the Italian sage Benedetto Croce. Though of a temperament marked by "an almost Goethean serenity and composure," as Gramsci put it, Croce in his quieter way accepted the vitalist or historicist philosophy, the philosophy of praxis. He had fought his way out of both Hegelianism and Marxism as systems, relentlessly criticizing both, as indeed he thought they demanded: were they not philosophies of dialectical movement, the march of ever-changing ideas as they interact with reality? They therefore necessarily were themselves imperfect statements requiring development and correction. Croce attacked the fatalistic, mechanistic sort of "economic determinism" that often masqueraded as Marxism. The spirit creates ever-fresh and unpredictable modes. "For Croce," Antonio Gramsci wrote, "every concept of the world and every philosophy to the extent that it becomes a norm for living and a morality, constitutes 'religion.'" The spirit is self-creating and self-justifying. Certainly the great Italian thinker regarded history as "rational," as much as Hegel and Marx had. But when one has given up any element of determinism in favor of an open dialectic which proliferates ever-fresh and unpredictable forms of life and culture, one accepts whatever happens as rational. The war, when it came, had to be rational, and Croce accepted it as such. One does not judge history by some exterior yardstick, as Marxists of the more doctrinaire sort did, and do. The yardstick *is* history.

Croce's support for the war was as remarkable for its absence of rancor as it was for its warmth. In the feverish Italian debate about entering the war, which went on from August, 1914, until Italy took the plunge in May, 1915, Croce denounced those who disparaged German culture or painted the issue as Latin civilization versus Germanic barbarism—how ridiculous this was in an Italy herself dominated intellectually by Hegel, Marx, Nietzsche, Weber! During the war he refused to countenance the demagoguery of race hatred. He was appalled by the *credo bellicoso* and mistrusted enthusiasts such as the Futurists, D'Annunzio, Mussolini. He rejected the assimilation of culture to politics, holding German realism in politics to be right; the intellectual heritage is international and above politics.[25] Yet politics has its own place. Like Shaw and Hesse, Croce accepted the necessity of the war but deplored the hysterical chauvinist tone of the intellectuals. He divorced his scholarly and intellectual work from his duties as an Italian citizen, while fully respecting both roles.

It was a rather unusual position in this war; but it did not mean that Croce lacked martial enthusiasm. His creed required him to accept that which happened "spontaneously," as the war clearly did. No one ever went to war more soberly, yet he thought Italy should participate and was happy when she decided to join "in this tragic and solemn struggle which the old Europe now fights within herself and nourishes with her best blood, to ripen many old forms of civilization . . . . Just as in the life of Europe we are bound in peacetime to noble duties of the common tasks, so in this war we ought at any cost to prove worthy of the sacred duties of our national individuality." With "the coolest Italian lucidity of mind" Italy should pay her respects to the historical process and take her part in whatever act was unfolding.[26] There was "nothing to be said" about the war, one just fought it.

To acquiesce in whatever it is that's happening seems an unthinking, irrational creed more suited to adolescents than to great thinkers; but the bankruptcy of past creeds, the crisis of consciousness and of language, the weariness with earth-bound scientisms, and the yearning for new experience combined to deposit European thought on these shoals at the beginning of the twentieth century. Ludwig Marcuse, who later found his 1914 patriotism hard to explain, had learned from Rudolf Eucken and Ernst Cassirer that the world spirit brings forth a new age in its own good time.[27] Troeltsch wrote in "Die Krisis des Historismus" that "in endless and always new individualization . . . State, law, morality, religion, art are all dissolved in the flow of historical becoming and are comprehensible only as ingredients of historical development." "Carried away into the whirlpool," as it later seemed, this flow into a fuller future was something to welcome before 1914. Amid the feeling of cultural chaos and the need to reunify a fragmented, valueless civilization, both of which found frequent expression, there were many manifestations of spiritual revival; the age hardly lacked vitality, when one considered all the exciting new ideas, movements, writings, artistic creations. A joyous affirmation of energy, *élan vital*, will-to-power, had seized the minds of young people, replacing the tired, decadent mood of the 1890's. "The search for the most extreme manifestation of energy is man's destiny," as Georg Kaiser wrote.[28]

He must be awakened, violently if need be, so that he may pursue the ideal. The weakness of this was the tendency to worship energy for its own sake, myth *qua* myth—anything with vitality must be hopeful. The year 1914 revealed how dangerous such a message could be.

There were other kinds of irrationalism. The mobs which raged in France during the Boulangist agitation and again during the Dreyfus Affair helped persuade Gustave LeBon, amateur social psychologist who won fame for his book *The Crowd* (1895), that the group mind is irrational and rather nasty. "Collective mentality" differs from individual. In the crowd the individual becomes totally transformed. His social unconscious emerges. (The "unconscious" was not an invention of Freud and Jung; they found it, as Freud said, in imaginative writers of the Romantic era.) Reverting to the primitive, descending in the scale of civilization, the individual in a mob is as one hypnotized: LeBon incorporated this nineteenth-century discovery of hypnotism, which was found first by Anton Mesmer and his followers, and was encountered by Freud in Paris in his early days as a psychiatrist. The crowd is impulsive, changeable, irritable, uncritical; it knows feelings of ecstatic, shamanlike omnipotence, and responds to incantations. It is little influenced by argument, much by force or action. It is prone to hero-worship and acceptance of leadership authority. "A group is an obedient herd, which could never live without a master," was Freud's paraphrase of LeBon, who he said had written "a brilliantly executed picture of the group mind."[29] (We know that Adolf Hitler read LeBon.)

A "group," however, might be conceived in the benevolent image of Durkheim's communal solidarity, or the religious congregation, or an Anarchist natural association. It is only when deeply disturbed by unnatural tensions and pressures that a group becomes a mob, its emotions worked up to bloodthirsty levels by hysterical leaders; this happens in the uprootedness and anomie of the great cities. Discussing the nature of the mob leader, LeBon saw him as a "true believer," fanatically committed to ideas whose power he exploits. Seeking a word for the quality which such leaders have, LeBon called it "prestige," a term carrying more connotations of magic and illusion in French than it does in English. Max Weber was to supersede this with "charisma."

One might think that LeBon would have seen in the August, 1914, situation a mob spirit which repelled him; but he did not. He took delight in pointing out the triumph of irrationalism: "The European conflict reveals to the rationalists what they forgot, how feeble a role reason plays in human actions."[30] A longtime opponent of the Socialists, he noted with some glee how their doctrines of class war and internationalism—which were merely ideas—went down before the deeper instincts of group solidarity. In 1914 LeBon saw in patriotism the "social cement" that was needed to restore France to health. She had looked into the depths of negation and drawn back, terrified; she sought to regain the foundations of unity.[31] The mob is an excrescence on the unsound social body; the whole people, reunited in a worthy cause, transcends mobbism.

III

Scientific naturalism was too powerful and too recent a force to have subsided altogether under the counterattack of "soul" and "spirit." Materialism, scientism, and agnosticism had climaxed in the 1870's, the hour of Darwin, Spencer, Marx, and Zola. ("In my youth almost all people of the same age, rich and poor, were socialistic in the Marxian sense," Richard von Kralik wrote of his Berlin youth in the 1870's.) This strong current of "naturalism" was by no means dead in the 1900's, despite being somewhat outmoded. Arnold Bennett in England and Heinrich Mann in Germany, as well as Theodore Dreiser in the United States, were still trying to write like Zola, hero of the Dreyfusards in his latter years. When Stefan Zweig went to Berlin from Vienna in 1901, he found Ibsen and Zola the idols rather than Mallarmé and Baudelaire. The disciples of Marx, organized in the great International Workingmen's Association, were far more numerous than they had been in Marx's lifetime, and generally paid tribute to a *more* scientifically positivist creed than he had evidently sanctioned. Philosophical naturalism continued brilliantly in the thought of George Santayana as well as in the more vulgar Society of Monists, founded in 1906 by the celebrated proponent of scientific materialism, Ernst Haeckel. Though Sigmund Freud and Carl Jung sneered at the *Monistenbund*, they were themselves firmly committed to a method they regarded as scientific, not literary or metaphysical. (Yet the chief grounds for rejecting Freudianism, on the part of professional psychiatrists, was in their view its excessively speculative, unscientific character.) The same was true of sociologist Émile Durkheim, as much an idol at the Sorbonne as his rival Bergson. In the *Methodenstreit* of the social sciences, strong voices upheld Durkheim's positivist methodology.

Herbert Spencer, under whose banner radical agnosticism had rallied in Victorian times, retained popularity with the general public, though by 1905 the advance guard had passed him by. It was still normal for young men to be atheists. In 1914 the young C. S. Lewis was citing Frazer and Lang to show that Christianity is only a myth of human invention, its Last Supper just another fertility rite; nature is so wholly diabolical, the future author of *Mere Christianity* and *That Hideous Strength* then thought, that if God exists He must be somewhere else, quite unaware of what is going on in this literally god-forsaken section of the cosmos. As for the soul, if such there be, we have no way of knowing it, since it cannot be stretched out on the laboratory table. Such views were those of many intellectual young men in their salad days, though likely not to last. Darwinian agnosticism in most respects was more characteristic of a generation just passing in the 1900's, those who had been young in the sixties and seventies, the generation of Thomas Hardy in England.[32]

As the basis for a warlike mood, Darwinism had relatively little to do with the events of 1914. It is true that statesmen shared the commonplace (much older than the nineteenth century) that, in the words of Austrian Chief of Staff Conrad von Hoetzendorff, "men and nations alike are dominated by the struggle for existence. Force is the law of life, and the statesman must shape his course accordingly." Max Scheler (in *Der Genius des Krieges*) noted that Darwinists were found among *both* the extreme pacifists and the most ruthless partisans of war. Herbert Spencer himself, along with such disciples as the American businessman–peace leader Andrew Carnegie, had held war to be an obsolete form of competition, replaced by the peaceful processes of industrialism; as a form of natural selection, it is disastrous, for it kills off the most vital people. On the other hand, Social Darwinists Karl Pearson and Francis Galton accepted and approved the competition between whole peoples, a relentless struggle in which the more vigorous and better organized push the weaker peoples to the wall.[33] Darwinian science seemed, to a contemporary observer, to have "waged war . . . with such schemes of social and political amelioration as tend to peace and equality between nations, cooperation between classes, and mercy and tenderness for the weaker brethren."[34] Maurice Bowra describes his father's Huxleyism as typical of his generation: "life as a struggle for the survival of the fittest," stress on "race and heredity" accompanying a vigorous belief in the superiority of Anglo-Saxon government.[35] (The Germans he dismissed as "not true Nordics but largely Slavs"!)

Such views already seemed curious to the young. In a letter to a Fabian colleague in 1905, Shaw referred to "a violent reaction against Darwin," entailing the "utter collapse of Natural Selection as a basis for political or social action."[36] He mentioned the work of Oliver Lodge; Bergson's attack on mechanical evolution, in *Creative Evolution*, lay just ahead. As a popular ideology, "a basis for political or social action," Darwinism was no longer in fashion, whatever scientific biologists did with Darwin's work within their own strict confines. It is significant that in his rousing defense of war in 1914, Max Scheler detached the war rationale entirely from any Darwinian animal-like struggle for existence, as much as he did from a Marxian economic competition. Almost every conceivable argument for war found its way into Scheler's presentation, but this one he rejected; war is a specifically human institution, unknown to the animal world, and its roots in human nature have nothing to do with merely seeking food or other economic sustenance. It rests on a will to power which is not reducible to anything material but is a motive in itself. It is an indispensable part of the historical process, impelling peoples to win their freedom, create cultures, establish values.[37] Péguy's "test of peoples" and Stravinsky's "necessity for progress" were a spiritual challenge, not a material one.

By 1914 the latest exciting developments in science, which switched the scene from biology to physics, seemed to bring even the laboratory in line with the fashionable irrationalism. The common-sense picture of the physical universe so widely accepted in the nineteenth century, not least by scientists themselves, had begun to disintegrate, as a grasp of the principles of that universe passed beyond the average cultivated understanding. Rutherford typified the Victorian scientist in his belief that the laws of physics should be simple enough for a bar-maid to comprehend. In 1911 he proposed a model of the atom as a miniature solar system. Still taught today to college freshmen as a kind of desperate tribute to the last century, Rutherford's model was actually in trouble at the moment of its birth, and within two years Niels Bohr proved it wrong. In 1911 C. T. R. Wilson's cloud-chamber revealed light acting in this milieu as particles, whereas elsewhere it seemed to behave as waves. The duality or basic ambiguity of matter had been revealed; indeterminacy and probability had begun their reign. Max Planck's discovery of the emission of energy in sudden jumps shattered all the traditional laws of motion.

If this news did not reach the front page of newspapers until after the war, educated people were frequently aware of it before 1914. Gramsci referred to it as a reason for rejecting determinist versions of Marxism. "Science has resumed the examination of her ancient certitudes, and has proved their fragility," LeBon wrote in 1913.[38] "Today she sees her ancient principles vanishing one by one." LeBon seemed to rejoice that the savants were joining his irrationalist cause, but a dismayed scientist in 1912 complained that Einstein and Planck "substitute mathematical symbols as the basis of science and deny that any concrete experience underlies these symbols, thus replacing an objective by a subjective universe."[39] This was in perfect agreement with Cubism and Expressionism, as artists delightedly pointed out. The Futurist Manifesto declared that "Time and Space died yesterday."

In a not altogether successful book of 1912, in which he included other fashionable messages of the era of the soul such as emergent evolution and phenomenological investigations, Walther Rathenau dealt with the need for some kind of *Mechanik des Geistes*, a science of the soul. To embrace all these novel irrationalisms within a scientific methodology, thus reconciling the two great modern modes of speculation, clearly would constitute the greatest of all achievements. As we noted, Edmund Husserl aspired to it for a time, philosophically. Sigmund Freud's alleged mechanics of the mind was still relatively obscure in 1914. "We are going through a critical period," Freud wrote to Jung in 1910. His *Leonardo da Vinci* had "aroused horror"; "we went ahead too fast."[40] The small International Psychoanalytical Association, regarded as a scandal by the great majority of professional psychiatrists at the time of its founding in 1908–10, was weakened by Adler's secession and then the quarrel between Freud and Jung in

1913–14. The latter's resignation as president of the IPA occurred three months before the start of the war. Thomas Mann later saw Freud as one who "developed the darker side of nature and the soul as the real determinant and creative force in life, in opposition to rationalism, intellectualism, classicism."[41] Freud found his predecessors among the poets and philosophers, as he freely conceded, not least the dark philosopher of unreasoning Will, Arthur Schopenhauer.[42] But, as a practicing doctor, Freud sought to make the mere ideas of the poets and philosophers scientific. The combination of tough-minded scientific method with extreme speculative boldness, along with his energy, accounts for Freud's extraordinary power and appeal. But on inspection his empirical testing of the daring hypotheses looks dubious; he did indeed draw them from the evidence of his practice, but he dealt with a small number of highly selective cases, and his ardent imagination frequently outran the data. After 1914 he became more speculative.

In any event Freud welcomed the war at first, then, as he grew increasingly depressed, found that war confirmed his gloomy views of humanity, filled as it is with aggressive atavistic instincts which it works in vain to repress. "Men are not gentle . . . . a powerful measure of desire for aggression has to be reckoned as a part of their instinctual endowment." To exploit one's neighbor, to seize his possessions, humiliate him, cause him pain, torture and kill him, Freud wrote to Einstein, are constant temptations to man. "Who has the courage to dispute in the face of all the evidence in his own life and in history?"[43] Seeking to dam these primal urges, civilization only builds up a torrent of discontent which in one way or another must find an outlet. Thus in the name of science Freud seemed to confirm the view that the war had been an outburst of irrationality, long suppressed by an overly calculating civilization which, proud of its efficiency and its niceness, forgot that deeper springs of mysterious violence nourish human nature.

It is worth repeating that the death-wish did seem to be present widely in the European intellectual consciousness on the eve of 1914. "Fascination with death was a key feature of the period," Donald Fanger writes in his perceptive study of the Russian avant-garde novel just before the war.[44] The same could be said of Expressionist Germany, as we know, as well as of Péguy's France and Brooke's England, to only slightly lesser degrees than in St. Petersburg's frenetic atmosphere. "An absolute longing for death" appears at this time (1912–14)

81

in Franz Kafka's diary.[45] Freud's curious idea, as many have thought, of Thanatos to be paired with Eros came to him from solid empirical evidence, though evidence perhaps germane not to humanity in general but to one moment in the evolution of the civilized European consciousness.

In 1914 it did not seem to matter much whether one was a Idealist or Realist, Dualist or Monist; almost everybody rejoiced in the war. But when we think of Russell, or the disciples of G. E. Moore, who showed some resistance, we are inclined to give the edge to the Idealists for belligerence.[46] A little later in the United States, William Hocking supplies an example of an Absolute Idealist seeing the war as a struggle of the human spirit for righteousness. But thinkers hostile to Idealism (e.g., John Dewey, Santayana) identified this tradition with Germany, found it appalling, and used it as a reason for joining the war to crush the infamy.[47]

IV

"The triumph of emotion over reason" is not of course adequate as an explanation for the war. This assumes that war is irrational and peace rational, that war came because people lost their reason and began to act without regard to logic and reality. This was hardly the case. In a sense the war was all too rational, the result of a deadly logic of power which men could not escape. It is not irrational to defend yourself when attacked, if you have or think you have something valuable to defend. It is not even irrational to forestall attack by striking first; such actions are shocking because they offend *feelings* (of honor, gallantry, etc.) more than they do logic. (In a game of chess one would quite naturally seek to nip an opponent's offensive in the bud by taking preemptive action.) If war were simply an irrational act, it would scarcely have lasted so long or occurred so widely. The eighteenth-century Age of Reason thought it sensible not to abolish war but to limit it by de-emotionalizing it. If there are rational wars, there certainly have been irrational decisions for peace, as most would, for example, judge the policies of the Western powers in the 1930's when, moved by a quite emotional repugnance to war, they disarmed and allowed Hitler to seize control of the Continent. Many wars have been entered upon with cool calculation, and many peaces have been surrenders to mass feeling. We may speak of the "herd instinct" to draw together in time of danger, or of blood lust spreading through crowds like a contagion. But there is also the collective panic when people fling down arms and flee in a wild *sauve-qui-peut*. Emotion may be on the side of either war or peace; it is not necessarily committed to either.

In 1914 why should emotion have been on the side of war? One can visualize the possibility of a great unreasoning sentiment for peace, with people rushing into the street shouting "We won't fight"—as has happened more recently, and as happened among the Italians at Caporetto, a rare case in the 1914–18 war. That people's emotions had been so remarkably mobilized on behalf of war in 1914 was because their reason had been captured, too. They believed in the necessity, the justice, the value of the war, and these were partly rational calculations. One should not omit the closely reasoned arguments for war that appeared before 1914, of which one example is Solovyëv's *War and Christianity* (1900), cast in the form of a debate between pacifists and those who, effectively, argue that pacifism leads to surrenders to injustice, abandonment of the weak, allowing the world to go to the Devil. Péguy offered similar arguments in his writings in 1913: to refuse to defend the Republic is madness. Tolstoyan attempts to justify pure pacifism force one, of course, into such corners as refusing to defend one's loved ones against attack, or refusing to place any value, such as justice, honor, life itself, above the negative value of nonviolence.

Nevertheless, this having been said, we recognize the extent to which in every belligerent country emotions and sentiments were involved which would generally be called nonrational. Powerful feelings welled up from the depths of the psyche. The war was a roar of protest against the kind of life that Europe had been living, and a grasping for another and better kind of life. The search for heroism, nobility, unselfishness, as well as adventure, danger, and even death, registered a protest against the rationalized, specialized society, the *Ameisenwelt*, or ant-world, as Georgists called it. And accompanying the rebellion-adventure urge, the most powerful, somewhat paradoxically, was the urge to group solidarity. The paradox is only apparent, for the ant-world of urban industrial society had lost the instinctive human kinship of old; it was as anomic as it was specialized. It is to this quest for community as a feature of 1914 that we turn next.

"Human reason was tired," Rolland's Jean-Christophe reflects in the last book of this pre-1914 epic. "It had just accomplished a mighty effort. It surrendered to sleep, and like a child wearied by a long journey, before going to sleep it said its prayers. . . . Even philosophy wavered. . . . Even science manifested signs of this fatigue of reason." So strong was this current that the rationalist hero of Rolland's saga did not try to combat it; he could only wait and hope it passed. These winds of the spirit have been exceedingly powerful in this century, and just as fleeting. The mystique of 1914 antirationalism was as mighty in its day as it was later to be incomprehensible. "Weary of peace and of ideas," Rolland added, "they celebrated the anvil of war upon which the pounding of bloody fists would reforge the power of France." Those to whom he referred, those who shared this mystique, would not have agreed with his diagnosis of fatigue or weariness; they thought themselves released from enslavement to rationalism.

—5—

The Quest for Community

I

We have already noted as the foremost theme of 1914 the joy which hailed the "union of hearts," the sacred union, the rediscovered community, in all the belligerent countries. "It is the tremendous significance of August," Ernst Troeltsch wrote, "that under the impact of danger it pressed the whole people together in an inner unity, such as never before had existed."[1] Max Scheler greeted the war as a return to "the organic roots of human existence":

> In this hour it was generally felt that a special national destiny reached into everyone's hearts, the greatest and smallest alike, and decided what each of us is and is worth . . . . We were no longer what we had been—alone! The sundered living contact between the series individual-people-nation-world-God was restored in an instant.[2]

Some intellectuals, he noted, were bewildered and shattered by the collapse of their entire world of the moment before, yet only a few attempted to hold onto that world; the great majority gladly let it vanish amid feelings of a new strength flowing into poetry, philosophy, religion, and politics from the regained solidarity.

The psychologist Otto Binswanger also wrote on this ego-submerging and merging phenomenon.[3] The war "established a newly felt connection between the individual and the entire nation," sociologist Georg Simmel wrote, while the young Franco-British avant-garde sculptor Henri Gaudier-Brzeska, who was to be killed in the war, approved it as a remedy against "arrogance, self-esteem, pride."[4] In Italy, upon that country's joining the war, her foremost philosopher Benedetto Croce spoke to his fellow Neapolitans:

> Divided in our political and administrative views, sometimes among the collisions of opposing opinions rendered almost ignorant of unity and of the goal toward which everyone really strives, we have now in this grave moment, suddenly rediscovered the awareness of that unity and we all seek the same goal in the same form.[5]

In his examination of how Russia greeted the war, Hans Rogger includes "a welcoming of it for having freed Russia of narrowness and pettiness and for opening new perspectives on greatness. Some viewed war as a spiritual awakening, the end of a moral crisis which had long separated the intelligentsia from the people."[6] "All differences of class, rank and language were flooded over by the rushing feeling of fraternity"; individual egos became incorporated into the mass, and in this way "his hitherto unnoticed person had been given meaning," so Stefan Zweig observed.[7] Any complete phenomenology of 1914 must make a place for this experience of lonely atoms finding relief in joining a purposeful crowd which included everybody. Arnold Zweig pointed out that "what normally separated average Germans from each other, making every single one a fortress of deep insecurity . . . this veneer of embarrassment and false refinement fell away."[8]

Le sens social, Émile Durkheim thought in France, revived by the war, was its most notable result, one "without parallel in history."[9] The sudden sense of community, such a startlingly intense and pervasive feature of the August spirit, was felt most by the intellectuals, the evidence strongly suggests. One might accept "the instinct of the herd," as Trotter called it in his wartime book of that title, as natural for the less sophisticated common herd, requiring no great amount of explanation; hardly so for that jaded set which had just recently thought itself at the end of civilization and beyond all novelty. But from poets to pedants, few escaped its appeal. True, it is often difficult to separate the exaltation of the "union sacrée" from other features present in the August mystique of war, for it blended into the thrill of danger, the excitement of combat, the sudden call to an apocalypse. To Stefan George, this seizure "in the grasp of the world's great storm" comprehended holiness, a new start, release from a "trash and triviality" civilization, but also embraced the magically rediscovered community.[10] Even those whose reaction to the war stressed adventure or apocalypse or some other motive had trouble keeping the word "community" out of their statement. Thus Ernst Junger wrote that the war

> ist die Hammerschmiede, die Welt in neue Grenzen und neue Gemeinschaften zerschlägt. Er ist das glühende Abendrot einer versinkenden Zeit und zugleich Morgenrot, in dem man zu neuem grösseren Kampfe rüstest.[11]

Images of hammering the world into new shapes, of glowing twilight and the dawn of a new day are thoroughly Nietzschean, but the word "community" slips in.

The comradeship of the trenches carried on and sustained this initial surge of tribal solidarity which was the result of suddenly standing together in danger. The war threw men together in a permanent fraternity of danger. "During the war I used to feel that this comradeship which had developed among us would lead to some new social order when peace came," Herbert Read recalls.[12] "It was a human relationship and a reality that had not existed in time of peace. It overcame (or ignored) all distinctions of class, rank or education. We did not call it love; we did not acknowledge its existence; it was sacramental and therefore sacred."[13] The sacrament hovers in the background of virtually every war novel, of course, in this most literate of wars. "I was preoccupied with an attachment, the sentiment of belonging to a living entity," Guy Chapman recorded in his war memoir.[14] Today, alas, this is likely to remind us of the "new social order" Adolf Hitler transformed into a hideous reality; but the brotherhood of the trenches, the classless society of the front line, among the private soldiers and junior officers (sharply marked off from the "scarlet majors at the base" who drew up blunderingly lethal battle plans and stayed out of range) appealed to many idealistic people at the time as a precious experience. It became the cliché of war memories: "War promoted working together into something good and true and rare, the like of which was never to be met in civilian life."[15]

The appeal of military life at all times has been its providing a simple and purposive framework for action. Of Rousseau's admiration for the military life, Judith Shklar writes that "Here, as in on other form of endeavor, the individual loses his personal identity and becomes a part of a purposive social unit."[16] The view that hapless slobs could be transformed into men by the military experience runs through nineteenth-century British thought from Ruskin to Kipling, of course.[17] Ernst Jünger explained that in the army

> Everything is simple. My rights and duties are prescribed. I need earn no money. My food is provided, and if things go badly I have a thousand fellow-sufferers. Above all, the shadow of death reduces every problem to a satisfying triviality.[18]

"The trenches made us feel larger than life; only there was death a joke rather than a threat," Robert Graves declared in *Goodbye to All That*, noting that men were *glad* to get back to the trenches from a home furlough.

Doubtless the fact that intellectuals succumbed so easily to this life of simple, clear structure implicates a large number of factors. The prewar intellectual, we know, entertained images of self-hate at times, as in Thomas Mann's classic story of the impotent artist, Tonio Kröger—who was introspective, fearful, weak, lacking in self-confidence because he was obsessed by ideas and unable to act spontaneously—and in Eliot's J. Alfred Prufrock, whose life was thrown in magic lanterns on a screen. To this apprehension about his fate of alienation, the intellectual added an equal hatred of the bourgeois "calculating machine," the *Zweckmenschen* whose actions were a mechanical response to accounting calculations.[19] *That* kind of purpose was abhorrent. This kind was at least free from the clammy grip of Gain, its goal was serious and real, whether or not noble. Carl Schmitt explained that war is existentially real, not abstract: there is a real enemy, and the stakes are life itself.[20] The gulf between reality and consciousness is bridged. We are reminded of those bewildered youngsters of more recent years who declared, with an obvious sincerity, that in the violence of street-fighting with the police (war, as such, they no longer accepted) they found out "who they were"; or of Frantz Fanon's thesis, in *Wretched of the Earth*, that the downtrodden and oppressed must fight back with physical violence to regain self-respect. Certainly many a youth in 1914–18 (if he survived) surmounted his identity crisis and became a man.[21]

At the same time, yearnings to be somehow reunited with the common man, an end blocked by the gulf in consciousness that previously existed, were apparently fulfilled. "No more rich or poor, proletarians or bourgeois, right wingers or leftist militants; there were only Frenchmen" (Roland Dorgeles). Martin Buber found that "for the first time the People appear quite real in my life"; his letters repeatedly stress the *Wirklichkeit* of what had been only an idea of human community.[22] There is evidence that the soldiers kept the 1914 spirit much longer than the people at home. In the course of the war an estrangement took place between the front-line soldiers, who knew "how it was" there, and the others who didn't—a bitterness that was by no means as simple as a reaction of the cannon-fodder against the scarlet majors or the generals who died in bed. It was, in fact, sometimes the opposite. Guy Chapman reprints a letter from *Nation* (October 21, 1916), the burden of which is that "we have not changed and you have"; we, the soldiers, are still ruled by the old sentiments of solidarity; you, the onlookers, have lost touch with that spirit.[23]

A part of that community of the trenches was a lack of hatred for the foe, who were also soldiers doing their duty; resentment against the hate propaganda exuded by home-front scribblers has been interpreted as war-weariness, but it was much more a keeping faith with the front-line soldier's code of quasi-chivalry, which required you to respect the enemy as you tried to kill him. The "jerries," C. M. Bowra recalls, were "regarded as men very like ourselves, condemned to an unnatural and hideous existence."[24] What led soldiers to do their duty was not a hatred of the enemy but a wish not to let one's fellows down. That this experience was in itself a good one, quite apart from the many features which were not, the testimony of a cloud of witnesses in all the armies proves. Bowra describes it as "a love for the comradeship that comes from living with people and sharing their interests and their work." If only, as so many sighed, a peacetime "moral equivalent" for it could be found!

Unity—if it exists in a great modern nation compounded inevitably of diverse (and ever more diverse) interests, occupations, temperaments, and above all ideas—has to be based on something simple: "such external functions as the millions have in common" (René Fülöp-Miller). The simplest of these is a struggle against a common enemy. If a man is proud of being a German, a Frenchman, or a Jew, Schopenhauer once remarked, he must have very little else to be proud of; but this is something that all men can share, when they can share nothing else, no longer being of the same religion, ideology, moral values, tastes. In the religiously divided, secularized state, even prayer leads to controversy; Germany's *Kulturkampf* and France's bitter debate over laicization had marked the previous decades. Only nationalism is a common denominator. Most of the European states were ethnically and linguistically diverse; though living under a common law and government, they did not speak the same language or practice the same customs. This was true in Russia, the Dual Monarchy, Great Britain, Belgium, Germany, even to a degree in France.[25] The sacred union healed all manner of breaches.

Hannah Arendt (*On Violence*) has called these hopes that "the strong fraternal sentiments collective violence engenders" can produce "a new community together with a 'new man'" an illusion: "for the simple reason that no human relationship is more transitory than this kind of brotherhood, which can be actualized only under conditions of immediate danger to life and limb." It was indeed a precarious and transient brotherhood, but this did not prevent it being deeply felt and highly valued while it lasted. To understand this, it helps to revisit the prewar history of ideas.

II

The nineteenth century, of course, had been at work destroying human communities in various ways. Much of its "progress" was almost deliberately designed to efface the forms of human association inherited from an immemorial past. As Robert Nisbet wrote, the new economic order of capitalism was "indifferent to every form of community and association," destroying the customary associations of village, guild, peasant community (though, it would appear, strengthening the family in some social areas, by way of compensation).[26] This vast process of "modernization" had been going on for several centuries, no doubt, at differing paces in the various parts of Europe, and is too complex to begin to describe here. (Its impact in all parts of society today engages the attention of whole schools of social historians, demographers, cliometricians.) Already, in 1843, Carlyle had announced the "social question" as the question of the century, in the aptly titled *Past and Present*, basically the issue being that "We call it a Society; and go about professing openly the totallest separation, isolation. Our life is not a mutual helpfulness; but rather, cloaked under due laws-of-war, named 'fair competition' and so forth, it is a mutual hostility." And Carlyle borrowed freely from Saint-Simon, from Coleridge, from many others of the post-revolutionary ferment. The reproach against "capitalism"—that it ruthlessly sacrificed human customs and values to a "cash nexus," dissolving everything into rationally calculable units of work and efficiency—was of course repeated by Karl Marx and John Ruskin and echoed through the whole century.

Since mid-century this process, which created unprecedented wealth and technological improvements, generally delighting the common man if not the intellectuals, had enormously accelerated, and reached areas such as Russia not then involved in it. The statistics of urbanization, which never can convey fully what happens in the human mind, suggest its progress. In 1900 there were seven European urban areas of more than a million people and 140 of more than 100,000. In 1801 less than 10 percent of the population of Great Britain lived in cities of 100,000 or more; in 1900, in this most urbanized of European countries, 27 percent inhabited cities above a quarter of a million. But the absence of any well-developed peasant villages in Britain, as compared to Germany or France or Russia, may account for the smaller amount of urban shock in Britain. In 1830 Germany had only two cities over 100,000; by 1910 there were forty-eight. Only about 6 percent of the Russian people, compared to nearly 40 percent in Britain, lived in cities larger than 100,000 at the end of the century; for an individual Russian, in Moscow direct from farm or village to study at the university, the impact was possibly greater than in London, long a multimillion constellation. In 1960 there were no fewer than 327 cities in Europe with more than a million. And "conurbations" such as London, Paris, or the merged Dutch cities reached to five, eight, twelve million. But there is a critical point for the psyche in this process which figures cannot reveal, and for articulate Europe it came in the later nineteenth century.

Intellectuals did not always experience feelings of bewilderment and dismay in the great city; like Adolf Hitler, they might well be dazzled and delighted at a Vienna contrasted with a provincial town like Linz, the latter large enough to be rather dehumanizing for the schoolboy migrating there from a village, but small enough to be uninteresting. Lenin's grandfather was a serf, his father something of a local grandee in a small-sized city, from which environment young Ulyanov was glad to escape (Isaac Deutscher describes Simbirsk as a "wretched and dull provincial hole"[27]). A dreary provincial city of 50,000 to 100,000 could do the spirit more damage than the metropolis. Intellectuals were natural urbophiles, more likely than not sharing Marx's contempt for rural idiocy and Flaubert's scorn for outlying philistinism. Of Thomas Hardy, Robert Gittings remarks, "In novels, he might extol the instinctive rightness of the peasant; in life, he always sought the company of the educated."[28] ("Truly, shepherd, in respect of itself, it is a good life; but in respect that it is a shepherd's life, it is naught.")

Such ambivalence ran through much of prewar thought; but a distinct movement of nostalgia had developed. In England the "Georgian" poets sought out the simplicities of an older England. The influential French novelist Maurice Barrès dwelt on the "deracination" of modern man. The great Russian poet Vladimir Mayakovsky regretted that

> iron rails oozed urban
> infection into the village sunburn.

Yet Mayakovsky, Boris Pasternak wrote, "was the poet not of nature like Esenin, but of the labyrinth of the great modern city in which the lonely spirit of our times, whose passionate, dramatic and inhuman situation he describes, has become confused and lost its way."[29] (Compare Andrey Bely's novel *St. Petersburg* [1913], with its themes of madness, death, and revolutionary apocalypse.)[30] Georg Simmel, in his famous essay on the city, drew the balance sheet of urban advantages and disadvantages: "The deepest problems of modern life derive from the claim of the individual to preserve the autonomy and individuality of his existence in the face of overwhelming social forces."[31] The city offers freedom, opportunity for expansion of consciousness, infinite opportunities; but also rootlessness, loss of social ties, opportunity for the destruction of personality through a surfeit of chaotic impressions. ("Stormed by a flood of random and unrelated impressions, urban, factory man is neurasthenic, bored, unable to endow any experience with value.")[32]

"In a coherent and animated society," Durkheim explained, "there is from each to all a continual exchange of ideas and sentiments—a mutual moral support—which makes the individual, instead of being reduced to his own forces alone, participate in the collective energy and find in it sustenance for his own life when he is spiritually exhausted." "Profound changes have been produced in the structure of our societies in a very short time. . . . Our faith has been troubled; tradition has lost its sway; individual judgment has been freed from collective judgment. . . . The new life which has emerged so suddenly has not been able to be completely organized."[33] It is notable that Marxists and Nietzscheans of this generation showed a greater concern for community than had the masters. Friedrich Tönnies, one of the great pioneers of German academic sociology, and famous for *Gemeinschaft/Gesellschaft*, drew on both Nietzsche and Marx.

All the great pioneers of this heroic age of sociology began, it would seem, with a profound sense of the crisis of modern man in terms of his "emancipation" from "traditional society," in which the community-regulated life had provided unquestioned values. Now the released individual ego had learned to question these values and demand autonomy. The communal "we," Max Scheler said, is in our consciousness before the individualized self, which is the artificial product of a cultural tradition and a historic process. ("Our fathers did not have the word 'individualism,'" Alexis de Tocqueville wrote in *L'Ancien Régime et la Révolution*.) The rise of the self-conscious individual sets formidable problems. For one thing, "person" and its spiritual acts cannot be objectified in knowledge, thus the individual consciousnesses—radically different forms of being from other kinds, as Hegel and the phenomenologists pointed out—can never really be known by other minds; they are condemned to loneliness and isolation. These were philosophical concerns; the sociologists chose more objective indices of social disintegration: Durkheim's anomic suicide, Weber's bureaucratic structures. (It should be noted that the line between philosophers, social scientists, economists, theologians, and other *Hochgelehrter* was not then so great. Durkheim and Weber, for example, mixed more philosophizing and prophesying into their "sociology"—a field not yet recognized by academic chairs—than would most inhabitants of a sociology department today.)

The German mind seems to have lain deeply under the spell of Tönnies' famous distinction between the natural community and the artificial society. Tönnies himself had pretended no scientific neutrality: "City life and *Gesellschaft* doom the common people to decay and death . . . the doom of culture itself."[34] The more extreme haters of the rationalized and fragmented society, such as Paul Lagarde, included among their *bêtes noires* educational specialization, science, liberal democracy, the whole urban industrial society, and the new German state of the Second Reich.[35] Students have named this strain "radical conservatism" and considered it a forerunner of Nazism; Hitler did indeed draw upon it as he did eclectically on many another creed, but it affected all sorts of people, Left and Right, in the pre-1914 Germany. It was not confined to Germany. Just before 1914 the Guild Socialists were on the rise in England along with the "distributivist" ideas of G. K. Chesterton and Hilaire Belloc, both trying to avoid socialism of the statist variety by returning to guilds, cooperatives, or local communes in some way: a tradition that led back to John Ruskin, quite as thorough a hater of modernism and preacher against destruction of wholeness as anything produced in Germany.

The drama of past and present played itself out in every great nineteenth-century social ideology and movement. Karl Marx himself, the most ruthless of modernists in his received dogmas, admiring capitalism for its destruction of the traditional society and sneering at sentimental peasant-lovers, was not so clear about this in his later years. The remarkable correspondence with Vera Zasulich and other Russians expressing some hope for the preservation of the peasant village is a case in point.[36] Among Marx's epigoni in the 1890-1914 generation, Werner Sombart, especially, in his study *Modern Capitalism*, focused attention on its abstract and inhuman characteristics as being the mode of uprooted, decultured, depersonalized modern man. In his distinction between the cultural aspects of early and late capitalism, a good and a bad type, Sombart nearly strayed off the Marxist reservation. Sombart was one who experienced severe trauma as he moved from his student days into the great society, and he wove this into his studies.

Georges Sorel betrayed the same inclination to admire a courageous capitalism, though he found his heroes in American freebooters of the recent Gilded Age, rather than in merchant-adventurers of the late Renaissance. Sombart and Sorel are not dissimilar from Robert Michels, one-time left-wing Socialist, who finally shed the class-conflict theory by deciding that even an Italian capitalist is better than a German proletarian.[37] Concern with the general process of "modernization" as both soul-killing and community-destroying tended to push out class conflict and class oppression as the leading preoccupation of social thought.

Anarchists, Syndicalists, Guild Socialists, and Russian Populists agreed in finding salvation in the small organic community rescued from the grip of the leviathan state. In *The Napoleon of Notting Hill,* Chesterton offered an answer which somewhat corresponds to those offered in more pedantic terms by the sociologists Durkheim and Max Weber: if you cannot feed your spirit in the great society, love your own neighborhood. Gustav Landauer's "Romantic socialism" combined anarchist, Buberist, and nationalist elements in an interesting mixture, obligated as well to Wagner, Nietzsche, Schopenhauer, and Ibsen.[38] Landauer's position is somewhat reminiscent of that Austrian circle which, originally of Nietzschean and Wagnerian inspiration, led in one direction to the popular, nationalistic Marxism of Viktor Adler and in another to the right-wing *deutschnational* extremism of Hitler's mentor, Georg Ritter von Schönerer.[39] These wings could agree at least in rejecting the economics of Manchester, the reigning liberal order of competitive individualism.

Richard Wagner, of course, had stressed the wholeness theme: art should fuse all the genres into a *gesamt* work, which itself should become a public ritual, as in ancient Greece; a hero such as Siegfried should embody the spiritual aspirations of the whole people. Nietzsche was less easily communalized, obviously, for hatred of German nationalism as well as the mass man marked his extreme esthetic individualism; his superman hero seemed to stand with Ibsen's "Enemy of the People," and communion with the "noisy dwarfs" was evidently possible only if they were placed firmly under the spur of high-spirited aristocrats. Still in *Schopenhauer as Educator,* while denouncing "money-makers and military despots" as "the current and worst forces" in present society, Nietzsche had cried that they would cause society to fall apart in an orgy of selfishness, an "atomistic revolution." He surely suggested Yeats'

Things fall apart, the centre will not hold

and in one sense was the enemy of "mere anarchy"; those who like D. H. Lawrence followed Nietzsche into a neoprimitive "religion of the blood" accepted neotribalism as well. The popularized (and vulgarized) Wagnerism *cum* Nietzscheanism of Jules Langbehn's *Rembrandt as Educator* (1890), which occupies so curiously significant a place in the intellectual history of this German generation, preached the creative rebirth of Germany in an organic society under a social monarchy. *The Greening of Germany* of its day, with the message such evangelism always contains of mastering selfishness and greed for the good of the whole community, Langbehn's book was a favorite of the Youth Movement.

The Youth Movement mixed together all the partly contradictory yearnings of those alienated by the urban-industrial-commercial-bureaucratic society, but most prominent was the quest for *Ungespaltenheit*. "A full life is above all a life in community," the *Wandervoegeler* declared. They were in rebellion against organization; they trusted only the spontaneous and the intuitive; and in other ways, such as their flight to the woods and fields and their antiintellectualism (they protested against false education, "growing up absurd," being treated as cogs in a machine a half century before college students discovered these targets in the 1960's), they seemed radically individualist. Nietzschean antidemocratic elitism entered deeply into the movement, for their prophet was certainly Zarathustra and their joyous wisdom indeed a release from the idols of the Christian tribe. Nevertheless, communalism of the kind "hippies" would later embrace was seen as a panacea.

Young Jewish intellectuals at the turn of the century were led sometimes to Zionism but more often to acceptance of the national culture, in flight from a feeling of insecurity and the rootlessness of urban society. "If one reads through the many analyses of the 'sickness of Judaism' written by Jews at the turn of the century, the same themes recur. Judaism is sick because Jews have lost contact with the genuine realities of life. They have become cut off from the nonintellectual, noncompetitive sides of human existence."[40] Jews took part in the Youth Movement. Martin Buber's important ideas of Hasidic communalism belong to this milieu. In the rich world of Viennese culture especially, it was common for Jewish artists and intellectuals to shed their traditional religious faith, less as a religious than as a cultural gesture: such was the case with that caustic critic of the Hapsburg establishment, Karl Kraus, as also with Mahler, Schoenberg, the Wittgensteins, and others. (Alban Berg, in a kind of secondary alienation, crossed over to Protestantism after having exchanged his Jewish patrimony for a Roman Catholic one.) Walther Rathenau, in Germany, was influenced by Buber in 1906 but never became a Zionist, turning his brilliant talents instead to the cause of German nationalism. "My

Germanism and Judaism do not harm one another, but rather do each other much good," Gustav Landauer thought.[41] French Jewry also rejected Zionism and remained deeply loyal to France.

Communalism, of course, did not necessarily mean nationalism. One might see in the image of a united people the desired cure for egoism and anomie; the state, however, appeared *gesellschäftlich* and bureaucratic-rational to many, and the whole nation perhaps too large for community. In whatever size the idealized community might be seen, it had the same shape. It was a vision of social harmony and solidarity, a curing of alienation and isolation, a society marked by distributive justice and by fulfillment for each unique individual within a harmonious whole. It was Marx's vision of Communism, "the solution to the riddle of history," which resolves the conflicts of existence and essence, contingency and necessity, individual and society. It was, in brief, both the Kingdom of Heaven to come and the Golden Age *in illud tempore*, transposed into secular terms. Herman Kutter, in a book published in 1903, *Sie müssen . . .*, told the Social Democrats that the reign of God was working through them, a proposition they disputed only formally. Karl Barth, famous for his later criticism of this-worldly kingdoms of God, became a Christian Socialist in 1911 and a Social Democrat in 1915. Conservatives, Socialists, Christians, Christian Socialists, Radical Conservatives, Zionists, Germanized Jews, Anarchists, Syndicalists, and others joined in a confused vision of what Fichte had verbalized at the dawn of the Romantic era, and during another world war:

> When no selfseeking purposes any longer divide mankind, and their strength is not exhausted in battle with each other . . . ; no longer separated by private ends, they are bound together in a single, common goal.

Written originally in 1800, Fichte's *Bestimmung des Menschen* was read throughout the century in Germany, and the prophet of heroic unity in the teeth of aggression made a reappearance in 1914, being much cited and discussed. A Romantic yearning for the lost unity of mankind filled the nineteenth century, even as nationalism waxed and selfish individualism prospered.

97

III

When they looked at the existing state of human relations, most intellectuals found them profoundly unsatisfactory. Instead of men "bound to each other by hereditary and unalterable ties," British social theorist L. T. Hobhouse put it, "we have merely fellow citizens, who have no special ties but those which they form for themselves."[42] Hobhouse as an optimistic British liberal worried about this far less than Continentals, seeing the advantages of being released from the restraints of ancient custom, status, tradition, authority. His liberal antecedents went back through Herbert Spencer to Bentham and Locke. Even in England that tradition was under attack, unless severely modified by the "new liberalism" of paternalistic state welfare then being adopted (1911). Spencer was no longer a prophet in good standing. The "society of strangers" accepted with such equanimity (or was it stoicism?) by Jeremy Bentham aroused little but uneasiness there.

To be sure, the message of the greatest of German sociologists was apparently one of resignation to the inevitable fate of "rationalization." Max Weber plainly felt an almost unbearable nostalgia for the lost wholeness and could express the pathos of modernism incomparably, as in his celebrated lectures on "Science as a Profession" and "Politics as a Profession." Yet as a social scientist—capable of a considerable impatience with the dreams of *literati*—he knew there was no escape from the hard bureaucratic world. Walther Rathenau echoed him in seeing mechanization as "man's fate."[43] Those who condemn the technological society would be helpless without its products and services. And technology entails specialization, professionalization, rationalization, bureaucratization. One may hope to mollify the monster but not to kill him.[44]

Impatient with illusions, Weber's hardness took the form of a grim acceptance of the "fate of our times," which is disenchantment —loss of religion, romance, magic. The creative statesman immersed in the real world of power, which is what Weber yearned to be, works with materials that are at hand. The world is as it is, at this moment in its long history, and our ability to reshape it is limited at best. Weber could not agree with those historicists and emergent evolutionists who saw total freedom and openness. But no more could he agree with determinists who enslaved history to some external prewritten destiny. We will never attain utopia. With the "elitist" school, including Gaetano Mosca and Vilfredo Pareto, he shared the belief that "the people" can never rule, the state will never wither away, power will not be exorcised from the world by any poetic incantations. The realization of Christian ethics is not possible in human society. The world is always at work destroying the ideals it produces. But there are countervailing forces. Charismatic leadership is so deeply rooted in human nature that it can arise in the modern society to counteract those all-too-potent elements of bureaucracy and legalism, helping us out of the Iron Cage. So too can democracy, as the plebs who respond to a leader, hoist him on their shoulders to power, and follow him blindly, so long as he *is* a leader, then ruthlessly reject him when he ceases to be.

Weber accepted nationalism as the given vehicle of modern politics and welcomed Germany's quest for a world role. Power exists, in a world inevitably half demonic. If Germany had not wanted to face the risk of war, she should never have made the decision to become a major nation. Having done so, she had the responsibility, not merely the right, to offer posterity another choice of culture, one different from Russian despotism, French dilletantism, and English dullness! Weber's feeling for the war as unifying agent broke forth at the beginning of the war, as we have previously noted. He shared with the Naumannites a vision of 1914 as an "uprising" realizing the dream of a *Volksstaat*, a people's state. But during the war his critical intellect came to regard the "1914 ideas" as too sentimental. Germany's political structure did not equip her to be a *Herrenvolk*; not unless the people participate in the political process does national unity truly exist. The will to power externally is incompatible with internal powerlessness. If only the Kaiser were charismatic! But he was not, and Weber saw Germany failing in her great test for want of adequate leadership. The Western democracies could produce great demagogues like Lloyd George, a product of a vital system of parliamentary democracy. Weber entered the great debate among German scholars about war aims and war policies on the side of those who would accompany realistic moderation in annexation goals with domestic reform, a distinguished group that included historians Meinecke and Delbrück along with Ernst Troeltsch; it was opposed, however, by a majority who feared that raising doubts about Germany's monarchical constitution and unquestioned rightness during the war would weaken morale.[45] Weber's doubts, of course, came two years after the beginning of the war, when lack of adequate civilian leadership manifested itself in blunders such as the U-boat decision.

IV

The yearning for *Gemeinschaft*, despite Fritz Ringer's plausible claim that German intellectuals reacted to the crisis of industrialization with peculiar intensity,[46] seems to have been equally as great in France, where the great sociologist Émile Durkheim made group solidarity *the* key to his thought, more so than Max Weber, and where Maurice Barrès erected "deracination" into the leading literary idea; where also the Nationalist Movement attracted at least as much eager support among outstanding writers (Claudel, Péguy, Maurras, Bourget, etc.) as in Germany. German counterparts, such as George, Mann, Hesse, Musil, are obsessed by the need for community; but they are far less explicitly nationalist, perhaps because they could less easily acclaim the existing political order. The *Alldeutscher Verband* (Pan-German League) was an affair of obscure schoolmasters and crankish ex-officers, largely outside the realm of serious intellectual movements. (The French parallel was the *parti colonial* led by Paul Bourde.) In 1913 celebrations of the centenary of the German "liberation" from Napoleon at the Battle of Leipzig found the Youth Movement and the intelligentsia vaguely dissatisfied with the official patriotism; there were counter-ceremonies, like those in the United States in 1976, in which struggle and sacrifice were accepted while being dissociated from the existing national Establishment. Despite the many bitter political divisions, above all over the Dreyfus *affaire*, and despite the characteristic disunity even of France's nationalist prophets, French unity was more assured and French patriotism more unitary, which ensured a whole congeries of post-Dreyfus patriotic "leagues." There was a deeper insecurity about German national unity.[47] In both countries, there was a thirst for unity accompanied by all too many indications of its absence.

The role of *l'affaire* can never be overstated; it was an intellectual *coup de fouet*, as Georges Guy-Grand remarks, that transformed everything. While Péguy, originally a Dreyfusard, hoped to repair the frightening divisions that tore France apart (striking *within* classes and even families), the affair propelled Charles Maurras into a lifelong hatred of democracy, to scepticism, moral anarchy, and national disunity. The founder of the nationalist *Action Française* differed on quite a few accounts from the Romantic Barrès. The archenemy of everything Romantic, Maurras agreed with the American Irving Babbitt in holding that Rousseau had poisoned the wells of French life. His paradigm was the Grand Monarchy of the *ancien régime*, era of the classical tragedians and the rationalist intellectual position founded by Descartes. Barrès wanted a democratic Caesar, Maurras a restored monarchy. Barrès made a Romantic cult of the fields, scenes, legends, and customs of France, and celebrated the simple countryfolk. Maurras discovered in his youth that nationalism was in fact the religion for modern man (he learned this at the first modern Olympic Games) and built a discipline, a structure around it, without himself much believing in French nationalism, certainly not romantically (his heart, if he had one, was in his native Provence). The disorder of modern life—its "sick hurry and divided aims"—needed to be cured by resort to some principle of order.

Maurras's invoking monarchy, church, and classicism reminds one of Arnold Schoenberg's adopting the deliberately artificial convention of twelve-note serialism in music: there must be a structure, but it doesn't really much matter what. Personally Maurras was one of those who, he said, "have an urgent need to lack God"—a Comtean atheist. But life must have rules, peoples must have clearly defined cultures. Catholicism is the traditional religion of France, rooted in her past and grounded in her character. And, in general, to be civilized is to be Latin. The universal rules of classical reason passed from Rome's universal empire to France as its legatee. This was a different stress from that of Barrès, to whom national cultures are unique, rooted in history and the land, untranslatable into other idioms; there is a French truth which is not at all like the German, English, Russian, or Italian. No one was better prepared than Maurras to identify modern Germany with Teutonic barbarism, whose murky mists he contrasted with Mediterranean sunlight; a view he shared with the otherwise incompatible Péguy.

On the eve of World War I French university students were under the spell of Maurras's militant, dogmatic, vigorous pen. Members of his French Action Movement, small in number but intellectually distinguished, gratified their yearnings to attack parliamentary pettifoggery, bourgeois cowardice, self-interest, disloyalty. The group's *esprit analytique* clashed not only with French Romanticism—Hugo and Michelet lay as much under the ban as Rousseau—but with Bergson and Péguy, whose stress on intuition at the expense of intellect seemed all too Germanic. When the war came, Bergson accused the Germans of being mechanical men without soul, almost the opposite of the Maurrasian analysis, French *clarté* versus German mystification!

Of these unseemly disagreements within the ranks of Integralism, Maurras was all too aware. One of them was on socioeconomic policy, Maurras favoring the Social Catholic idea of a "corporate state" while Paul Bourget wanted to destroy the trade unions and Barrès was generally more "populist." Yet somehow the spirit of the *renaissance nationale*, resurgent since 1905, pulled together Maurras, Barrès, Bergson, the Socialist-Republican Péguy, the pious Claudel; Catholics and freethinkers; republicans and monarchists. After 1912, with the German menace mounting, Maurras's group rallied to defend the republic in the higher cause of the homeland, *patrie* over *régime*.[48]

The path of Maurice Barrès had led from early fastidious estheticism to a rejoining of the national life via traditionalism. There were other ex-dandies who converted to rightist politics; Guy-Grand, in *La Philosophie nationaliste* (1911), commented that the literary nationalists were formerly "refined literati, subtle philosophers, conscientious professors," mentioning, in addition to Barrès and Bourget, Jules Lemaître and historian Jacques Bainville. They were marked as much by their distaste for democratization as by their affected taste for French traditions. Barrès was drawn into Boulangist and anti-Dreyfusard politics, and became intermittently a member of the Chamber while continuing his literary career. His Nietzschean immoralism, at a peak in *Of Blood, Voluptuousness and Death* (1894), which out-D'Annunzio'ed D'Annunzio, he discovered to be a dead end, a not uncommon experience for Nietzscheans—one might compare Merezhkovsky in Russia at about the same time. A vigorous personality found it hard to live in such an exile. *The Uprooted* (1897) signaled his conversion from the hyperindividualist *culte de moi* to the cult of the fatherland. That too could be beautiful!

From then on, the talk was no more of the *niaiserie* of the masses and the boredom of superior souls, but of those healthy peasants who lived in the immemorial customs of their country. With Paul Dérouléde, Barrès founded the League of the French Fatherland (*Ligue de la Patrie Française*) in 1898. The two tried a rather ludicrous coup d'état in 1899, leading to Déroulède's temporary exile. Maurice Barrès was re-elected to parliament in 1906 and made himself the spokesman for national unity against the German threat, while he became the literary idol of young France. A whole school of works about the sufferings and the heroism of the lost provinces (Alsace and Lorraine) was spawned, led by Barrès' *Colette Baudoche* (1909).[49] His was a truly remarkable career, a virtuoso performance; this transmogrification of master writer into major politician was reminiscent of Chateaubriand, and in more recent French times only André Malraux has emulated it. These French supermen were driven by the very Romantic, Balzacian dream of experiencing everything, living many lives—life as the supreme adventure. (A youthful admiration for Scott and Dumas links Barrès to Romanticism.)

Less flamboyantly, author Jules Romains invented "Unanimism" in 1905, celebrating collective actions and feelings, an idea influencing the Futurists via Romains' poem *La vie unanimiste* (1908). A thirst for solidarity with the masses, imaginary more than real, of course, may be seen in the Whitmanesque long poem by Edward Carpenter, *Towards Democracy*, reprinted several times between 1882 and 1905. "If I am not level with the lowest I am nothing. . . . The craziest sot in the village is my equal." A sort of *Thus Spake Zarathustra* in reverse, Carpenter's rhapsody sought immersion in the masses as a cure for spiritual desiccation. The gesture reminds us of that of a much greater writer, Count Tolstoy, at about the same time. Rolland's *Clerambault* must "run with the herd, rub against the human animals his brothers, feel like them, act like them." The religion of social service sent conscience-stricken rich folk into the ghetto to expose the scandals of poverty. The urge to break away from a life-killing egoism often led to affirming one's organic connection with the great collectivity. If their mystic "people" was still largely a Romantic abstraction, these late-century rebels did often embrace actual specimens of derelict humanity. One thinks of Dostoyevsky, and of those poet drop-outs who from Arthur Rimbaud to Francis Thompson and Ernest Dowson sought the gutter, communed with the damned, went "underground." Zola's gallery of wretches, *Of Human Bondage, Crime and Punishment:* the imaginative literature of the *fin de siècle* teems with portraits from the lower depths sympathetically drawn by the greatest artists in the image of a common humanity. In England, George Gissing's *The Nether World* (1880) was perhaps the first literary work

103

to really enter a working-class world.[50] "Solidarisme" was the slogan of even so bourgeois (!) a politician as Leon Bourgeois. The whole socialist mood in this most socialist of eras (judged by popular acceptance) is related to the same urgent desires. The future socialist society should bring a "fusion of souls," Maxim Gorky declared. Russian symbolism was flavored with an unusual element of populism.[51] In Russia a mystic Christian philosopher like N. F. Fyodorov could influence Dostoyevsky, Tolstoy, and Mayakovsky with a message of brotherhood and integration, healing not only divisions of nations and classes but all dualisms of knowledge—a yearning which suggests reasons why Hegel and then Marx made such an appeal to the Russians.[52]

At the opposite extreme of temperament, the drily disabused Italian economist, mathematician, and political sociologist Vilfredo Pareto saw the era of "foxes" reaching its appointed term, and the second of the great human "residues," the "persistence of aggregates," about to reassert itself. Translated into less pretentious terminology, the need for heroism and wholeness, Sparta as against Athens, was due for a return as part of that cyclical course human history runs, the focal point being the psychological qualities of ruling elites. Foxiness, the "instinct for combinations," was a trait all too evident among the "demagogic plutocracy" which plundered and misgoverned Italy in the disillusioning aftermath of the Risorgimento. It was not exactly socialism that Pareto looked forward to, nor a sentimental bathing in community. (His *Systèmes Socialistes* [1902] was said to have cost Lenin more sleep than any other book.) The few always rule, democracy being only a particular form of elitism. The unmasking of ideals, reducing them to mere "rationalizations," not primarily, as with Marx, of economic interests but of political power based on psychological temperament, delighted Pareto, satisfying no doubt his own bitter resentments and unsatisfied wishes for power. As social scientist he posited what *au fond* was a rather familiar cycle of decay and renewal. The foxes with their instinct for combinations grow too clever by half, and corrupt; despite their wiles, which include buying off or co-opting potential revolutionaries, a wave of disgust welling from the aggregational instinct overwhelms them; lions arise to slay them with weapons they do not know how to use. His friend Georges Sorel, Pareto said, meant the same thing by intellect versus "myth": the two basic residues which we might perhaps translate as the modernized community versus the (supposed) premodern organic one.

V

Thus in one way or another the thought of this era seemed always to come back to a preoccupation with social disintegration and longed-for reintegration. Community and Society; Myth and Intellect; Dionysus and Apollo; Charisma and Bureaucracy; Aggregates and Combinations; Solidarity and Anomie; Integral Nationalism and Deracination—these were some of its formulations, at bottom close to stating the same duality; to which one might add Freud's Id and Superego, Jung's Collective as opposed to Individual Unconscious, and Henry Maine's Status versus Contract. These varied and fumbling attempts to conceptualize the problem all derived, surely, from what was happening and had happened during recent decades.[53] Capitalism substituted the impersonality of the marketplace for custom, ritual, and ceremony, destroying ancient social structures. At the same time, town and village dissolved into the "great society," governed bureaucratically and not by personal, human relationships. In great cities the society of strangers tended to supplant high-context neighborliness. These new social units were too big by far for meaningful participation; democracy, if it meant only voting for representatives in parliament, did not satisfy the need for community feeling. (Each man, Georges Sorel remarked, is one ten-millionth a tyrant but every bit a slave!) The state was a cold and remote monster; but even institutions such as trade unions, spontaneously arising to fill a social need in the urban-industrial situation, became too large to be governed except by a small elite cut off from the mass of members. Ideals, when they arose, whether of reform or revolution, were quickly swallowed up by the sheer size and complexity of this society; *mystique* evaporated into *politique*, the rationalized world became disenchanted.

That in such a frustrating situation violence could be tempting is revealed in the wave of militant and often bloody strikes which swept Europe at intervals, particularly from 1910 to 1914; in the Russian Revolution of 1905; in feminist aggressiveness in England and the Irish troubles which threatened civil war on the eve of the 1914 war; and in other ways. "If simple anomie is present," Sebastian de Grazia concludes, "the prospect of a war will augur for its relief."[54] Surprising to those who looked at the situation from a simple Left-Right perspective were about-faces by, for example, Russian strikers, who went straight from their picket lines into the trenches, and militant

British suffragettes, who had been fighting the government tooth and nail, immediately becoming (in most cases) superpatriots lending their full energies to the crusade against the Huns.[55] Psychologically, if not ideologically, such transfers made sense; the constant was combat against a tangible foe, knitting together the band of brothers or sisters in common cause. Durkheim pointed out that suicide and other indices of social disintegration decline in war because collective passions are stirred; his disciple Halbwachs attributed this lessening of anomie to the simplification of life patterns that occurs in war and crises.[56]

Nostalgia for community might be in plentiful supply, but needless to say few if any really wanted a return to the ancient days, if these were conceived as medieval, feudal, or peasant. Hierarchical and authoritarian, the old society sacrificed the free individual ruthlessly to the demands of an organic order backed by an intolerant religion. "This whole order of ideas has vanished from the civilized world," Bertrand Russell rejoiced, adding that he hoped it had vanished forever. "The old order has been destroyed by the new ideals of justice and liberty."[57] Less approvingly, Durkheim remarked in *Le Suicide* (1897) that "people view any attempt to dam up the flood of their desires as a sort of sacrilege." The free individual, including the free woman, concerned with her own "growth" and fulfillment as a creative person, had rebelled against the demands of organicism which forced self-sacrifice, familialism, subordination.[58] Those intellectuals who pined for something nobly communitarian could never accept any elimination of the free individual. They could only hope for some future "re-integration" that managed to conserve the emancipated ego while somehow providing it with that solidarity or *Gemeinschaft* it missed.

Durkheim offered the sociologist as demiurge of a postmodern socialization. Marxists dreamed of the kingdom of freedom-in-community which would somehow combine an even more efficient technology with the ability to hunt, farm, and intellectualize. Marx's ideal of the free citizen may be traced to the ancient Greek *polis*, reasserted in Renaissance humanism. Such an ideal could be no more than a wistful hope. In twentieth-century Europe the only practical kind of community was nationalism. And the need for a "moral equivalent of war" remained as great as when William James wrote his essay in the United States in 1898.

—6—

"La Patrie Est en Danger":
Socialism and War in 1914

I

On the puzzling question of why the European Socialists succumbed to Mars in 1914, immense amounts of ink have flowed, much of it inevitably polemical but a great deal by honest and industrious scholars seeking painstakingly for truth amid the multitudinous records. In a controversy as old and as mulled over as this one, we realize that there is no escape from subjectivity: no "final synthesis" awaits us, satisfactory to all parties and all points of view. Nevertheless the questions frequently asked even by one's fellow historians suggest that clarification has not been achieved, and needs to be. "Why *did* the Socialists cave in?" is still likely to be the bewildered cry emanating from those with an interest in the period, or in peace, or socialism.

The average uninstructed posing of the question has always been somewhat misleading. The Socialists, it is frequently said, had time and again vowed that they would oppose war under any circumstances, and that they would defeat any effort to launch war, by refusing to fight, summoning the proletariat to resistance, or calling a general strike. They based their position squarely on Marx's "the proletariat has no fatherland," being completely opposed to nationalism and viewing a national war as inevitably hostile to the interests of the laboring masses. Any Marxist must hold (so we are often told) that under capitalism any war would have to be one unleashed by seekers of profit at the expense of the exploited toilers; a war moreover to prolong capitalism's miserable life, by injecting a shot of illicit profits and destroying the glut of constant capital. The workers' enemy is at home; if he wants to fight he should choose his own employer, not his fellow toilers abroad. Leaders of the working class therefore cannot have been in doubt about where their duty lay. If instead they rallied to their own country's cause and allowed the toiling masses to slaughter each other, it must have been because they totally lost their wits, or were corrupt, or were unaccountably swept away by strange tides of irrational emotion.

The Socialists, it is further assumed, had the power to stop the war. At a peak of success just before the war, the Second International counted twelve million members, and had an effective international organization. The German Social Democrats became the largest single party in the Reichstag in 1912; the French Socialist party with 103 seats in the Chamber became the second largest party in 1914, and the premier of France was an independent Socialist. It was widely believed that in November, 1912, the International had in fact saved Europe from war, when a ringing proclamation from its meeting at Basel seemed to rally the forces of peace at a time of serious crisis following the First Balkan War. The prominent Belgian Socialist Hendrik de Man, writing in 1910, assumed that everyone knew that if the German government contrived a war this would lead immediately to social revolution in Germany.[1]

Many of these assumptions are questionable. If we examine the record of socialist utterances and action reaching back to Marx and Engels, we find much more ambivalence. To begin with, the founding fathers bequeathed no consistent theoretical guidance on the subject of war, nationalism, or imperialism. A definite theory in Marxist terms that rivalry among industrial countries would lead to war was apparently first discussed by Karl Kautsky in 1901.[2] And Kautsky eventually rejected this view, accepting the more logical one that capitalists would join together to create a world cartel, the better to do away with painful competition and collaborate in fleecing the noncapitalist peoples. (Lenin himself, when he came to compose a theory of capitalist imperialism as leading to war, *after* the event in 1914, decided that "International capitalist monopolies *share* the world among themselves.") Marx and Engels assumed that both capitalist and precapitalist societies naturally had wars, which would disappear along with all other imperfections in the future classless golden age. But they did not tie war to capitalism in any specific way—i.e., they did not compose a theory of the necessity of war because of the dynamics of a capitalist order. (The nineteenth-century evidence was scarcely persuasive.)

It was in their youthful thunderbolt *The Communist Manifesto* that Marx and Engels said "the worker has no fatherland" and also hinted that wars would increase as class conflict mounted.[3] But in their mature years the founding fathers were much more nationalistic. They were staunch supporters of German unification under Prussian leadership down to the war of 1870, which they supported. (Not until the annexation of Alsace and Lorraine did they stop cheering for a Prussian victory over France.) No one has ever suggested that Marx was a "pacifist"; he preached struggle, conflict, and war as the law of life. His attitude toward nationalism is perhaps less well understood. A short discussion of elementary Marxism in relation to the problem of war and of nationality may not be amiss.

Doubtless one can draw from the master much more subtle and sophisticated ideas than his organized disciples of the Socialist Movement did—a fact of which they were more aware than recent commentaries would have us believe. (A highly sophisticated mind such as Viktor Adler's deliberately created a vulgarized Marxism, so that the masses might easily grasp it—who could deny that Marx wanted them to understand and act on his thought?) Among the elements of popular Marxism, the most important was the belief that history is a rational, orderly progression, meaningful and purposive, from lower to higher, passing through various definite stages and headed toward an ultimate completion marked by the full development of both material and spiritual powers. Almost equally important was the conception of truth and value as dependent on the phase of social development, every position being true only for the historical moment, to be absorbed in the next, higher truth. The "mode of production" *determines* social, political, and cultural forms. History is a record of class struggle; but class struggle is only the engine that drives the great machine, onward and upward, dialectically, which was construed as meaning sudden changes from one basic social mode to another, changes which have been ripening for a long time but happen all at once (like the air in a tire gradually building up to an explosion). We had feudalism, we have capitalism, we shall have socialism or communism: nothing much in between. And unto each its own laws.

This is no place to expound Marxism, popular or unpopular; but the "mechanical" or dogmatic type purveyed in this era seemed the most specifically Marxist, meaning "scientific" (deterministic, exact, impersonal, heedless of mere human emotion or will). The progression of stages, with the last act soon to begin after a crashing penultimate climax, dominated popular socialism, because it offered assurance of success, a clear guide to action, a dramatic vision of history. But of this apparently simple idea, as in Christianity, there were interesting and often puzzling implications.

The inevitable-stages-of-history theory committed one to accepting all the horrors of capitalism, as well as its blessings, so long as its writ still has time to run. Like adolescence, or like the long hot summer, capitalism has to be gotten through, with little chance of escape from pimples or heat strokes. Any effort to force the norms of a higher stage onto capitalism would be as bizarre as trying to bring snow in July. And capitalism, like all the other stages of human history, the mechanical Marxist conceived as an organic whole, glued together in a single ball of wax, all of whose portions related. If war is a part of capitalism, then in the capitalist stage war will come. It can be used as an opportunity to hasten the end of capitalism, conceivably, if capitalism is in its latter days. But even a capitalism not yet decrepit might have war, in which case should or must socialists support it? The flow of history is always forward; to accept what is as right, tempts Marxists as much as it does other kinds of historicists.

Moreover, the gains of the past have to be conserved. Marxism held capitalism to be an advanced stage of human history, indeed almost the last stop before the Blessed Kingdom; it contains much that is good, much that must pass into the next and highest stage, transformed and transcended but preserved. Mankind struggled *up* to capitalism from savagery through long eons of travail, reaching through slavery and serfdom. Capitalism is higher than feudalism, and in any struggle between these two, the progressive man must be on its side. Marxists in their way could agree with the crude remark of an American statesman who once said that he was on the side of the Negro against the alligator but of the white man against the Negro. They were on the side of the Russian against the Oriental but of the European against the Russian. (Engels said that in the beginning one should have been on the side of the slaveholder against the tribal chieftain.) Many Marxists and other socialists were on the side of the

European imperialists against African "savages." Most English Socialists, for example, backed the Boer War. Jean Jaurès supported French
penetration of Morocco.[4] Marx himself had supported the United
States against Mexico in 1849, the "energetic Yankees" over the "lazy
Mexicans."

Above all, capitalism bears in its aging womb the precious hope
of the future, and must live long enough to deliver the child safely.
What if a socialist is living in the era of a fairly mature but not yet
pregnant capitalism, or one, say, only about three months along?
Suppose she is attacked by some brute of a premodern culture? Iras-
cible and mean-spirited mother though she may be, she carries the heir
of tomorrow and must be defended.

Implicated here is one of Marxism's central problems. "In combining the two ideas of the necessity of further development of the
established order and a necessary and inevitable proletarian revolution
at some indeterminate future date," a recent historian (R. Tiersky)
notes, Marxist doctrine was condemned to an ambivalence: it is necessary both to advance the existing society, which means defending it
and, even to a point, helping it, preventing its retrogression, preserving
it; yet also to revolutionize it and supplant it. In this era, against
Anarchists and Syndicalists committed to an emotional faith in revolution, Marxists stressed the scientific character of their philosophy,
which turned out to mean chiefly the need to traverse and exhaust the
bourgeois stage before entering the last and highest one.

The above picture was complicated for Marxists by the bothersome
fact that we have a number of separate states or nations not only at
different phases of development along the feudalism-capitalism-social-
ism road, but each also with certain peculiarities not entirely dependent
on socioeconomic conditions. It was with difficulty that any Marxist
could be brought to admit the latter, for it does not square with the
theory of "superstructure" and economic foundation.[5] Yet as "superstructure," if not basic structure, such national differences were too
obvious for anyone to miss. *Languages* differ. On a famous occasion
in the future, Josef Stalin was to fly into a fury and decapitate a poor
savant who preached what he thought to be the correct line, that
language is "superstructure," determined by the underlying socioeconomic realities. Faithful "dialectical materialist" though he was,
this was too much for the robust common sense of the Georgian.
Clearly language is *not* "superstructure," since it does not basically

depend on or vary with the class system and mode of production. Russians speak Russian under capitalism as they spoke it under feudalism and will speak it under socialism; they will not start using French or German when they arrive at the higher stage, though small changes will be made. And from language comes literature, bestowing upon each people precious treasures of poetry and prose which eat their way into the deeper consciousness of all. What of the Pushkins and Goethes and Hugos, the Shakespeares and Molières and Emersons? Were they simply feudal or capitalist entertainers paid to distort or distract the minds of the underlings? Whatever the requirements of theory, few German Social Democrats really believed that Schiller and Heine belonged to the bourgeoisie and not to all the people. Nor could French Socialists forget that they were not merely the heirs but in some sense the products of past French literary giants. "They love France because of St. Louis, Joan of Arc, Pascal; we love it because of Voltaire, Hugo, Blanqui, Zola, Jaurès" (Gustav Hervé, 1914).

Marx's theory of history stressed preservation, rather than annihilation, of previous epochs: socialism as the dialectical reply to capitalism includes it while surpassing it. History turns the instruments of the bourgeoisie into socialist assets, altering them but not abolishing them. Great factories, of course, created by the capitalists, will be used even more effectively under the socialist order, which having thrown off the shackles of private ownership causes the machines to work for humanity instead of for a few. Similarly, nationalism is a potentially valuable bourgeois creation, destined to realize its value *fully* after the revolution: national culture for all, not just the upper classes. Bissolati, the Italian "revisionist" Socialist, spoke of "the stupid legend that socialism means the negation of the Fatherland." In the Marxian-Hegelian sense of the word, there would have to be a negation. But a negation is not a destruction; it is much more nearly an addition. "The nation is a step on the road to the great human *patrie*," Jules Guesde declared. "Nations are not only useful but necessary elements of human development," agreed Édouard Vaillant, his fellow French Socialist who more often sided with Jaurès than Guesde, the fraternal disputers of the movement.[6] All the past consists of necessary steps, in the Marxian view. If at the top of the stairs lies the ultimate fair haven, one had to climb them to get there, and the stairway remains for others who have still to complete the ascent.

As for war, Marx saw it as the midwife of revolution. He sided with Prussia in 1870 on the grounds that a Prussian victory would advance socialism. In 1874 he remarked that "We must go through a general European war before we can think of any decisive external effectiveness of the European working class." Whenever wars occurred, Marx and Engels tended to take sides on the basis of judging which was the more progressive, within the Marxist evolutionary scale. Engels regarded the French conquest of Algeria as "a fortunate fact for the progress of civilization." Almost nothing of the later socialist animus against "imperialism" appears in the thought of its founders, who ordinarily took it for granted that backward, primitive, "barbarian" peoples did well to submit themselves to the more advanced and enlightened Europeans. Marx and Engels were infatuated with the pronouncement of military theorist Clausewitz that "war is a continuation of politics by other means." In other words, war is a continuation of the social process at an accelerated pace. (Little difference exists in principle between war and peace, there being violence in both.) Acceleration is a most desirable thing, for the engine of history is en route down the track toward paradise and ought to be speeded on its way.

Engels, whose nickname was "the General," took a keen interest in military affairs, on which he was considered something of an expert, though he wrongly predicted the outcome of the Austro-Prussian War of 1866. The founders of scientific socialism delighted in the hard-headed debunking of Romantic illusions, the exploding of innocent sentimentality. War, therefore, in itself did not bother them. Some wars were obviously bad: thus after 1871 Marx feared a war between France and Germany because in his view they were the two most advanced countries with growing Socialist movements. His "almost pathological hatred of Russia" lasted most of his life. He and Engels agreed that the German Socialists would eagerly defend their country against Russia and, Engels subsequently added, against France if she is Russia's ally. "*Possibly* the French Republic might represent the bourgeois revolution against the German Kaiserdom. But against the Republic in the service of the Russian tsar, German Socialism unquestionably represents the proletarian revolution. . . . Should the thirst for conquest of the Tsar and the chauvinistic impatience of the French bourgeoisie attempt to hold up the victorious but peaceful advance of the German Socialists, the latter are ready to show the world that they are not unworthy heirs of the French sans-culottes of a century ago, and that 1893 can stand comparison with 1793."[7] This was right after the bombshell of the Franco-Russian alliance, of course; but the note of hostility to Russia and the robust German nationalism is quite consistent with most of the lifelong pronouncements of Engels and, to a considerable degree, of Marx.

II

Nationalism had been a Good Thing, down through the great Italian Risorgimento and German unification of the 1860's, for all European radicals and Socialists. It still was, for those people such as the Poles, who suffered from lack of national independence. While Marx never clearly faced the issue, he may well have seen nationalism, freed from the incubus of the bourgeois-dominated state, as the natural community for modern man. At the same time, he and Engels showed little patience with the claims of smaller peoples; like Hegel they valued only "world-historical peoples" and could sound as ruthless as any pan-German in contemptuously dismissing the pretentions of various sub-Slav groups to independence. Marx and Engels thought that the Germans and Hungarians should absorb the Slavs within the Dual Monarchy; Engels spoke of "a war of extermination of the Germans against the Czechs" in 1848 and called for "determined terrorism" against the South Slavs. Great national states, Engels wrote, are "the unavoidable precondition for the harmonious international cooperation of the peoples" under proletarian rule. Only large political units can develop the large-scale industrial economies which are capitalism's bequest to the future socialist society. In the future utopia, the *state* will wither away or be superseded, but not the nation—i.e., the cooperative political community with its own language and culture.

It may be noted that Marx's great Anarchist rival in the First International, Bakunin, was also an enthusiastic nationalist; his rival within German socialism, Ferdinand Lassalle, was even more so, since he retained Hegel's view of the state (rejected by Marx) as transcending class and individual interests, destined therefore to survive even in a classless future. Lassalleanism did not entirely die within German socialism despite Marxism's general triumph; it was represented by Ludwig Quessel and others.

Indeed, Marx was not the only socialist prophet and oracle, especially in France, where the movement, fragmented until 1905, featured five or six kinds of socialist or working-class ideologies and factions. An anarchist or syndicalist wing of significant dimensions stood well to the Left of the Marxists (Guesdians) measured by militancy, proneness to violence, revolutionary energy. It was one of these who boasted that "We are eternal rebels, men truly without god, without master, without country, the irreconcilable enemies of every form of despotism, whether moral or material, individual or collective . . . and passionate lovers of the cultivation of the self."[8] Far from the Marxist style, this was more nearly the schoolboy idea of the romantic rebel. Marx and Engels had fought it, as Blanquism or as Nechaev-style anarchism. Such incurable enemies of all authority, even their own, were unacceptable to the Marxists, who expelled them from the International whenever possible. (The author of the above encomium to anarchy, Fernand Pelloutier, was so treated in 1896.) *Le syndicalisme contre le socialisme* (1907) was the title of a book directed against the Guesdists (by Gabriel Terrail); for even the rather precarious unity achieved by the various Socialist factions in 1905, creating the Federated Socialist party (SFIO), left out the Anarchists or Anarcho-Syndicalists.

It cannot be said that any of these were pacifists. Proudhon, sometime friend but more often foe and rival of Marx in the early days of *le mouvement social*, had been a notable glorifier of war (see especially his *La Guerre et la Paix*, 1861). Proudhon does look forward to the sublimation of war into other kinds of struggle, but does not see an end to conflict; the first part of the book presents war as "the discipline of humanity" and "the most solemn and sublime form of justice." The Socialist Victor Considérant in 1847 had recommended a war between France and Prussia on one side against Austria and Russia on the other, "civilization against barbarism." Just wars, wars to annihilate despotism and enthrone righteousness, were always attractive to the emotional radical, who dreamed of some heroic climax—the last war, no doubt, but a rousing one, freeing all the oppressed and vanquishing all tyrants. He was excitable and easily aroused to a frenzy of hatred against some monstrous injustice.

The archetypal nineteenth-century revolutionary Auguste Blanqui, who spent half his life in prison, ended his turbulent career by crying out for the defense of France—*la patrie en danger*—and of the Paris commune against Prussia. This great radical event in French history, which Marx himself hailed as the dawn of the proletarian revolution, and which indeed was an authentically popular uprising, was a patriotic response to the existing French government's surrender to the Prussians, rather than a socialist revolution. But it contributed more than its share to the potent French radical myth of the citizen soldiers rallying to save the revolution from a foreign invader. That these reactionary interventionists had been Prussians in 1792 and 1871 was significant for 1914, the myth being only slightly marred by the fact that at the start of the Franco-Prussian war in 1870 the French regime was not a republic but an imperial despotism, and the Communards fought their fellow Frenchmen, not the Germans.

The epigoni of the pioneer socialists lived in an era of apparent socialist success—the era of the Second International, founded as the organization of world socialism in the centennial year of the French Revolution. During the years from 1889 to 1914 socialism achieved both legal recognition and a mass following, at the cost of that revolutionary élan which never is consistent with size, organization, and respectability. Certainly some pacifist tendencies showed themselves in this relatively sunny period; but at the same time nationalism also grew, a product of socialists' enhanced feelings of belonging, of having a stake in society, of being prepared to take over the nation and thus wishing to defend it. Jean Jaurès, a pillar of the Peace Movement, was equally well known for his fervent attachment to France. He was, Milorad Drachkovitch aptly remarks, "a mixture of workingclass internationalism with jacobin patriotism."[9] Incurably optimistic ("all his verbs are in the future tense," one fellow parliamentarian complained), the great orator did not see war as inevitable and could even accept Norman Angell's celebrated demonstration that capitalism makes for peace, not war. Jaurès was known for his attachment to the International and his close friendship with the German Social Democrats. Without renouncing the desire to recover Alsace and Lorraine from the Germans, he would not raise the issue of the lost provinces, either; and certainly, like the German Social Democrats, he aroused deep suspicions on the Right as a man who would betray French national interests. And yet, at the same time, Jaurès the Jacobin patriot characteristically averred that "The nation is the treasure house of human genius and progress, and it ill behooves the proletariat to smash to pieces this priceless vessel of human culture." And "The notion that the proletarians, enslaved by capital, could not through invasion and conquest fall into a *worse* slavery is childish."[10]

Jules Guesde, Jaurès' rival in the dialectical debates among the

116

French Socialists, harbored a deeply emotional patriotism underneath the hard exterior of scientific Marxism.[11] But he kept the argument on an unsentimental plane: the logic of social evolution within the framework of different political communities at different stages on the path. Suppose, at the extreme, that the proletariat *won* in France, while Germany remained capitalist (or vice versa, though it must be confessed Guesde did not prefer to put the case this way). Would not everybody agree that France could justly defend itself (or even attack)? Is the case any different in principle when the proletariat in one country is *closer* to power than in another? The German Social Democrats, Guesde conceded, had a duty to defend Germany against Russia. It is evident that Guesde thought France a more advanced country than Germany, a proposition the German Socialists would scarcely have accepted. What if two countries were at the same level of development? Guesde and Paul Lafargue tended to fall back on the argument that if war comes, as it probably must under capitalism, then *che sara sara,* and history's course is accelerated, drawing closer to the inevitable happy ending.[12]

The German and Austrian Socialists were equally nationalistic. Karl Kautsky remarked on the "intense German nationalism" of the Austrian Socialists, who were heavily Jewish, and the most cultured of all the European Socialists—made up of professional people, doctors, lawyers, musicians, journalists. Viktor Adler was in many ways the most remarkable specimen of socialist culture ever produced.[13] A doctor, he was the friend of Gustav Mahler and other Austrian artists, musicians, and scientists. Wagner and Nietzsche had influenced him almost as much as had Marx. It was his vivid imagination, inspired by Wagner and Nietzsche, that led him to invent the socialist spectacles to appeal to the feelings of the working masses: the May Day parades and the famous procession in 1905 on behalf of universal suffrage, which dressed the proletariat in colorful medieval *Volksfeiertag* costumes. Adler had had ties early in his life with the *deutschnational* movement, likely today to remind us of Adolf Hitler's first teachers. (There was a curiously fervent German cultural nationalism among many educated German Jews.) Adler prided himself on his knowledge of mass psychology, and as politician was an artist with a keen sense of the possible as well as a strong desire to give dramatic and esthetic shape to mass aspirations. He reminds us strongly of Jean

117

Jaurès, likewise a combination of great actor ("Sarah Bernhardt," Kautsky caustically called him), nationalist, and man of culture.

A work by one of the leading Austro-Marxists, Otto Bauer's *Die Nationalitätenfrage und die Sozialdemokratie* (1907), was probably the most important theoretical statement on this question that Marxism produced before the war. The Austro-Marxist did not think that nationality would vanish with the arrival of socialism. On the contrary, it would evidently increase. "Socialist society . . . will mark off entire peoples sharply from each other, as today only the educated strata of the different nations are separated." As the masses gain culture, this will inevitably be culture within a national context. Colored by the situation within the multinational Dual Monarchy, Bauer's views were admittedly criticized as too nationalistic by Kautsky and then by Josef Stalin, but they were influential. That the *Sonderleben*, the special life of nations, would not cease even after the goal of a "socialist world economy" was reached became standard doctrine among the German Socialists. The rhetoric of August Bebel, speaking for the mainstream of the Social Democratic party (SPD), stressed making Germany a great *Kulturstaat* by freeing it from the Junkers. Thus purified, *Deutschtum* would be the valued inheritance of the future socialist society. That this view was not confined to the party's right wing is suggested by Franz Mehring, who wrote in 1906 that "Every national working class today needs the independence of the nation to which it belongs, in order to emancipate itself, and it is prepared to defend this independence with its blood and bones."[14]

When the question arose of defending their countries in 1914, the European Socialists discovered this distinction between land and regime as a vivid reality. The Social Democrats, Eduard David exclaimed, "love this land of their fathers, which is also the land of their children, and will not let its culture be destroyed and trampled on by enemy powers."[15] David, a right-wing Social Democratic member of the Reichstag, was one of the most ardent of the social patriots, but in this statement he spoke for the great majority of his fellows. Guesde, the veteran French Marxist, expressed it in the metaphor of a house on fire: "If a workingman lives on the fifth floor and the owner of the house on the first, the former won't refuse to help put it out."

Neither did the thought die from socialist minds—it was too much a part of basic teaching—that war could be a means of furthering the social revolution. Juarès remarked that "the Revolution can spring

118

from a European war," while Otto Bauer in 1908 declared that "the future imperialist war will bring the Revolution." This was standard doctrine.[16] The ways in which this might happen, according to the usual account, point to an ambivalence which largely went unrecognized. As Karl Kautsky (the leading German theoretician) put it, war will either "compel the governing class to grant concessions to the aspiring class which they might not be able to attain without the war," else, if the governing class does not do this, "war can easily lead to defeat from without carrying with it a collapse from within."[17] Granted that one or the other of these things might happen, the strategy they dictated was surely quite different. The latter alternative pointed to the path Lenin was to take quite early in the war: change the war somehow from one between nations to a war between the ruling and oppressed classes within each nation, therefore try in every possible way to bring about internal collapse, by sabotaging the war effort. The former alternative was one of class collaboration and of reaching socialism by peaceful and legal means; it indicated wholehearted support for the war in exchange for equal partnership in governance. How could one pursue both goals simultaneously, or even readily switch from one to the other? Parenthetically, it might be noted that both strategies faced an awkward problem of timing. Suppose one Socialist movement sabotaged, and another, on the opposite side of the war, collaborated? The former country would face defeat with consequences likely to prove disastrous for everybody *including* the workers. In any case, whatever the workers decided to do, the side that won the war would see to it that no socialist revolution took place among their defeated foes. (Suppose both Socialist movements tried to sabotage: there still might be a victor who would feel no obligation at all to support its defeated foe's socialists, having none in its own government to plead for them.)

Such uncertainties were seldom if ever explored; Marxists preferred to wait for experience to decide these matters. But they continued to view the coming of war with considerable theoretical equanimity, as (a) inevitable under capitalism, (b) certain to advance the course of historical development in some way, (c) likely to lead to the socialist revolution one way or another.

It was by no means standard doctrine that revolution must come catastrophically and violently. Such a view, associated with Lenin and a few others, was the opinion of only a minority within the Marxist camp before 1914. The revolution would come, but it might steal in quietly, like a thief in the night. The capitalist edifice would crumble and collapse of its own weight. When this might happen was any-body's guess in 1914. Many socialists were perhaps secretly half per-suaded of the error of their position in predicting an early demise of capitalism and birth of socialism. They had predicted this, time and again, only to be forced into embarrassing explanations for the delay, rather like Christians awaiting the end of the world. Bebel had an-nounced the Great Day in 1893 and again in 1899. Every time capital-ism had one of its periodic recessions or depressions (this is true down to today), Marxist determinists sprang up to say "Aha!"; then recovery and boom would force them back into their holes for a season, busying themselves with the discovery of reasons why the apocalypse had again misfired. An erosion of credibility was bound to occur, despite all the strength that faith could muster. Eduard Bernstein had already cre-ated a scandal when this old Marxist (in truth one of the first apostles, directly out of the master's circle) boldly declared in his celebrated "revisionist" tract of 1899, translated as *Evolutionary Socialism*, that Marx's prophecies had all proved wrong, his science was a sham, Dia-lectical Materialism was mumbo-jumbo (Bernstein was one of the first to notice that this term came from Engels and not Marx); the ethical imperative for socialism remained, but it must be taken as a humane goal which one chose to work for, knowing, moreover, it would be achieved only little by little, not in a grand dialectical leap.

This was apostasy, and Bernstein was crushed. The counterpart of this debate in Italy, touched off by Saverio Merlino at just about the same time, had the same outcome, Merlino being driven from the field under heavy attack even from those who like Antonio Labriola were not exactly "orthodox," and in time would (arguably) silently accept the revisionist points. Again in 1912 the "reformists," led by Leonidas Bissolati, were expelled from the party. In France, Alexandre Mille-rand sacrified his party standing (because of class collaboration) when he accepted membership in a bourgeois cabinet. But the controversy left its scars. Despite clinging formally to the dogma of the revolution ahead, and to the laws of capitalist self-destruction, for most Social Democrats of the 1900's such credos had become as mechanical as twentieth-century Anglicans mumbling the Thirty-Nine Articles. They did not, perhaps, really believe them. Perhaps capitalism was indeed here to stay, making a tolerable place for the workers.

120

III

These were among the great socialist debates of the 1900's, making for much interest and excitement among the socialist intellectuals. They bore on the decision of 1914 that lay ahead. Meanwhile, in their party conferences and congresses, the Socialists tried to frame a policy for dealing with the war that might come. Their basic ambivalence was that on the one hand they expected war, in a certain theoretical way: "not until the end of capitalism can we reckon on peace" (Wilhelm Liebknecht) was a socialist truism. They normally attributed wicked designs and devious methods to the "ruling class" which, being "capitalist," was always in danger of overreaching itself from greed. In commenting on the various crises and conflicts which overtook European diplomacy in the years before 1914—Morocco crises, Bosnian crises, bickerings about railroads, not to speak of the real wars that occurred in Manchuria, in South Africa, in Libya, in the Balkans—the Socialists adopted a moralistic and self-righteous tone, which infuriated their opponents; they denounced these scandalous carryings-on as the shameful depredations of profiteers, or else the immoral maneuverings of a corrupt set of decadent diplomats. The horror with which Socialists regarded the "sinister intrigues" of the Foreign Office was very similar to that of British "radicals" or Gladstonian liberals. Often innocent of any real knowledge of the situation, and finding the whole subject distasteful, they retreated into invective and spoke of "sordid deals," "imperialism," of "knavery, chicanery and dishonesty" (Keir Hardie), of "butchery to satisfy capitalist ambitions" (Edouard Vaillant). Similar outcries arose particularly from the left wing of the German SPD as represented by such persons as Rosa Luxemburg and Franz Mehring. There was enough real scandal, in the form of the Congo exposures of E. D. Morel and Roger Casement, for example, to satisfy any appetite for it.

And so Socialists knew that the combination of bourgeois greed and aristocratic cynicism, unbounded in their capacity for evil, might well plunge the world into chaos at any moment. We must not forget that these were the years in which the theory of imperialism as "the highest stage of capitalism," brought on by a last desperate quest for diminishing profits and leading inevitably to clashes between competing capitalisms, received its attractive if loose formulations by the British Socialist J. A. Hobson, by the Austro-German Rudolf Hilferding, and by others (from whom Lenin would later borrow).[18]

And yet Socialists, sharing in the general optimism, agreed with Jaurès and Dickinson that war couldn't happen, or failed to believe that it could even if theory suggested otherwise. They wavered in their attitude towards it. Was it legitimate defense of the fatherland or wicked capitalist plot to be fought root and branch? Their pronouncements reflected this ambiguity. The opinion, still frequently found, that in 1914 the European Socialists of the International went back on their pledges not to go to war is doubtful. Briefly, the socialist resolutions usually affirmed the right of all nations to self-determination and the concomitant right of every nation to defend its independence against outside attack.[19] In the important debate of 1907 at Stuttgart, the International rejected the doctrine then associated with Syndicalists, above all with the Frenchman Gustave Hervé, demanding a pledge to armed resistance in the event of war. French Socialist party congresses voted down Hervéism in 1906 and 1907, the two rival leaders Guesde and Jaurès joining forces on this. Hervé's amendment calling for commitment to a general strike in the event of war lost by 251 votes to 41 in 1907. When he carried the issue to the International meeting at Stuttgart, he got nowhere, and had no better luck the next year at Copenhagen. In France his resolution was again buried in 1910 by 210 to 34. The approved resolution, drawn up by Jaurès and Vaillant in 1907, stated that if war broke out Socialists should try to bring it to an end, and also to use it to overthrow capitalism, but it did not mention the general strike. At the same time it reaffirmed the right to self-defense.

The coldly logical Guesde aimed his sarcasm at this compromise which, he said, contained contradictory utterances, one insurrectionist and the other superpatriotic. Another critic called it a combination of anarchism and opportunism united under the banner of confusionism. While paying lip service to the emotional feeling against war, the debate of 1907 made it clear that few Socialists of any major country wished to rule out a war in defense of the homeland. Bebel raised his respected voice to repeat the point that "what we fight against is not the Fatherland as such—that belongs to the Proletariat much more than to the ruling class—but rather the condition of the Fatherland at the present time." The French were equally unequivocal in affirming that "if France were threatened by an invader . . . the French socialists would defend to their last breath the last inch of soil where liberty was born and social justice nurtured." It is clear that the authority of Marx could be invoked against the general strike: he had written to Engels of "the Belgian stupidity of wishing to call a strike against war," an idea which he attributed to Cesar de Paepe. It was almost always found among Anarchists or Syndicalists, not orthodox Socialists. And one of the most remarkable stories of 1914 was to be Hervé's conversion to passionate patriotism, after having preached the opposite between 1904 and 1912 in his paper *La guerre sociale* and having spent a term in jail for it.

Thus the myth that the Socialists had solemnly pledged themselves to resist war at any cost, and betrayed their own principles in 1914, should be laid to rest. *However,* after years of shying away from it, the Socialists seemed about to accept the general strike against war in 1914. The SFIO (French Socialist party) voted approval of it on July 15, 1914, though it was a doubtful victory: the vote of 1,690 to 1,174 indicated a distinct lack of unanimity, especially as the trade unions seemed the least enthusiastic. The great Jaurès had been converted. The masthead of *Humanité* carried the program of international arbitration, reconciliation between France and Germany, and a citizen army. Jaurès had written his *New Army* (1910) expounding the philosophy of a citizen army (long familiar in socialist thought, favored by Marx and Engels) that would act defensively but not offensively—able to repel invaders but incapable of aggression—as a means of squaring the circle, overcoming the contradiction between patriotism and hostility to war. In 1913 the French Left was fighting the battle of the three-year law, which aroused a storm of opposition and seemed a glorious issue. This attempt to lengthen the term of obligatory military service from two to three years, in order to keep pace with German military strength, struck Jaurès as a "senseless and perilous law"—not, however, because he wanted to leave France defenseless: his citizen army would take care of that. (Jaurès' plan, as embodied in an act he introduced on June 17, 1913, which was heavily defeated, included two weeks' service each year after one initial training period of eighteen months.) A violent parliamentary debate punctuated by mass rallies marked the progress of the three-year bill, which eventually passed by a substantial majority though some radical and radical-socialist (left liberal) deputies joined the Socialists. One of these was Joseph Caillaux, whose wife assassinated the editor of the leading newspaper *Le Figaro* in the most spectacular incident of this highly charged controversy. When the Socialists won over a hundred seats in the 1914 elections to become the second largest political party in the Chamber, their campaign featured antimilitarism, an evidently popular platform.

In the 1914 party debate, to the Guesde question, "If France were attacked, would you let her be crushed by a general strike?" Jaurès answered, we would defend the country if attacked, but the general strike might be used in advance to nip the threatening war in the bud. Hervé had now turned patriotic, and the Guesdists still opposed the threat of a general strike as "high treason against socialism." But Juarès and Vaillant secured approval for the resolution favoring a strike against aggressive war. The tenth congress of the International was scheduled to meet at Vienna in August.

This projected convention never took place, of course. Faced with the suddenly worsening diplomatic crisis, the Bureau, or executive committee of the International, met in Brussels on July 29–30 to prepare a peace strategy. It decided to move up the date for the coming congress from August 23 to August 9 and to move it from Vienna to Paris—too late still, as it turned out. Meanwhile the distinguished group at Brussels produced some antiwar rhetoric, pleaded for mediation, and agreed to try to persuade their respective governments (French and German) to restrain their allies. The French Socialists did ask Premier Viviani to hold back the Russians; but France was already committed to support her ally, and it was difficult to see how she could not do so, if Germany backed Austria-Hungary. Meanwhile the German Social Democrats made it clear that they would defend their country against Russia, which on July 31 switched to general mobilization, from the partial mobilization it had decreed on the previous day to indicate an intent to fight only Austria. At the Brussels meeting the German Socialists promised that while they would vote to defend the fatherland against Russia they would not vote to attack France. In the event, they found it impossible to separate the two actions.

Jaurès thought "it will be settled, somehow." ("Even when we stood in the shadow of war, optimism continued to prevail," the Belgian stalwart Vandervelde recalled.) The next day Jaurès was dead, the victim of a crazed rightist. His friends went from his funeral to vote approval of the war credits. "They have assassinated Jaurès, we will not assassinate France." Though on August 1 a representative of the German SD's had assured the French that his party would never vote for war credits, they did so at *exactly the same hour* as the French vote, on August 4.

It seems almost certain that Jaurès would have approved, for he was at bottom a fervent French patriot who had never questioned the need to defend France. In his last writings he stressed that there could be no sabotage of the war unless there was "assurance and certitude" of this happening on the other side too. His last article in *Humanité* (July 31), refusing to believe that the situation was beyond rescue, hoped for "vigorous demonstrations" by the German Socialists. But it was just after this that events began to overtake everybody. His close associate Vaillant and Guesde and other Socialists "threw themselves into the war with a wild chauvinism" (Robert Wohl) and on August 4 Vaillant clasped hands with the clerical reactionary Alfred de Mun, to whom he had refused to speak for twenty years because Mun had fought against the Communards in 1871.[20] The war was to revitalize old Socialists, as it did so many others. They channeled all their energies into the crusade to save the republic and crush "Prussian militarism."

They did not outdo the erstwhile revolutionary pacifist Gustave Hervé, editor of *La guerre sociale*. Hervé's conversion from militant pacifist to equally militant warrior is one of the most remarkable stories of the times. A glance at the course of his thought in the crucial few days before the war began is illuminating. The man who once went to prison for preaching the general strike as a weapon against war asked on July 28, "Where is our beautiful dream of a general international strike against war?" We dreamed of raising peoples against their governments, of forcing governments to arbitrate their disputes, of founding a new republic of international justice and beauty. But "our wings are broken from the shock of harsh reality and we fall to earth, each on his own native ground, with the single preoccupation, for the moment, of defending ourselves, as did our ancestors, against the brutalities of invasion."[21] Hervé reproduced the career of his idol, the great nineteenth-century revolutionary Blanqui, in turning from insurrectionist to patriot when he saw *La patrie en danger* (the title of Blanqui's call to rise against the German invaders in 1871, the journal of the Commune, a phrase which Hervé repeated as the book title for his own articles in *La guerre sociale* from July 1 to November 14). He was pro-Serbian after Sarajevo, admiring the revolutionary spirit of the Serbs. But at the same time, he confronted what had been a bugbear for every French leftist, the alliance with despotic Russia. The strangler of Finland, the muzzler of Poland, the persecutor of the Jews of Kiev and Odessa—what an ally for which to fight and die! (But after the war started, Hervé discovered hope for Russia, who he expected would free the Poles, give the Jews equality, evolve toward a more modern political order now that she was one with the Democracies. His editorial of September 12 cried, "Vive le Tsar!") "Rather the rupture of our defensive alliance with Russia than the shame of taking part in an offensive war against Austria!" On the twenty-ninth he again turned on Austria, who had played the part of a brigand against the "valiant little Serbian people," but he again showed ambivalence, seeing no reason for France to intervene: if Russia wishes to defend Serbia, she has our sympathy, but let her not have our arms. If it is going to lead to war, down with the Russian alliance!

The same day, he explained his two-year-old renunciation of the general strike. He had noticed during the Balkan Wars that people were simply not prepared to go on strike with the country in danger; and that the German and Austrian Socialists were not going to do it. At this moment, it is not in our interest to sabotage the French government which, he thought, sincerely wants peace. "Who does not know that our government is as sincerely for peace as we are?" That the French government was one of the moderate Left, with a sort of Socialist as premier and two independent Socialists in the cabinet, undoubtedly was important. Hervé's editorials several times repeated the point that if this were the government of a Clemenceau or Delcassé the case might be different, but everyone knows the present ministry does not seek war. Later the same day, he saw "our duty" as "to defend the home of liberty as our fathers" had defended the revolutions of 1789, 1792, 1848, 1870. "Between Imperial Germany and Republican France, no hesitation, our choice is made."

On the thirtieth, Hervé was as hopeful as Jaurès that peace might be saved, and complained that antiwar demonstrators had received rough handling from the police. But he noted again the total demise of the general-strike idea: neither the trade unions nor the parliamentary Socialists were ready to deliver the country to the Kaiser. "Finish with the monstrous and foolish legend which represents us as saboteurs of national defense." On the thirty-first, Hervé announced "La patrie est en danger!" In a Saturday editorial on the death of Jaurès, he has the fallen leader say from the grave, "They have assassinated

me. In wishing to avenge me, do not assassinate the fatherland!"
Jaurès died nobly, a martyr for peace; but the assassination "changes
nothing in our political situation." On August 2 Hervé is asking to be
accepted into the army, despite his forty-three years (as he was careful
to point out) and bad eyesight. "Before the spectacle of this national
union, of which one has never seen a similar example, the specter of
war recoils in fright." The myth of the *union sacrée* was already
born. Much of Hervé's writing in the first days of the war is a celebration of this "moving unanimity." And this was, after all, a socialist
desideratum.

IV

Each of the socialist groups found it alarmingly easy to justify its
country's cause. Since the case against the arrant aggression of "Prussian militarism," entailing the defense of democracy, is more familiar
and seems more defensible to most Anglo-American readers, it might
be well to recall the German-Austrian case. The Austrian Socialist
Kurt Renner argued that a victory for the Entente side would be a
victory for imperialism and monopoly capitalism, while a Central
Powers victory would lead to socialism.[22] The logic of this was perhaps no more strained than similar exercises on the Franco-British
side. Which country had the largest, best organized, and most pres-
tigious Socialist party? Or the most advanced social services? No one
between the Rhine and the Oder had any doubts, and a fair share of
the world's disinterested minds would have agreed with them. Though
Germany was famed for her state welfare program, it is worth noting
also that according to Edward Crankshaw "the Austrian half of the
[Austro-Hungarian] Empire enjoyed a very high level of freedom for
the individual and a much higher level of social welfare than, for
example, England."[23] Max Brod, the antiwar Prague intellectual, said
this was the freest society he ever encountered.[24] On the other hand,
which country was the bellwether of world capitalism? Clearly, Great
Britain. Which countries had been the most imperialistic, swallowing
up the great bulk of the Afro-Asian colonies? Britain followed by
France far outstripped Germany in colonization. Who had thrown
down the gauntlet in Morocco, shaped an alliance encircling Germany,
and egged on the Serbs to churn up the Balkan waters? All this was

apart from the strongest German socialist argument, that of the need to stand guard against the brutal despotism of Tsarist Russia. Even the Belgian Socialist Émile Vandervelde (writing in the American *Independent*, December, 1914) conceded that the German Socialists were in the position of having to vote for the credits at the risk of leaving their country defenseless against Russia, and could not avoid voting also for the war in the West. Russia was the country Marx and Engels, followed by Liebknecht and Bebel, had claimed was not only ruthless and bloodthirsty, but always expanding, a distinct menace to all the world and to Central Europe in particular. Her rule there would be a disaster to the cause of progress. On the other hand, a German defeat of Russia would overthrow the tsardom and lead to revolution in Russia.

It did not look that way from Russia. Kropotkin argued that if Germany triumphed, all revolutions would be put down; German hegemony would mean the end of the whole order in which revolutionary hopes were embedded. The Anarchist Prince's dislike of Prussianism included not only its militarism but its socialism!—the authoritarian, statist brand of Marxism, which Anarchists always disliked, dating back to Marx's quarrels with Proudhon and Bakunin. He had said as early as 1906, "If a war between Germany and Russia begins, I would sling a rifle over my old shoulders and go off to kill Germans." He now perceived "a war of liberation from Teutonic barbarism." A majority of the Russian Anarchists followed him into the "defensist" camp.[25]

Plekhanov was in Paris when the war started, having attended the Brussels meeting of July 29. The dean of Russian Marxists said that he would join the army if not so old and sick (he was fifty-seven). His *O Voine* (*On the War*, 1914) pointed out that to declare "capitalism" responsible for the war was an answer empty of content. *Germany* was the aggressor, in any comprehensible statement, not "capitalism." The International itself had recognized the legitimacy of self-defense. A military victory for Germany would be a disaster for socialism, as well as for Russia, since the German right-wing militarists would be the winners and would surely crush progressive movements everywhere. Certainly no social progress would be possible for Russia under the heel of the Germans, who would ruthlessly exploit her. The disaster would affect all Russians, not just the ruling class. To refuse to defend Russia meant handing her over to a *foreign* ruling class, with far worse consequences for the masses than at present. He found himself arguing that a German defeat would aid revolution in Germany, while a Russian defeat would have the opposite effect in Russia. But no matter: Plekhanov did not hesitate, and his paper *Prizyu* (*The Call*) issued a clear call from Paris for Russian Socialists to defend their country. Joined by Ida Axelrod and Alexinsky (a former Bolshevik) among other Russian SD's, he formed the Right to Lenin's Left, with most of the Socialists somewhere uneasily between. It was much more difficult for a Russian to justify national defense by the "stake in the country" argument than for Western leftists. Yet a deep love of country had long been characteristic of Russians who hated the regime, as witness, for example, Tolstoy. Russia belongs to all the people, not just the Tsar and the nobles. The people who will one day inherit it cannot be indifferent to its fate. Like the Germans and French, the Russian radicals felt "Russia" as something far bigger than the regime that happened at the moment to run it.

The venerable party heroine Vera Zasulich was among the "defensist" Social Democrats. The populist Social Revolutionaries were represented patriotically by Ilia Rubanovich. The Russian emigrés in Paris, including some Bolsheviks, were ardently pro-Allied and many volunteered.[26] Not until September did the Russians who opposed the war find their voice. The emigrés in Switzerland were also divided, but initially the "defensists" had little opposition. Lenin defined his views in September, not with entire clarity but already with a tendency to see a Russian defeat as "the lesser evil." Yet he criticized the German Socialists and defended the French. Not Lenin but Leon Trotsky gave the clearest call in the first months after August, to those Russians who thought a victory for their own country would be disastrous.[27] The report of the Russian Social Democrats' Organization Committee conceded that "The struggle against German militarism, against the mighty power of German capitalism, the question of freeing the oppressed nationalities [i.e., Slavs within the Austro-Hungarian state], the participation of democratic France and England in the war as Russia's ally—all these factors . . . worked on the masses and made the war popular."

Lenin, of course, welcomed the war for other reasons: a golden opportunity for revolution. He didn't think "Franz Josef and Nikolasha would do us the favor"; when they did, he was delighted. To which it may be added that Polish Socialists, who stayed away from the July 29 meeting of the International at Brussels, also saw possibilities in a war involving Russia: the defeat of their oppressor and the liberation of Poland. So likewise did many subject-peoples from the Dual Monarchy as well as the Russian Empire. Max Brod relates how he and his friends sought the help of Thomas Masaryk in Prague in 1914, only to find the Czech leader quite happily resigned to the war. Masaryk clearly looked forward to the break-up of the Austrian Empire in defeat. In Ireland a large majority of the people followed John Redmond in supporting the war, the rationalization being that collaboration would bring the reward of freedom. But, as did the Socialists, one might think that either path could lead to the desired result.

Whatever their rationalizations, the Socialist leaders felt a tide of spontaneous patriotism welling up from below, and responded to this. A French Socialist later said that "if we had wanted to try to resist it, we would have been swept away." Adler, his ear to the ground as usual, quickly saw that the war was too popular to resist in Austria. Watching from a neutral corner, the Dutch Socialist Henriette Roland-Holst thought that the proletariat's "rational interest" had been overwhelmed by "feelings, moods, instincts, emotions which break forth from the subconscious with irresistible force."[28] Their democratic instincts (or in some cases, their opportunism) pulled the Social Democrats along toward the war. They wished desperately to become a part of the body politic from which they had so long been alienated, and which had deeply mistrusted them. In Germany, the chief reproach against the SD's had long been not that they were socialist but that they were *Reichsfeindlich, Vaterlandlos*: "this forms the deepest rift between you and us," Bülow had said in 1905. "The desire to belong, or, negatively stated, the urge to escape from the pariah position in which the Social Democrats had been held" was "a psychological factor of great importance," as Carl Schorske writes. "We German Social Democrats have learned to consider ourselves in this war as part, and truly not the worst part, of the German nation," wrote the Socialist pedagogue Konrad Haenisch during the war.[29] Equally, in France, where in 1914 the Socialists sensed the possibility of becoming the majority party, they wished to be released from that "monstrous legend" of their hostility to the nation.

The urge to bring socialism into the national body, to cease being an alien element, was a strong factor in Italy, too. Paradoxically, the most humanitarian and warm-hearted of the Socialists were also the most community-minded and most sensitive to public opinion. They were also the most inclined to sympathize with the democratic cause of the Entente. After all, the goal of socialism was to become the nation (eventually to "*be* the human race"), not to remain a sullen minority. In Italy as in Germany, the 1912 elections had brought to the Socialists an upward surge of electoral strength, lending support to gradualist or revisionist views. (Universal male suffrage, unrestricted by the literacy requirement, operated for the first time in this election.) The PSI maintained its purity in 1912 by expelling the distinguished Bissolati and others, who set up a rival Parti Socialista Riformista Italiano; it could not prevent a feeling among younger members that the old party leadership was a bit stodgy.[30] Currents among the younger socialists in the years just before the war flowed against dogmatism. In France, Guesde was far less popular than the more flexible and humanistic Jaurès. The voluntarism of a Sorel or the revisionism of a Bernstein was a welcome relief from mechanical Marxism.

The younger and more radical, the Syndicalists and semi-Anarchists often were among the most patriotic in 1914. War appealed to men as adventure and as hope of revolution, as well as because of feelings of community and solidarity. The fact is that in the years just before the war Europe was stirred from one end to the other by violent strikes. Such was the case in Italy, as well as in England and Ireland; in Russia, a desperate rebellion among the industrial workers, housed in prisonlike barracks with hopelessly inadequate community or recreational opportunities, gripped the capital city just as the war began. The workers immediately turned from the violence of the strike to the violence of battle, diverting their wrath from their own class enemies to the Germans. Theories that governments deliberately whipped up a war to distract their discontented subjects are implausible. But war was decidedly an outlet for all kinds of frustrations, social as well as individual.

V

Their naïveté about the causes and origins of wars victimized the Socialists. In general, along with other unsophisticated students of international relations, they supposed that war would begin as a deliberate act of aggression, long premeditated and easily recognizable. The

1912 Manifesto from the International at Basel, which appeared amid the war scare of late 1912, included denunciation of "intrigue," and "great power maneuvers," with strong implications that all this was most sinister if not criminal, but with obviously only the vaguest grasp of its details. It also referred to "capitalistic anarchy" and was replete with vows to rebuke "warmongers," keep up the "struggle for peace," etc. Such rhetoric came nowhere near facing the question of what Socialists would do if confronted with an actual war, particularly one in which one faced the stark alternative of letting the foreign invader walk in or taking up arms to repel him. Every socialist party was pledged to reject a war of aggression but equally committed to defend its country from attack. In 1914 they were unable to distinguish; each nation, including its socialists, honestly supposed itself to be the victim and the other side to be the predator. If the French and British pointed to the assault through Belgium, which seemed to make the Germans a peculiarly ruthless kind of aggressor, the Germans pointed to the encirclement which forced them, surrounded and greatly outnumbered, to act before being crushed between the excellent French army and the vast manpower of Russia.

All the socialist plans for stopping a war by some kind of protest or strike supposed that aggression would be plain. Jaurès, replying in 1913 to Charles Andler's doubts about the German Socialists' internationalism, expressed faith that "four million German socialists will rise like one man and execute the Kaiser if he works to start a war."[31] But the four million German Socialists did not think that the Kaiser had worked to start this war, any more than the French Socialists thought their government had started it. After the war began, the German reply to those who asked why the German Socialists had not defied the marching orders was a *tu quoque*: why didn't the French, British, and Russian workers do so? They noted the lack of coordination: if the Germans decided on a strike against the war, and their fellow workers in France and Russia did not, then they would secure the downfall of Germany.

> Once the matter has developed so far, that a population is threatened by invasion of foreign armies, then it becomes a question of what Karl Kautsky wrote in April, 1911, in *Neue Zeit*: "Then everybody turns into a patriot, and if individuals of unusual courage should dare to oppose sending soldiers to the frontier and

provision of military materials, the government would not need to lift a finger to make them unpopular; a furious public would spontaneously strike them down."[32]

As we have seen, there *were* socialist attempts to meet and coordinate the tactics at the beginning of the crucial week of July 29–August 4. The reason for failure was not lack of time or opportunity for communication, obviously, though this was a frequent excuse: "We were confronted with the fact of war," Dr. David exclaimed; "on August 1 the war was there." (On August 1 the German government, having received rejections from Russia and France of its ultimata of the previous day demanding that Russia cease mobilization and France state her intentions, declared war on Russia, as France issued mobilization orders.) Granted that events moved fast, if the Socialists could have agreed on fundamentals they would have emerged from their meetings of July 29–30 with a plan and forestalled the fatal day.

Nor was it adequate to say that Socialists did not control foreign policy, which was made in secrecy by a handful of state leaders, though this also was a popular excuse, given not only by Socialists but by many liberal organizations who worked during the war and after for "democratic control" of foreign policy. To make closet diplomacy the scapegoat was easy. Comrade Chaustoff cried in the Duma on August 8 that "the people," not the experts, should conduct affairs. This is impossible; but the "people" could have refused to accept the decisions of the leaders; instead they enthusiastically approved them. They were not driven sullenly to a war they did not want but gladly accepted war. More to the point, the Socialists always knew that under the present dispensation the "ruling class" makes policy and might make war; their plan, such as it was, for stopping war rested on their ability to refuse to carry out its orders.

In brief, the French and German Socialists could have decided on and coordinated a strike against the war; they failed to do so because they believed in defensive war and each side thought its posture was defensive. The subsequent allegations of the postwar far Left, that the Socialists in 1914 had grown slack, were eaten by "opportunism," had become "lackeys of capitalism," etc., are at best the juggling of words, in itself highly opportunistic, not to say devious. That the Socialists in 1914 went with the masses is surely a strange matter for reproach, from one Socialist to another. They opted for no bed of roses, but for war which meant hardship and death for many a comrade. They were guided by the precepts of the socialist sages and prophets; and above all they saw no alternative save destruction of the European socialist movement. One may pick many flaws in their arguments, but no one who has studied them carefully with an open mind can believe they were corrupt or cowardly. On the contrary, they poured an intense idealism into what they wrongly but sincerely believed was their only real socialist choice. They usually arrived at this decision after much agony of soul; once they reached it, they threw doubt aside and plunged in with the usual fierce enthusiasm of the social activist.

No one, it has been said, is so bloody-minded as a radical turned patriot. These embattled ideologues contributed not a little to answering the real question about World War I: not why it began (for accident and miscalculation can trigger conflict, as was obviously the case on July 29–August 3, 1914), but why it went on its bloody way four and a third terrible years, defying all attempts to resolve it by diplomacy and compromise. For, contrary, to what is widely believed, most of the Socialists never wavered in the faith with which they began the war. Dissenters grew in numbers as the slaughter went on, but nowhere did they become a majority among the Socialists, not even in Russia.

One attractive quality might be noted: in the beginning at least, the French and German Socialists showed an appreciation of the other's position and refrained from recriminations. Refusing to reproach them, Dr. David wrote that the French comrades "did what they had to do as good Frenchmen." Gustave Hervé, for his part, pointing out that the German Socialists "have never said they would not fight in case of war—never!" opposed propaganda which depicted Germans as barbarians and lashed out against the violence perpetrated against German civilians in France. Mourning the death of a German Socialist on September 13 (just at the time of the Battle of the Marne), he showed sympathetic understanding of the German socialist dilemma on the war. Viktor Adler likewise said that the French Socialists did their duty, as the Germans and Austrians did theirs.[33]

This sort of gallantry, which admittedly underwent severe attrition as the war became steadily grimmer,[34] deserves note. It rested on the whole prewar debate during which most Socialists had agreed in the International that their own nation was worth defending if attacked, and even that war might be regarded with some equanimity.

VI

We have discussed primarily the French and German Socialists, who were indeed the heart of the International, and on whose close connections Jaurès had relied for peace. In Great Britain, the Marxist element counted for less, but was equally patriotic; the venerable leader of the British Socialist party, H. M. Hyndman, said he would enlist were he not seventy-two.[35] Almost all the Fabian Socialists supported the war, on grounds that it was necessary to "overthrow aggressive militarism" (Sidney Webb). Those popular individualistic Socialists H. G. Wells and Arnold Bennett threw themselves into the "war to end war" with a fine fury. And Shaw, though he was flippant about the war, did not really oppose it.

Mary Agnes Hamilton, biographer of Arthur Henderson, estimated that 90 percent of the rank and file of Labour backed the war. Labour leader John Burns joined the aged Gladstonian liberal John Morley in resigning from the cabinet as the war began, chiefly on the grounds that Russia, not Germany, was Britain's real enemy. Ramsay MacDonald, in resigning the Labour party leadership, became one of the very few European Socialists to renounce the war, but in doing so he was aware that he was opposing "the most popular war the country has ever fought," and he did not do so militantly. Like Rolland, he lapsed into silence, which perhaps covered confusion, and in any case there does not seem to have been anything particularly "socialist" in his rejection of the war.[36] Keir Hardie, soon to die, disliked the war but was unable to make any impact on an overwhelmingly warlike public opinion.[37] The October 15 prowar Manifesto of Labour MP's bore the signatures of most party stalwarts, including Henderson, J. H. Thomas, and J. R. Clynes. Henderson assumed the party leadership and joined the government. Robert Blatchford, independent Socialist editor of the popular *Clarion*, had been preaching the need to prepare for the inevitable war with Germany since 1909; he thought the Germans "a race of militaristic bandits" who in fact, half crazy from beer, wished to come to London and murder everybody.[38] This caricature of Germany was typically lower class and popular.

Sidney assured Beatrice Webb that "the Great War will seem to future generations a landmark of progress."[39] Beatrice was less certain. The war soon threw her into despair, as she brooded on how little her social science had prepared her to cope with it. "The war is a world

135

catastrophe beyond the control of my philosophy. Such social philosophy as I possess does not provide any remedy for racial wars," she confessed in her diary. But, watching George Lansbury and Keir Hardie attempting to rally the pacifists, she thought it "an undignified and futile exhibition," and consoled herself with the reflection that "war is a stimulus to service, heroism, and all forms of self-devotion." The response of this brilliant pair, surely among the finest of the socialist brains which the 1890–1910 years had produced in such abundance, may well sum up the socialist failure. Sidney's historicist outlook had convinced him, as much as it had the Marxists, that history drives onward and upward on a predestined course toward the collectivist utopia; a war not only could not interrupt this but might advance it. The war, he believed, not without reason, would bring the Labour party to power, and what other consummation was there to look forward to? He threw himself into the task of making sure that this happened. As for Beatrice, more sensitive to the sheer human tragedy, to "the horror and insanity of the killing and maiming of millions of the best of the human race," she was helpless, lacking an answer to this "racial war" for which socialist theory provided no solution.

Amid all the talk about social betterment within the nation, Socialists had overlooked the sheer power of the group instinct in time of danger. Gustave LeBon, the old irrationalist, in his *Premières conséquences de la guerre* (1916) noted with a good deal of *Schadenfreude* that the Socialists had found that the bonds between men are not those of class, a merely cerebral matter of interest, discerned by those incorrigible intellectualists, the Marxists; but rather are bonds of country, touching ancient tribal instincts. As Croce put it, "The war has demonstrated that the international struggle always takes precedence over the social, that the actors of world history are peoples and states, not classes."[40]

—7—

Images of Hate

I

It was a *Glaubenskrieg*, an ideological or religious war, Werner Sombart rightly claimed; the one-time Marxian materialist saw the physical foci of rivalry, whether colonies, Alsace-Lorraine, the Balkans, as mere epiphenomena of deeper forces emerging from the soul. The British scholar A. E. Zimmern agreed that it was "a war of ideas," "a conflict between two different and irreconcilable conceptions of government, society and progress."[1] Certainly the two sides assailed each other with words as much as guns, and the battle for morale was critical, not least in the search for allies. "The task of the spiritual leaders, the so-called intellectuals, was to strengthen courage and plead the rightful causes of Germany," Rudolf Eucken wrote.[2] "Turn words into bayonets," Ernst Troeltsch urged.

The intellectuals in all countries fell to with a will. They delivered lectures, wrote books and articles, made poems and posters, served as ministers of information or propaganda. Eucken says he gave thirty-six lectures the first year, sometimes speaking to thousands; by 1916, the audiences had dwindled. The lecture circuit burgeoned everywhere. An aloof Oxford literary don like Walter Raleigh would publish his war addresses (hardly to his enduring credit), as did many others.[3] The eloquence of Gabriele D'Annunzio was to play a large part in precipitating Italy into the war in May, 1915. *King Albert's Book,* published by the *London Daily Telegraph*, an example of the collector's-item commemorative book designed to raise money for war relief as well as bolster Allied solidarity, contained contributions from French and British authors, composers, and artists (Debussy donated a piece of music). There was also the *Book of France* (1915), undertaken on Gide's initiative, with pieces from Kipling, James, Hardy, Gide, Barrès, and others. Kipling separately apostrophized *France at War*. In Britain C. F. C. Masterman, John Buchan, and Arnold Bennett served in turn as exuberant directors of propaganda, writing tracts themselves and goading others to do the same. Bennett's pamphlet *Liberty!* proved that Germany was out to enslave the world. "Burke said you cannot indict a whole nation, but you can," said Ford Madox Ford, who attacked Shaw and produced two effective pieces of white-hot propaganda before going off to fight in the war he later so brilliantly fictionalized.[4]

While German literature and music were banned, the city of St. Petersburg was rebaptized Petrograd in an effort to escape a German word—which did not succeed, as Georg Brandes pointed out, since "grad" also goes back to a German root. Besides dropping Brahms and Beethoven from the concert stage, the British changed the name of their royal house.

Russian avant-garde artists drew patriotic posters for which poets, including the great Mayakovsky, supplied jingles. Arnold Bennett's *Over There* (1915) tried to bring encouraging news from the front, though this proved less and less rewarding. If exercises continued such as French Jewish actress Sarah Bernhardt's "Inspiring Experience at the Front," reported in *Current History*, December, 1916 ("What wonderful spiritual progress the experiences of these men have created for them! ... We have arrived at the epoch in the history of the world when fear of death is no more"), there surely was some erosion in their appeal. Celebrations of courage and heroism in battle did remain a staple—"a courage," according to D'Annunzio, "which was unknown to Rome and Sparta, to lions and eagles." "The *Poilu* feared nothing; his very appearance struck with terror the Barbarians, the Huns, the Boches."[5] Conceived in the initial euphoria of battle, which seems to be a common war phenomenon,[6] such extravagant heroics could not maintain their full credibility. A law of diminishing returns affected these hosannas to battle. What other content could invigorate war writing, strengthening the national cause?

The lowest common denominator was simple vituperation of the foe, or, contrariwise, self-praise. The former was doubtless momentarily bracing but quickly palled too, and moreover could land one in contradictions. Professor Raleigh spoke of the Germans' "passionate devotion to the State, their amazing vulgarity, their worship of mechanism and mechanical efficiency," accusing them also of filthiness.[7] But others claimed the Germans were obsessively clean, and impossibly idealistic. The Germans in turn accused the English of vulgarity in the form of a *kaufmännisch* mentality that valued only material things. The Oxford don categorized the Germans, presumably *en masse*, as "highly emotional and excitable people," yet they were "organized and regimented like an ant-hill or a beehive," in contrast to the free and easy-going Englishman. Bureaucratic by nature, these inhabitants of the *Ameisenwelt* only follow rules and hence were unfit to govern, as opposed to the confident, relaxed British habit of command. But habits of command were what others found all too evident in the Teutonic temperament. Raleigh accused the Germans of lacking a sense of humor. Americans entertained the same illusion about the English, humor being the least translatable form of expression; Englishmen evidently knew no more about Munich cafés than Americans did about London music halls. *Simplicissimus* was as idiomatic as *Punch*. Straying into these well-trapped fields of national character, one fell into pitfalls of contradiction and might be forced into more careful analysis, for which there was hardly time—or need, if making words into bayonets was the goal.

Self-praise also could be dangerous. To argue that man's fate depended on the preservation of Britain, France, Germany, or Russia, of democracy, liberalism, Orthodox Christianity, or *Kultur* boosted the spirit as much as the claim that the enemy represented some principle inimical to civilization itself. The Germans, D'Annunzio alleged, were trying to destroy "a great civilization for the benefit of an unworthy one, a great history for the benefit of one which does not equal it, a great state of consciousness for the benefit of one that daily proves itself base"; but such appeals to ancient Latinity might leave one uncomfortable, especially when one thought about the British or Russian ally. Intellectuals who had often in the past criticized their own national institutions could hardly forget these imperfections overnight. A typical British line was "Yes, we have all too many social ills to cure; but at least we have the will and the means, and shall get at them immediately the war is over, whereas autocratic, authoritarian, and militaristic Germany can never reform"; while a German one was "Much remains to be done to secure the ideal society here, we admit, but at least our hearts are sound whereas the materialistic and corrupt British/French . . . ." One could then proceed to the congenial task of cutting up the foe. "Our civilization has been based on selfishness, our commerce on competition and the unrestricted love of wealth," Bishop Charles Gore cried in a burst of *nostra culpa*.[8] "Every nation has blots upon its scutcheon, and the cynic may point to the Irish Union, the destruction of the Danish fleet, the Cyprus Convention, as proofs that we have richly earned the name of 'Perfidious Albion,'" a British writer conceded, quickly adding that now, at least, the British stand on the side of right against might, the sanctity of treaties against international lawlessness.[9]

Naturally, the Allies exploited the German violation of Belgian neutrality. They were also able to make the most of the "atrocity" charges, since German troops stood on Belgian and French soil, not vice versa, and most of these claims of outrageous mistreatment involved military handling of civilians in time of battle. By comparison to World War II, this was mild indeed. British accounts of atrocities were driven to exploiting Turkish cruelties against Armenians, and then, in what would cause a postwar scandal, to manufacturing stories of abominations.

One could, of course, go over the events leading up to the war with an eye to blaming them on the foe and exhibiting the unblemished record of one's own country. This occupied a good deal of time. Closely connected (by way of Germany's violation of Belgian neutrality, for Allied writers) was the question of brutality, violation of the laws of war, "atrocities," which brought one back to national character via reflections on "a natural and brutal barbarity of character" attributed to the Germans.[10] The series of "Studies and Documents on the War" produced by French scholars (Paris, 1915) was translated into English. Durkheim, the famous sociologist, oddly was assigned the historical portion; his book *Who Wanted War?* was included as well as volumes by J. Bedier on *German Atrocities* and *How Germany Seeks to Justify Her Atrocities*; by R. A. Weiss on *How Austria-Hungary Waged War in Serbia* and *The Violation by Germany of the Neutrality of Belgium and Luxembourg*; and by Ernest Lavisse and Charles Andler on *The German Theory and Practice of War,* invoking Clausewitz, Treitschke, and Bernhardi to build a view of Germany committed to total ruthlessness in the methods of warfare, as well as aspiring to rule the world; and one by Durkheim again, *Deutschland über Alles*, in which the German mentality of violence and domination was proved with the aid of the indispensable Treitschke and a mistranslation of the national anthem. Charles Seignobos, another venerable historian, sketched the diplomatic history of the nineteenth century with a special concern to build up the Russians ("a pacific spirit is the basis of the Russian character"). Andler, a leading Socialist intellectual, wrote also on *Pan-Germanism*, inflating the role of Heinrich Class' little band of fanatics.

The Germans talked about a secret conspiracy fashioned over many years, in which the chief or at least the most sinister role fell to the English. The "blind revenge-hate of the French" and the "pure barbarism" of the "Cossacks" and "slave masses" of Russia were the materials on which the cold calculation of Perfidious Albion operated. Watching and weighing, the piously hypocritical nation of Pecksniffs saw Germany becoming too strong and threw herself into the scales on the side of France and Russia for a war she preferred now rather than later; so asserted leading representatives of Germany's famed historical profession.[11]

So one always returned to the national character of the foe. In this contest of imagery, the Western Allies pressed home an advantage. The Germans even admitted this, confessing frequently to feelings of the world being against them, of being misunderstood, of having trouble getting their case across. "A monstrous campaign of slander and aspersions" against Germany had been "all too successful," Troeltsch thought. "From all sides come the harshest and most extreme attacks on the German character. . . . We have been spiritually isolated."[12] The foe appropriated the slogans of democracy and humanity, and was winning the battle of ideas. Writing after the war, Eucken thought this moral defeat had been decisive, costing the Central Powers Italy and the United States, along with much of neutral opinion throughout the world.[13] This was unfair and hypocritical, Germans cried. In fact the Allies maneuvered them into the war, they felt, then convinced the world that Germany started it. The democracy of the Allies was really a fraud, yet the Germans, who invented and perfected the idea of freedom, were accused of being under the yoke of tyranny, their virtues twisted into vices. "Militarism" to Germans was honorable service to the free state, not an Asiatic barbarism. The "arch-imperialists" had the gall to accuse Germans of imperialism, they complained.

Yet the tar of militarism, despotism, and imperialism stuck, as all too much evidence testifies. The Germans sought desperately to stem this tide of defeat in the *Glaubenskrieg*. Eucken's reflection that "throughout the war we did not sufficiently value the *seelische Element*" does not appear to be true; the effort was made, but failed to convince many outside the German world, which was evidence, no doubt, of that estrangement between Germany and the West to which Benedetto Croce (by no means an enemy of German culture) so notably called attention.[14] The Germans knew themselves to be misunderstood but could not correct the misunderstanding, and only made matters worse by trying, like an accused person crying "No, no, you've got it all wrong!" but managing only to dig himself into a deeper pit by his excited efforts to explain.

Clearly, national images are highly selective if not subjective concoctions, stereotypes that are not so much false as misleading because fragmentary. In the United States, the older settlers made jokes about first the Irish, then the Italians, and finally the Poles as slobbish, drunken, stupid, because these groups were an impoverished peasantry in the process of adjusting to urban American society. But at other times these people had a dashingly romantic reputation. "You have only to point out a precipice to a Pole and he will throw himself over it," Balzac remarked at a time when Frenchmen knew Poles as Chopins and Ciezkowskis, romantic artists and libertarian thinkers— actually an emigré upper-class intelligentsia. The Italian whom white, Anglo-Saxon, Protestant Americans visualized as a grotesque pushcart peddler was elsewhere transmogrified into elegant lover, sophisticated politician, or star-struck artist. It has often been pointed out that the world's image of the Frenchman—voluble, volatile, argumentative—is based on the Parisian and is actually an international urban type, to which stereotype the rather dour French provincial makes a strong contrast. Savants point out that there are at least six French "families."

In the Romantic era of the earlier nineteenth century, Germans gained a reputation as impractical visionaries, earnest, poetic, and lovably foolish; their transformation into a grimly efficient race of mechanical monsters is one of the more extraordinary examples of the fickleness of "national character." The most superficial knowledge of

Germany reveals the presence of marked regional variations, making for the virtual hostility of Prussian and Bavarian. Of course, as Jules Romains pointed out,[15] all the European countries are racial mixtures, no nationality being based on any cultural homogeneity; and as for cultural differences, many other factors cut across that of nationality. Any modern people is a diversity of types, classes, occupations, levels of education and intelligence, membership in religious and intellectual traditions, etc.

A composite picture of Germany manufactured out of bits and pieces of German reality in the inflamed minds of Allied intellectuals included the goose-stepping soldier blindly obedient to the ferocious commands of his drunken *Feldherr*. Henri Bergson, especially, employed the negations of his own philosophy of freedom, vitalism, and spontaneity to picture a mechanical monster fed on materialism, a "predatory nation" which worshiped only "brute force."[16] Max Scheler simply reversed this, postulating soulful Germans against Cartesian Frenchmen and Benthamite Englishmen—idealism versus materialism or mechanism. German propaganda persistently stressed the *Händler und Helden* theme, heroes opposed to tradesmen. English people talked about English liberties while Frenchmen stressed Bergson's *élan*,* contrasting these qualities with the alleged bureaucratic slavishness of Germans, who, it was claimed, lagged behind the Western democracies in parliamentary government, who had a famous bureaucracy and were known for meticulous attention to organization. Russian anti-Germanism, articulated by those who had even more "soul" than the Germans, was inclined to stress the latter's atheistic, "spirit-killing" rationalism. But of course they could just as easily have turned this argument against rationalist France and utilitarian England, their allies, had they so desired.

"The Barbarism of Berlin," as G. K. Chesterton termed it, embraced regimentation (the Ant Hill); dreams of world domination; a natural brutality of character, marked by an "unhealthy activity of the Will" (Durkheim); worship of the state, to which Germans were slavishly obedient and which they elevated *über alles*, above all other values; deification of war, which they allegedly regarded as "needed to maintain the virility and courage of a nation" (Bryce), and which

---

* Bergson himself, the representative French philosopher, was the son of a Polish Jewish father and an English mother and was raised in Switzerland.

rendered them impervious to "ordinary morality and ordinary sentiments of pity." Germany, Arnold Bennett declared, is one vast military camp, a modern Sparta, "every male citizen a private soldier, and
every private soldier an abject slave."[17] At the same time, Germans
were admitted to be incurably "idealistic" in a way that was a bit
mysterious ("We shall never understand the Germans," Raleigh
sighed) but decidedly ominous, leading them away from common
sense to mystic flights of unreason. To John Dewey the chief source
of the poison was Immanuel Kant.[18] (It would surely have surprised
the author of the tract on perpetual peace to learn that he had fathered
a militaristic tradition.) Germans were "militaristic" because ruled by
a "military caste," a term repeatedly used in British and French war
writing; this caste was in fact said to be responsible for the war.
(Gilbert Murray saw the "specialized soldier" as a deplorable Prussian
invention, to which he contrasted "the human soldier, the Christian
soldier, or soldier with a sense of civil duties.") If the Allies had
armies, these were not "militaristic."

Germans were misled by other leaders whom they blindly followed. The extraordinary unanimity with which these guides were
identified has often been discussed: Nietzsche, Treitschke, Bernhardi,
the unholy trinity. To us today they appear an oddly assorted trinity:
a great poet-philosopher, who in fact hated German nationalism; a
nationalistic historian; and a crotchety retired military officer grum-
bling about the state of national security. Each had his counterpart in
other countries. Preachers of an inevitable war with Germany had
appeared in France and England in the years just before the war—e.g.,
W. T. Arnold and the Socialist editor Robert Blatchford, whose alarm
cries began two years before Bernhardi's *Deutschland und der nächste
Krieg* (1911). Charles Maurras had been assailing French ears with
the same message since 1905. Master of the era that he was, Nietzsche,
as we know, had as many admirers in France, England, and Russia as
in Germany. During the war the German philosopher Hans Vai-
hinger, in *Nietzsche als Philosoph* (1916), showed that Nietzsche was
neither a nationalist nor a militarist, and sales of Nietzsche's books
increased rather than decreased in England.[19]

Nevertheless, the opinion persisted that the unholy trinity had
combined to create a doctrine of inhumane power-worship and war-
madness in Germany. Thomas Hardy thought that there was "no
single instance since history began of a country being so demoralized

by a single thinker" as the Germans had been by Nietzsche.[20] (H. L.
Mencken, in the United States, reported being investigated by the
police as a suspected agent of "the German monster, Nietzky.") This
scarcely accords with Gerhart Hauptmann's boast that every German
soldier carried his Goethe and Schopenhauer in his knapsack, along
with the Bible and Homer: relatively few Germans, surely, had plowed
their way through *Thus Spake Zarathustra.*

Durkheim accused Treitschke of preaching a pagan and anti-
Christian doctrine of the state as power, a "madness" which in fact
Benedetto Croce recognized as closely akin to the great Italian political
thinker Machiavelli, so misunderstood by Anglo-Saxon moralists, and
which, indeed, Englishmen might have found in the legal positivism
of the Benthamite John Austin, in a tradition reaching back to Thomas
Hobbes.[21] Mix Nietzsche's immoralism and *Übermensch* with Hegel's
doctrine of the state, adding Treitschke's power politics, and you got
"a case of social pathology," as Durkheim called it: D'Annunzio's
"massive, mechanical beast" infused with the soul of a weird mystic
craving blood. The imagination could do much with such combinations of ideas. It could have done just as well with a Franco-British-
Russian constellation: Utilitarian rejection of natural law, say, joined
to Bergsonian irrationalism, Sorel's thirst for violence, British Social
Darwinism, Dostoyevsky's mystic nationalism, Maurras's dislike for
democracy, etc.

The Germans were said to wish to impose on the world their
vaunted *Kultur*, of whose superiority they incessantly boasted. About
this somewhat puzzling German claim, there was persistent discussion
in the Allied camp. A passage by A. E. Zimmern, the British classicist,
suggests how strange this claim was to the Anglo-Saxon mind. Zimmern reflects that these Germans really do seem to think that their
national glory lies in things of the mind:

> To the question, "What right have you to call yourselves a civ-
> ilized country?" . . . a German would reply . . . "look at our
> achievements in scholarship and science, at our universities, at our
> systems of education, at our literature, our music, and our paint-
> ing; at our great men of thought and imagination; at Luther,
> Dürer, Goethe, Beethoven, Kant."[22]

No such reply would occur to your true Briton! He would point to
"the things we have done," especially to the growth of the British

Empire. The German stresses knowledge, the Englishman character, Zimmern thought. Aware that this was hardly to pit pure good against perfect evil, he went on to argue that what mars *Kultur* is its alliance with the state, hence to the mailed fist of the Kaiser; this entails a standardization whereby all Germans are taught the same things in their national system of education. "Our real opponent is the system of training and education, out of which both German culture and German militarism spring." It is not German culture, it is not even German militarism which is the foe; it is this uniformity of public organization.

To make the widely admired German system of education the target of the Great Crusade might seem a dubious victory for propaganda. But Zimmern made the most of the contrast between British freedom and Prussian regimentation, which "dislikes the free play of human groupings"; and to the imperialistic connotations of a national view of culture, implying the inferiority of the lesser breeds without a Goethe. To the charge that their education stamped its statist seal on everybody,[23] the Germans replied in kind, one of the many examples of compliments repaid in the same coin in war imagery. French education was called standardized and fact-oriented, purely formal and not directed to original thinking. Robert Horn retrieved the old story about the French minister of education who rejoiced that "at this exact moment students all over France are learning the same thing." It is the Frenchman who had become a mechanical man.[24]

For the most part, however, the German ideologists preferred to train their fire on England. Not even the defense of civilization against Russia's barbarian hordes received as much attention in the Reich as did the hypocrisy, baseness, and hateful resentments of the nation of shopkeepers. "Gott strafe England!" "Germany's prominent men unanimously call England their chief enemy, the great tragedy's stage director," the Danish writer Georg Brandes noted, mentioning the theologian Harnack's diatribe: "England is hypocritical, England is mendacious, England is tortured with envy of Germany, and her actions are based on the violent passions of greed."[25] "All the German hatred goes against England," Stefan Zweig observed. Of twenty-five German historians polled, twenty-three agreed that the *Hauptfeind* was England. A Manifesto signed by more than three thousand teachers put England at the head of Germany's enemies.[26] "England alone among our enemies wishes our unconditional destruction," Professor

F. W. von Bissing thought.[27] Thomas Mann declared that "we do not hate the Russians,"[28] an attitude evidently reflected among the front-line soldiers, where the only really bad blood, it seems, was between British and German.

Sombart's book on heroes and hucksters set the tone of the German attack: British philosophers from Bacon to Bentham, Smith to Spencer, have been low hedonists and utilitarians. Love of creature comfort and respectability, absence of ideals, of heroism, and of community spirit—what else could be expected of a people without music? The German counterattack also attempted to exploit British smugness. Exasperation with a "what's good for England is good for the world" attitude was an old story, expressed by the Frenchman who said he didn't mind Gladstone having an ace up his sleeve but resented the implication that God put it there. Some Englishmen were aware of the weakness, and a recent student of their World War I aims concludes that "The leading British statesmen were only attracted to the principle of self-determination outside Europe as a matter of expedience and because they were convinced that it would work in their favour."[29] But the strongest charge in German war ideology was against the *bürgerlich* Englishman. Max Scheler spelled it out in a long table of about sixty contemptible Anglicanisms paired against their correct, presumably German opposites: Comfort against culture, calculation against thought, the useful as opposed to the good, prudery versus good behavior, bigotry versus piety, and of course *Gesellschaft* rather than *Gemeinschaft*.[30] A shallow creature, pursuing his selfish interests, the true Briton is capable of no higher philosophy than Utilitarianism (Bentham was the counterpart of Nietzsche in German anti-British imagery), has no feeling for religion, society, or intellectual culture, and goes about in a fog of canting self-satisfaction, confusing a moronic public opinion with the voice of God.

Such was the portrait for which, in fact, one might find excellent sketches in English writers themselves, from Defoe to Dickens, just as many German and Austrian intellectuals—not least, of course, Nietzsche himself—had earlier picked at the insufferable pomposity of their own bourgeoisie. Writing in later and calmer times, E. M. Forster put the case even more devastatingly.[31] But by then the Germans too were back to savaging their own militarists, as witness Kurt Tucholsky's or Bertolt Brecht's satires. Only for the war period did European intellectuals switch their targets and attempt to defend their

147

own country while assailing their neighbors—an inherently hazardous process, given the similarity of European society, not to speak of European intellectuals.

Many Germans were inclined to accept the "democracy versus militarism" or even the "civilization versus barbarism" formulation, if allowed a slight verbal adjustment. Werner Sombart picked up this gauntlet, altering it to *Händler* versus *Helden,* the money-grubber against the hero. Virtually to a man, the Germans found the "English spirit" an ignoble one. The British wanted to free Germans from their Kaiser, their army and heroes, so that they may be respectable burghers. The shopkeeper mentality could only categorize as "militarism" what was really the heroic ideal. Incomprehensible to mean-spirited tradesmen was the idea of battle as something quite different from mere brute force: sacrifice, community, idealism, not only guns and blood but "Faust and Zarathustra and Beethoven's *Eroica,*" touching "the life of the people, the life of the state."[32] When they thought about the *händlerische,* the *krämerische kultur* of the English, these Germans were inclined to take their chances with autocracy and even barbarism. The German Socialist Haenisch accepted the indictment of "militarism": yes, Germans admired the military virtues of discipline and courage, which is why in art they produced Beethovens and Goethes rather than Lockes and Mills (conveniently forgetting, of course, the Shakespeares and Miltons as well as the *deutsch kitsch*). German propaganda was nevertheless on the defensive about the charge of militarism which the foe pressed so ardently.

Thomas Mann thought it less easy to be a German than to be an Englishman or Frenchman. Deepened by struggle and suffering, the German soul plumbs below the surfaces to touch the irrational. Those who think the *deutscher Geist* wild and weird are philistines. Demonic and heroic, the German soul knows the Nietzschean struggle of Dionysus with Apollo toward a higher creativity. If Germany is misunderstood, that is because she is harder to understand, unlike those who can be taken in at a glance.[33] As Mann added in his celebrated *Betrachtungen eines Unpolitischen,* it is a German virtue not to be merely political, a matter of newspapers, elections, and "rights," but rather to be cultural, involving art, philosophy, and an inner freedom. Against the Allied disparagement of Germany for having no proper elections and parliaments, this reply dismissed such matters as essentially trivial (rather in the spirit of a great Englishman, Dr. Samuel

Johnson, when he remarked that "I would not give half a guinea to live under one form of government rather than another"). Yet one of Germany's greatest minds, Max Weber, thought otherwise: the Germans were a politically immature people, unable to produce the kind of leadership necessary for a *Herrenvolk*. They lost the war on the political not the military front, he thought. So the *Kultur* line was a failure even among a few German intellectuals. (In the principal debate among German intellectuals, that about war aims, Weber's moderate position was supported by an articulate minority of liberal historians and theologians.)[34] This high line made poor propaganda by insisting on aristocratic, feudal values in a democratic world, and by seeming to flaunt the superiority of German values over all other peoples'—hardly the way to win support outside Germany.

But if the Germans failed in their use of intellectual weaponry, the Allies often were equally unimpressive. One interesting insanity was the invention in France and England of a progressive Russia. Writers showed a positive enthusiasm for redeeming the Tsar's empire from calumny, perhaps because the task was so challenging. On the eve of the war in Britain and France, the intellectuals' hostility to an illiberal despotism had been a real problem; what British and French opposition there was to entering the war seized upon the frightfulness of being Russia's ally. But within a surprisingly short time, Englishmen as well as Frenchmen were discovering hitherto unsuspected virtues in the Tsar's regime. According to J. Dover Wilson, the persecuted Russian revolutionaries were actually miserable creatures, and Russian public opinion fully supported their elimination; the Jews were mistreated, yes, but one must understand the problem. The war would do Russia much good, for wars have always benefited her, and this time might lead to representative government and a liberal policy toward nationalities. He painted Russia as a kind of bucolic paradise inhabited by simple but sweet, religious peasants and kind-hearted landlords, living "in close communion with nature."[35] In any case, Russia was not "an aggressive military state"—her national character was deeply pacific. "The most Christian country in the world," with a "fundamentally democratic spirit," "socially more democratic than any modern country," the land which had once been presented as the abode of the knout and of unmitigated despotism emerged from this wartime bath of Franco-British propaganda looking even better than Stalin's USSR was made to appear during World War II.

II

This is perhaps enough about the endless foolishness of wartime attempts to convert ideas into weapons. The task was necesssary. "Each side is inspired by its own idealism," wrote the relatively neutral H. N. Brailsford, "for no Government can hope today to lead any people into war unless it can convince them it is fighting under dire necessity for the defence of right."[36] Each side, he added, "with the pitiless insight of enemies" can see how fatuous the opposing idealism is, but is blind to its own follies. "Nations are strangers to one another," Paul Valéry had written. "No matter how sincere their desire to agree and understand each other may sometimes be, the understanding always becomes obscured and stops at a certain point."[37] Determined in wartime to misunderstand each other, they found it all too easy. It was rare to find a Croce pointing out that war and philosophy have nothing to do with each other. Croce found it possible to support his country in the war quite enthusiastically, yet at the same time denounce the "lies, calumnies, and insults poured out against Germany, its culture, its poetry, its science, its philosophy." For the average person, this was too difficult. The myth of the enemy required that he be a personified unity.

The ultimate irony is that, so far as an intellectual or spiritual ingredient entered into the war equation, it was much the same for all the warring countries, on both sides of the battle. "Die Ideen von 1914" differed little from Britain to Russia. Merchants and heroes existed on both sides. When the Germans attacked bourgeois timidity and triviality as English traits, they were attacking their own countrymen as well. The British could have found a panting militaristic idealism in their own traditions, as well as in their own youth of 1914.[38] The rival national images set up for purposes of propaganda were phantasms, without substantial reality—like so much of this century's ideology.

—8—

Dissent and Disenchantment

I

It cannot be the purpose of this book to tell of the intellectuals during the war, as a subject in itself—it is too large a topic except as this casts some light on their motives in entering and supporting the war. But of course it does. The strength and seriousness of their motives are revealed in how firmly they held on to them, or how readily discarded them. At any rate, it seems legitimate for us to explore some significant instances of exceptions to the rule—i.e., negative responses to the war made either immediately (which was extremely rare) or relatively soon, and either forthrightly or confusedly. There were degrees of resistance to the contagion, and we shall be describing several types.

Some things, of course, wore off quickly. Herbert Read said that "one week in the trenches was sufficient to strip war of its lingering traces of romance."[1] For Jean Vigier, "Two months showed us the inanity of this way of looking at things"—i.e., the heroic image of the first days.[2] "Der alte Gott der Schlachten ist nicht mehr," Stefan George noted sadly. George Bernanos echoed, "The old glory is a lie," long before Wilfred Owen wrote his immortal poem on the same theme. "This dance of savages bears no resemblance to war."[3] No reality could have lived up to the extravagant expectations of the war's beginning, but the disenchantment of reality was particularly brutal.

Romantic illusions vanished in the grimness of trench warfare and mass slaughter. Shaw and Kraus, among others, made the most of a dreadful impersonality:

> . . . the utter divorce of the warrior from the effects of his soulless labor. He has no sight or knowledge of what he is doing: he only hands on a shell or pulls a string. And a Beethoven or a baby dies six miles off. . . . The notion that these heavily bored men were being heroic, or cruel, or anything in the least romantic or sensational, was laughable.[4]

The war was of course not that simple, and both excitement and heroism did exist. There was a grandeur in the incessant roar of guns, which reminded many of a terrible music, and even the immense sacrifice of blood fitted the image of an awful apocalypse: "the earth is hungry." But in general the mechanized mass slaughter of the Somme, and at Verdun in 1916, and on the Eastern Front, was to destroy forever the heroic image of war, which may have revived faintly in the tank battles of World War II: in World War I only a few somewhat ridiculous airplane duels smacked of chivalrous combat.

The trenches did in part fulfill the hopes of community, as we have seen, at the expense however of cutting the soldiers off from the home front, in a growing misunderstanding that became one of the war's chief psychological themes; a vague anger was directed against the journalists and politicians who mouthed slogans of high idealism, never visiting and not understanding the death-haunted and flea-ridden front lines. (The erotic potential of the war must have been disillusioning, too; there was enough sexual activity, but also a serious outbreak of venereal disesase, a consequence of unregulated armies of camp followers along the Western Front.) Under such conditions the public-spirited features of the war dwindled also, until soldiers decided they were fighting not for their country—the "old lie," *dulce et decorum est pro patria mori*—but for their mates, or themselves. "I have decided that my epitaph will consist only of these two lines," Bernanos wrote in September, 1915. "Here lies a man who fought and died for his personal satisfaction and to enrage those who did not fight and die"! Soldiers stuck it out with incredible endurance, moved more by such perverse logic than by the initial idealism of *pro patria*. But the later months of the war saw such secessions as the French mutinies, the wild Italian flight at Caporetto, and the ominous clouds portending revolution in Russia and Germany.

Vladimir Mayakovsky, the great Russian poet, was excited at first by the war, but like Maxim Gorky soon turned to "revulsion and hatred."[5] Clearly, Russia, suffering a succession of heavy military defeats and groaning under the burdens of a war she lacked the efficiency to conduct, was a special case. Yet her incredible perseverance in the war through more than three years of agony suggests the weakness rather than the strength of opposition. There was some confusion stemming from the widely held view that the expected revolution would come *through* the war and not against it. (Stravinsky, supporting the war in 1914, was confident it would lead to extinction of the Tsardom and a Slavonic United States.) When the first Russian Revolution in March, 1917, did overthrow the Romanovs, war opponents such as Bertrand Russell expected Russia to leave the war, instead of which the new republican regime tried to carry it on with a better will. Not until April, 1917, did Lenin experience anything but frustration and despair in his Swiss exile.

Meanwhile, a variety of other opponents or semi-opponents were equally ineffective. Of these, probably the best known among the intellectuals was the musicologist and writer Romain Rolland. Rolland's internationalism had been revealed in his most famous novel, widely read just before the war; its hero, Jean-Christophe, was a universal man, a German who lived in many other lands and used the cosmopolitan language of music (Cesar Franck was the model). Rolland was as great a fan of Beethoven as Shaw was of Wagner, a commitment which at that time put a certain gulf between them—both Germanophiles, but of different German cults. Finding himself in Switzerland when the war began, Rolland stayed there, trying to organize the intellectuals of the world against hatred and lies, not without feeling in some measure the allure of the August idealism: "O young men that shed your blood for the thirsty earth with so generous a joy! O heroism of the world! What a harvest for destruction to reap under this splendid summer sun!" He asked Gerhart Hauptmann to lead the German intellectuals in repudiating the attack on Belgium, a role which Hauptmann vigorously declined. In opposing the war, Rolland did not exactly cease to be a French patriot; his position was closer to those who sought merely to preserve some sanity against the day when the contagion would end. His influence was to spread widely among those unhappy with the war, including Einstein and Stefan Zweig, after publication of *Au-dessus de la melée* in late 1914.

Refusing to sign Rolland's petition against the bombardment of Reims, Shaw accused him of a lack of realism ("if I were a military officer defending Reims I should have put an observation post on the cathedral roof; and if I were his opponent I should have to fire on it").[6] Naturally, Rolland's stand seemed, to the Germans, not exactly "above the battle." Rolland lost friends, too, by his "above it all" stance. In the *Daily Chronicle* (March 17, 1916), H. G. Wells vented a long complaint againt Rolland, the result of *Au-Dessus* and other Rolland writings being used in England by "your Cambridge friends," in *The Cambridge Journal* and *Labour Leader*.[7] Standing above the battle, up there in Switzerland, Wells told Rolland, you adopt an irritating self-righteousness while those of us who mingle in the melee seek by sweat and suffering to find some practical solution; and what is your solution? Do you propose that we surrender to the Germans? Do you propose anything? You extract much literary ore from this pose of being noble while the world goes wrong; but this sublime detachment is futile and (Wells came close to saying) hypocritical. Wells would sign the anti-German protest, naturally; but at the same time, Rolland's desire to withhold approval from tsarist Russia annoyed him greatly.[8] Rolland was not the only one who discovered that standing in a neutral corner preaching moderation during a general affray is likely to be an exercise in futility. Italy and then the United States were to find that the only way to exert an influence was to enter the fight. And among the major foes of the war, Lenin and his followers were filled with contempt for the "pacifist" Rollandists.

Admirers of this gentle and courageous man, such as gathered at Vézelay in 1966 to do him centennial honor,[9] declared that he was "fifty years ahead of his time," but in fact Rolland seems as well placed a half century or more in arrears. The kind of warfare that spares historic relics was to be even more obsolete, by far, in 1941–45, when the Allies did not scruple to drop millions of tons of high explosives on German cities indiscriminately. And what spared Rolland participation in the 1914 mystique was a certain immersion in antique values, those roughly of the Enlightenment, as well as a certain innocence of practicalities. Along with Max Nordau (*Degeneration*), he had sensed decadence in Wagner ("poisoned by unhealthy notions reflecting the aspirations of the times," 1902), and his musician's ear heard in young Stravinsky an "intoxicating frenzy and burlesque hysteria" which he tied to the war. Jean-Christophe had observed the irrational- ist and bellicose prewar spirit "with curiosity" and incomprehension (though "he did not try to combat it").[10] It was because he was *not* up-to-date that Rolland was largely immune to the fever of 1914. Not the avant-garde, which was warlike, saved him, but Beethoven.

Rolland's *Journal of the War Years* is an invaluable source and a tribute to his energy and spirit. He received many sympathetic as well as hostile letters upon publication of his *Au-dessus de la melée*, which was followed by other writings, chiefly in the *Journal de Genève*, in 1914. But the tide of condemnation rose rather than subsided, at least in France. Severe attacks on him came from all directions; he noted the irony of an alliance against him of liberal freethinkers, Catholics, and conservatives of the Maurras or Barrès school. Well-wishers in France were soon telling him not to try to publish anything more there. *Le Temps* attacked him on December 17, contrasting him un- favorably with the patriotic Bergson. Rolland then fell silent publicly, for two years, "convinced of the uselessness of speaking to those who do not wish to hear," deciding "to disinterest myself in the ruin of these peoples, who *wish it* and even seem to take pleasure in it." Barrès, he groaned, is the only French writer of any distinction who has the ear of the French people—Barrès, preaching hatred of the Boche and war to the utmost, in the columns of *Echo de Paris*. Rolland thought most French Swiss hostile to him too, despite the loyalty of the *Geneva Journal*. "The French intellectual is in the grip of a delirium which equals or surpasses that of Germany in August and September," he wrote at the end of 1914.[11] Sharp attacks on him came from Germany, too, but for obvious reasons he found some welcome there. But in the measure he was accepted in Germany, he was bound to be an em- barrassment to his own countrymen.

Rolland was ambivalent about the Germans; he admired their energy and organizing ability as well as much of their culture. Like Bertrand Russell and Benedetto Croce, he felt outraged by the unfair- ness of the attacks on them. He kept many German friends, such as Richard Strauss. Among German Rollandists were Walter Schücking, Wilhelm Herzog of Munich, and the Alsatian René Schickele who edited the *Weisse Blätter*, whose contributors included Heinrich Mann —it was not militant in tone, but kept alive a flicker of sanity among writers. But Rolland disliked the "enormous egoism of race" which had developed in the Wilhelmine Reich.[12] Whenever he encountered a pious and philistine hatred of the Germans, as in the rather bizarre American George D. Herron, he bristled; he would even defend Wagner from Saint-Saens' self-serving campaign against the German master, whose music Saint-Saens called "a means employed by Germany for the conquest of souls."[13] Yet he conceded the "Dionysian brutality" of the German mood.

Rolland opposed Lenin's return to Russia in 1917 with German aid, on the grounds that it would contribute to a German victory and discredit the Leninists in Russia by associating them with treason.[14] This seems strangely inconsistent: if the Germans did conquer Russia, the fate of Lenin's movement was already sealed, while one wonders why Rolland displayed such solicitous concern for a man he did not at all admire, as well as such a fear of a German victory if this would shorten the war. His true lineaments as a French patriot, in spite of all, are revealed here. His hatred of war, and of hatred, was deep and real, and courageous. At the same time, his love of France prevented him from doing anything that would cause her to lose the war; his relative silence in 1915 and 1916, an accession to pleas that he was damaging the French cause, is evidence of this. One notes also, in the *Journal*, an ambivalence about American entry into the war, about which Rolland says little, a sign of conflicting emotions. (The *Journal* normally pays close, careful, and copious attention to anything relating to the war, which is what makes it so absorbing a source.) On the one hand, this was a widening of the war, drawing another piece of the world into the holocaust. His sympathies had lain with the martyred Bryan and with President Wilson's efforts to bring about a negotiated peace. On the other hand, American entrance obviously rescued France. In the end Rolland could not escape the cruel logic of choosing sides which war forces on everyone, and his "above the battle" struggle, carried on with such energy, was a failure. His subsequent career, one might add, revealed how little he was in fact by nature "above the battle"; he eventually became an impassioned supporter of communism. One thinks of his defense of Stalin's purge trials, a part of the "great terror" which in its totality may have taken more lives than World War I.

II

Dissenters came in different sizes and shapes. Ludwig Marcuse, in his autobiography, *Mein Zwanzigstes Jahrhundert*, tells of a friend who continued to think in the trenches that Kant's third antinomy was more important than the war. Jacques Rivière turned to religious meditations. Alain pondered problems of esthetics in his dugout. As Marx had done mathematical problems to take his mind off troubles, so many intellectuals used purely formal projects as a relief from battle, perhaps thus preserving their sanity. Teilhard de Chardin's wartime journal, which he began to keep in 1915 as a relief from boredom, is remarkable for almost totally ignoring the events of the war, being devoted to theological and philosophical speculations. (When he alludes to the war, it is to see it characteristically as a catastrophe somehow necessary to cosmic evolution, a crisis of growth.)[15]

Alexander Blok said rather proudly that his war record was to edit Apollon Grigorev, help to stage *The Rose and the Cross* (one of his plays), and write *Retribution*. Ludwig Wittgenstein, too, sleepwalked through the war, it would seem, thinking only of his *Tractatus*, which, he wrote Bertrand Russell, would be sent to England should he die. ("If I remain alive, I should like to come to England after the war, & explain my work to you by word of mouth, if you are willing.")[16] On a somewhat less elevated plane, the sexologist Havelock Ellis, according to his biographer Arthur Calder Marshall, considered the war as an irrelevance, his own work doubtless being completely absorbing. One finds many men, such as the Russian poet Osip Mandelstam, who seem hardly to have noticed the war. Bertrand Russell, however, was just the opposite, and there were many like him: his philosophy and mathematics now seemed empty, the huge drama of human history made all studies trivial. He could write and lecture about nothing except the war.

Paul Klee, born in Switzerland, was living in Munich, then "the center of the art world" as he said, where he had gone in 1908. He was drafted in 1916, at the age of thirty-five. The absurdity of Klee as a soldier being evident even to the military, the greatest of modern painters was given a job varnishing airplane wings. (After the death of Klee's friend Franz Marc, the royal family, it is said, gave secret orders that the talented artists of Munich should be exempted from battle.) "I have long had this war in me," Klee wrote in his diary.

"Therefore it does not concern me inwardly."[17] He saw it, as he saw all life, as a dream. Old picture books had come to life.

Intellectuals, especially those who remained at home, might soon weary of the highly charged emotionalism of the first days and, as the war dragged on, discover their own versions of ennui. Some grieved over the loss of freedom of the mind and diversity of ideas. "All discussion, all pursuit of truth ceased," Lowes Dickinson lamented. "To win the war or to hide safely among the winners became the only preoccupation. Abroad was heard only the sound of guns, at home only the ceaseless patter of a propaganda utterly indifferent to the truth."[18] Georges Sorel, the old *combattant*, delighted in intellectual combat, not the vulgar physical kind, and lamented that "Europe is going to sleep intellectually." Drawn into service as manufacturers of "propaganda," writers might eventually wonder about this dubious role, which trespassed in shady domains of misrepresentations, exaggerations, lies. These were uncommon cases, to be sure. Sometimes, also, the extremes of war glorification and hatred of the enemy caused a reaction; thus, Stefan Zweig found that Thomas Mann's diatribes against the French people put him off.[19] It was in fact the manifest unfairness and suspension of all critical judgment, in the rush to vilify the enemy, that played the greatest part in engendering disaffection during the early part of the war; so the cases of Russell in England, Rolland on the French side, as well as Zweig, suggest.

G. F. Nicolai, one of the handful of German scientists who signed Einstein's counter to the warlike Manifesto of ninety-three professors in 1914, proved to be one of the most stubborn war opponents. Arrested and imprisoned for his teaching at the University of Berlin in 1915, he wrote a book called *The Biology of War* while in prison, subsequently published in Switzerland (Zurich, 1917).[20] The German physiologist was dominated by a biological conception of the unity of mankind, and doubtless, like Georg Trakl, who committed suicide while in medical service on the Austro-Russian front, by a simple horror at human suffering. (Others whose exposure to treatment of the wounded disgusted them with the war included Roger Martin du Gard and Alfred Döblin.) Inducted into the army as a physician, Nicolai refused to wear a sword and fled to Denmark in 1916.

But of such eccentric if courageous figures effective antiwar agitation is not made. Tolstoyan pacifists such as J. M. Whitham in England could only conscientiously object on a purely individualistic basis. The trouble with the pacifist gesture, as Richard Aldington reflected, is that it is "simply playing into the hands of the opposing militarists," and "a futile gesture." That the war was, after all, a monstrous fact, armies locked in death grips, governments and peoples locked into demands for victory, made it impossible to contemplate simply laying down arms. Calling the war *inutile et mauvaise*, Jules Romains (in an article written in late 1915 which his publisher did not have the heart or courage to publish at that time) still thought the only possible and desirable outcome was Allied victory.[21]

There was a less active sort of opposition, a sort of "dumb insolence" which took the form of withdrawal, private mutterings, and flippancy. There were books which did not get published, like Max Brod's answer to Max Scheler, called the *Genius of Peace*, which he says he wrote but could not print.[22] A virtually licensed gadfly like Karl Kraus, having established his position from long and honorable service in satire, could get away with witty deflations of the war spirit, such as appeared in *Die Fackel* in Vienna during the war.

The so-called Bloomsbury circle in England may be taken as an example of a purely personal resistance, not altogether serious, which was tolerated because so obviously harmless. Quentin Bell says that "none of them, so to speak, 'believed in' the war, and they refused, resolutely, to be religious about it."[23] In the case of Lytton Strachey, they were positively frivolous about it. The Strachey stories include his reply to a reproach for not enlisting: "Madam, I am the civilization they are fighting to defend"; and his alleged answer to the Hampstead Tribunal, which asked what he would do if he saw a uhlan trying to rape his sister: "I should try to interpose my own body." Before 1916, of course, one could evade the issue by not volunteering, if one were able to resist or hide from public opinion; the introduction of conscription did not come in Britain until two years into the war. Clive Bell, who published a feeble pamphlet in 1915, *Peace at Once*, calling for ending the war "as quickly as possible by a negotiated peace," found refuge along with Leonard and Virginia Woolf, Bertrand Russell, and others at Garsington Manor, the estate of Philip and Ottoline Morrell outside Oxford. This famous entourage, marred by internal bickering and furtive sneering at the hostess, provided material for many memoirs and for Aldous Huxley's novel *Crome Yellow*.[24] Under provisions of the Military Service Act, they were allowed to work on the land. Duncan Grant and David Garnett (who served for a time with a Friends' ambulance unit in France) raised fruit in Suffolk, then joined the Woolfs in Asheham, Sussex.[25] Among these conscientious objectors Maynard Keynes, subsequently the famous economist, did not object to fighting but did object to conscription, on the grounds that the decision had to be one's own, not the state's. Virginia Woolf, in the throes of a mental illness begun in 1913, recovered in 1915; she was revolted by excessively patriotic propaganda and in 1916 saw the war as "a preposterous masculine fiction."[26] Her being out of the scene in the year 1914 constitutes an interesting situation for the study of the influence of the August ideas. The exchange of letters between Virginia and Lytton Strachey never mentions so dreary a subject as public affairs. (Her husband, Leonard, did not share the Bloomsbury cynicism or scepticism about the war, but believed it necessary to resist the Germans, who were "mainly responsible for the war.")[27] It seems a just verdict that Bloomsburyites tried to ignore the war, did not vigorously oppose it, hid from it, and joked it out of their minds. Lytton Strachey took subtle revenge by working on that deflation of heroic seriousness, *Eminent Victorians* (1918).

D. H. Lawrence, whose antiwar inclinations brought him into contact with Russell and with the Bloomsbury group, reacted with typical violence against their irreverence, their brittle egoism, their sophisticated prattle. His "black beetles, horrible and unclean" represented, as often suggested, a revulsion against their homosexuality (intensified by his own, which was suppressed, Quentin Bell alleges), but the whole Bloomsbury character-armor of aristocratic dandyism, their irony, cleverness, and affected world-weariness, had to offend Lawrence's intellectual personality. His bizarre wartime attempt to join forces with Bertrand Russell in a world-saving venture, uniting brain and heart, ended predictably in fiasco.[28] Lawrence's position on the war was ambivalent. Nothing was less pacifist than the Lorenzian *Blut und Boden* world-view. "He had no conscientious objection to the war," as Somers says in *Kangaroo*. Lawrence's whole ethos disposed him to accept struggle and conflict, even unto suffering and death: "the great adventure of death." "Humanity needs pruning."[29] He might well have accepted the war as eagerly as Péguy or Weber or Kokoschka. But Frieda barred the way; he had a cherished German wife and many German intellectual contacts, and unlike those Englishmen who hated a stereotype he knew something concrete about the enemy. This, rather than an instinct for intellectual fairplay, as with

Russell, seems the decisive factor. "I can't help feeling it is a young and adorable country—adolescent—with the faults of adolescence." Like some other critics, he settled his hostility on the "mob spirit" rather than on war itself—the bullying, the servile conformity, the loss of "manly isolation."[30] "War made a hell of his world," Edward Marsh said.[31] Defense of the private man against the crowd—"the living rock of a single creature's pride"—is a powerful theme in Lawrence, but so is its apparent contradiction, disgust with narcissistic self-love and petty egoism. His hatred of the mob and the mass-man accompanied a thirst for genuine community. But he could not find community in the war. "The War was not strife; it was murder," Lawrence later decided.[32] Suffering through the war, he extruded schemes for total reform of the human race and contemplated withdrawal to some utopian community. In 1916 he wished "there could be an earthquake that would swallow up everybody except some two dozen people." Yet he did not really oppose the war, and it seems evident that but for the accident of having Frieda he would have responded to much of its appeal.

Lady Cynthia Asquith says Lawrence recognized that the war brought "a slump in trifling." "I am English, English in the teeth of all the world—even in the teeth of England," he exclaimed. His friend Middleton Murry thought that Lawrence "repudiated the war because he had some deep sense of kinship with the war." Bertrand Russell divined in him "two attitudes to the war," and David Garnett suggested that "he hated the war because it was not war enough"—both of course unfriendly witnesses, but right in sensing the ambivalence.[33]

Lawrence learned to hate Cambridge intellectualism during the war, and was inspired to write his greatest novel, *Women in Love*, as a kind of search for the roots of the sickness. "It explores the nature of the deep-seated disease in the body politic of which war is the ultimate death-agony," he said. "This world of ours has got to collapse now, in violence and injustice and destruction, and nothing will stop it," he wrote to Lady Ottoline in February, 1916. His foes thought he welcomed the destruction, charging him with "a sort of blood-lust, a desire for destruction" (Garnett); but the evidence of his letters and other writings shows that Lawrence suffered deeply from the destruction ("the great past, crumbling down, breaking down—I can't bear it") while at the same time he had moments of hope that "the world will come through . . . and in the end it will be cleaner." As apparently odd as his abortive approach to Russell for a partnership in social salvation, his scheme for a utopia in Florida was his tribute to the community quest. "We must begin afresh—we must begin to create a new life together—unanimous."

III

Despite his reputation as a foe of the war, it is difficult to find a clear line of war resistance in George Bernard Shaw. He made no practical suggestions toward ending the war, and his insolence (as it seemed) in declaring one side no better than the other did not mean that he wanted Germany to win. He even confessed, "to my utter scandal," feeling an impulse to enlist.[34] Though the combatants were two pirate ships, he was on one of them! Shaw could not stomach the outpourings of sentiment and self-righteousness (which seem the inevitable tenor of popular opinion in time of crisis). Like Hermann Hesse, he objected to the tone rather than to the war itself, which he thought necessary. Colin Wilson, a staunch though discriminating admirer of Shaw, cannot muster any enthusiasm for his war role, for Shaw really had nothing to say yet insisted on saying it, loudly.[35] He played the "down with military castes" record, yet in *Common Sense about the War* thought that England should have had half a million men ready to defend Belgium, a deterrent it is hard to conceive of as existing without military leaders, and of course hard to imagine existing at all in a country traditionally opposed to standing armies. On another occasion, he declared that Germany's violation of Belgium had nothing to do with England's entering the war, "except to furnish Mr. Asquith with a presentable pretext for entering on a war to which he was already secretly pledged, Belgium or no Belgium."[36] Making fun of the Futurists' belief in "purification by artillery fire," he still believed that Germany had to be beaten and made to awaken from "a romantic dream." He pleaded for less vindictiveness, but complained that German prisoners of war were too well treated.[37]

In practice, after all, there was not much difference between fighting without hate and with it. Lytton Strachey called Shaw "our leading patriot." Shaw refused to sign Rolland's petition protesting the Reims bombardment, and urged the Irish not to be pro-German. While *Punch* chided his "devastating egoism," Blatchford demanded a parliamentary investigation of him, friends dropped him, and the Dramatists' Club threw him out, it is clear that Shaw thought Great Britain quite justified in going to war but had got the reasons all wrong. This was doubtless true; but it might have occurred to an imaginative writer, one supposes, especially one as cynical about mass intelligence as Shaw, that leaders of nations do not rally support for a war by talking about the balance of power.

If Shaw's attitudes toward the war amounted to a bundle of contradictions, so to a degree did Bertrand Russell's. Russell's argument for England's staying out of the war, as he gave it later, is really an argument for going in, as most people had to view the situation in 1914. Germany would have won, he explained, the war would have ended quickly, the world would have been spared Communism, Nazism, and many other horrors that resulted from the holocaust of 1914–18, compared to which the triumph of the Kaiser's slightly absurd but basically civilized Germany was a triviality.[38] Plausible though it may be in hindsight, frank defeatism of this sort was not anywhere near the bounds of possibility in 1914, and Russell's intimation that this was the line he then preached is not accurate. He was not a militant opposer of the war during the first several weeks. "We are all patriots in one sense, that we ardently desire the victory of the allies," he said.[39] If he soon felt himself isolated, horrified, "driven nearly mad with disgust,"[40] he reacted chiefly against the hysteria: "Every tale against Germany is believed—there is no hint or trace of justice or mercy." He thought his friend and collaborator Alfred North Whitehead, from whom he became estranged, "utterly wild and mad in his determination to crush Germany and in his belief in the quite special wickedness of Germany." "I suffer most from the absence of any attempt at justice, at imagining how matters look from the German side." His old philosophic colleagues, including McTaggart, helped get him ostracized. Separated from his lectureship at Trinity College, Cambridge, and in 1918 even imprisoned, though by his own account "quite agreeably," facing mobs on two occasions (his account in *Portraits from Memory* manages to be almost hilarious), Russell was certainly courageous in opposing—what? He first joined the Union of Democratic Control, then found a cause in the No-Conscription Fellowship; neither was against the war as such, but against an illiberal war, almost a contradiction in terms. He meditated much on the causes of war, talked about a postwar organization for peace (in com-

163

mon with many others), and declared that the present war was not one of principle or self-defense but of "prestige."[41] People ought to be rational; the war ought to have been settled by negotiation; the withdrawal of the Germans from Belgium should now be secured by negotiation (!); and yet Russell knew that men are not rational. Mankind has "an impulse to conflict rather than harmony."[42] "I discovered to my amazement that average men and women were delighted at the prospects of war."[43] "The old primitive passions, which civilization has denied, surge up all the stronger for repression," he noted, in agreement with Freud.[44] He turns on the pacifists and reminds them that no one would want to live in a placid utopia.

It is not true that, as Englishmen generally believe, Germany deliberately planned the war for many years.[45] Yet Russell accused the Germans of waging war out of jealousy of French culture (they wanted to kill the French intelligentsia, while presumably contriving to spare their own) and British wealth.[46] Russell wrote much on what must be done "if a better and saner world is to grow out of the horror of futile carnage," talking of reeducation, of the follies of patriotism, the delusion of "glory," the absurdity in general of war; he looked to the future and re-examined the past, but had nothing helpful to say about the present. The war did have the effect, for better or worse, of turning the great philosopher's attention to social and political questions. "The books of mathematics and philosophy that used to seem full of hope and interest now leave me utterly cold." *Principles of Social Reconstruction*, begun in a whirl of excitement about the challenge of war, broadened out to appraise property, the state, education, marriage, religion. The first two belong with war as embodiments of evil "possessive impulses," the last two ought to channel the "creative" impulses, "though at present they do so very inadequately." "The creative impulses in man are essentially harmonious . . . . It is the possessive impulses that involve conflict." (Earlier in the book, we had read that "Conflicts of party politics, conflicts between capital and labour, and generally all those conflicts of principle which do not involve war, serve many useful purposes and do very little harm.")[47]

Russell's antiwar propaganda probably lost effectiveness because of a characteristic hyperbole. Cowardice, love of dominion, and lust for blood he calls the only military motives. The war experience is rendering soldiers unfit for civil life: "We cannot hope that very many of them will ever again be as useful citizens as they would have been if the war had not occurred."[48] Privately, he wrote that the Foreign Office had committed a "whole chapter" of "crimes"; "I cannot discover an infamy in the whole wide world which the F.O. has not done its best to support." Every word the Germans say against the British is justified, he added.[49] Russell's pursuit of his own country's foreign policy crimes in 1915–18 compares well with his anti-American crusade fifty years later. Russell's often brilliant discussions of war's stupidity and immorality embraced diatribes against almost everybody from common soldier to government, accompanied by general moral strictures rather than immediate practical advice.

A curious mixed marriage of war resisters was that between Christian pacifists and Bloomsbury/Russell scoffers or Socialist atheists. Lytton Strachey paused to marvel at finding himself "on that fellow's [Jesus'] side."[50] Russell preached antiwar sermons at Friends' meetinghouses, at a time when he was engaged in divesting himself of his first wife, an American Quaker, and was of course a celebrated "agnostic."

The British left liberals ("radicals") had been left a shambles by the events which led to war in the early August days. Represented in the Asquith cabinet by Loreburn, Morley, and Harcourt, embracing a gallery of intellectuals such as Norman Angell, the Trevelyans, Arthur Ponsonby, and Francis Hirst, this group dominated the intellectually distinguished *Manchester Guardian, Nation*, and *The Economist*, but their forte was not foreign affairs. In this area they tended toward the radical innocence of opposing all use of force, all "secret diplomacy," armament expenditures, and involvement in other country's affairs; but in fact they were not even consistent in this, for like some more recent "pacifists" they were quite selective in their opposition to war. They traditionally favored righteous wars, among which were those of "national liberation," and so they cheered the First Balkan war of 1912–13, the rehearsal for 1914, as the liberation of oppressed peoples from the hateful Turk. Seeking to base their foreign policy on moralism and ideology, they were uncomfortable in the Grey era from 1905 to 1914 when Great Britain edged toward the Franco-Russian side, being generally pro-German, anti-French, and very anti-Russian. At that time they denied that Germany was an aggressive menace, questioned the commitment to defend France (though not unhappy with France as an ideological ally), and were moved to indignation at the mere thought of associating England with "despotic Russia."[51] But in August, 1914, the great majority of them confessed the bankruptcy of their principles by acquiescing in the war against Germany at the side of France and Russia, with only feeble and confused murmurings. Most of them quickly re-moralized the war, discovering that Russia was really not despotic at all but a great potential democracy, that the Germans were subhuman, that the war was a great crusade to save the world for liberal principles. But others regrouped after a time to form the nucleus of the "neutralist" Union of Democratic Control (UDC).

The German counterpart of the UDC was the Free Fatherland Association established in November, 1914, including Rathenau, Weber, Naumann, Meinecke, and Troeltsch, who opposed the extreme annexationists without much success, while in Italy a similar circle arose, the *Giretti*. Einstein joined the *Bund Neues Vaterland* also, along with business figures like Ernest Reuter and Hugo Simon. The goal of such groups was to keep alive hopes for an early peace—inevitably entailing some compromises, "the kind of a peace treaty which will not plant the seeds of future wars," as Einstein put it—and, as a means to this end, to keep down the temperature of war propaganda.[52] The task of encouraging an atmosphere in which rational adjustment of conflicting national claims might take place was of course a hopeless one. Against it stood the fear of courting a letdown of morale by "defeatist" talk, and the even more fearful logic which reasoned "having shed so much precious blood, we cannot now settle for no gains," thus admitting that the whole war was a ghastly mistake, and a million lives sacrified in vain. "We must be solidly indemnified." Obviously, too, one could not settle for the same amount of security possessed at the beginning of the war, since this led to war; to revert to the 1914 status quo or something like it was to restore the situation that engendered war. Nothing is less promising than trying to tell a nation at war that full victory is not its goal, though the truth may be that the demand for total victory is ultimately disastrous for everybody.

Organized as early as September, 1914, the UDC included public officials such as Charles Trevelyan and Ramsay MacDonald, who had never accepted the decision for war; Trevelyan resigned from the British government charging that the French had duped them, while MacDonald quit his post as leader of the Labour party rather than support the war. Arthur Ponsonby was a maverick Liberal MP. E. D. Morel had acquired a bitter hostility to France during his celebrated exposés of Belgian and French colonial practices. Norman Angell, whose peace publications were subsidized by Andrew Carnegie, was the only one of the original UDC founders who was not an activist. As noted previously, the UDC accepted, reluctantly, the need to repel Germany, but hoped for an early peace and specialized in critical post-mortems on British policy before the war, challenging the popular and official verdict which assigned all guilt for the war to the Central Powers.[53] (Most discourse on this topic, including that emanating from distinguished writers and professors, depicted an insane or brutalized German people, taught that Might makes Right, descending on their hapless neighbors like wolves on the fold to torture, maim, and kill.)[54] Russell and Shaw played this revisionist game too, though perhaps the best and most thorough example was G. Lowes Dickinson's *The European Anarchy* (1916). Enough had leaked out about the prewar British understandings with the French and other matters to provide the basis for challenges to the orthodox Allied version of brute aggression versus primal innocence. (Essentially, there is not much in the postwar autopsies based on a flood of documentation from archives and memoirs that is not in Dickinson.)

On the basis of its rejection of the Asquith-Grey secrecies, the UDC erected its sovereign remedy for war: an end to secret diplomacy. "Open covenants openly arrived at," with full and constant disclosure of foreign policy in Parliament, would forestall those Foreign Office plots which allegedly instigated wars. "Wars are not made because of the passions of the many, but because of the intrigues of the few," Dickinson claimed.[55] It was doubtless such simple-minded rationalism that led Russell away from this group after some cooperation with them.

But UDC publications shared with Russell's a disposition to talk about hypothetical past and future wars rather than the present one, and to annoy the majority by intimations of British and Allied war guilt. Not surprisingly, their influence was limited. Kingsley Martin put the circulation of the pro-UDC *Cambridge Journal* at 25,000. Had the UDC had a practical program, it surely could have expanded this base. There were internal problems. H. Hanak describes E. D. Morel, a courageous activist, as "a fanatic with absolute faith in the righteousness of his own cause," quite unwilling to compromise with anyone. He shared with Russell the honor of being imprisoned by His Majesty's government during the war. The rest of the UDC roster included brilliant leftist *feuilletonistes* like H. N. Brailsford, Leonard Woolf,

Phillips Price, J. A. Hobson, Lowes Dickinson—a type of political journalist merging into serious historical writer which enriched the literary world in this era but has since almost disappeared, or grossly deteriorated. (The late Walter Lippmann was a notable American example.) Their war-induced analyses are interesting and some of their work was fruitful. Woolf, Brailsford, and Dickinson became involved in trying to clarify the many vague ideas for a postwar league or association of nations which would prevent war by "collective security" agreements.[56] The UDC position on the League of Nations was that formal arrangements did not touch the root of the matter, which was to democratize foreign policy; particularly through Norman Angell, they exerted some influence on American president Woodrow Wilson.[57] Among other UDC participants were the subsequent Communist luminaries R. Palme Dutt and Hewlett Johnson, together with Labourites Philip Snowden and Arthur Henderson, also John Maynard Keynes and Viola Paget.[58]

IV

Protest only gradually increased, and in some ways in this war it never did get off the ground. By 1916 it was possible for Henri Barbusse to publish *Le Feu* and win the Prix Goncourt for it—a potent novel that under the guise of an honest naturalism projects an image of the little man as victim of a horrible war he has been duped into fighting. But this was an anomaly, opposed to which one might place the hostile feeling against Rolland in France, which was so great that even after the war was over, in 1919, it alarmed his publisher.[59] In July, 1917, the English poet Siegfried Sassoon in a letter to his astonished commanding officer conveyed his belief that "this war, upon which I entered as a war of defence and liberation, has now become a war of aggression and conquest." But a fellow poet, Robert Graves, recognizing the utter futility of the gesture, contrived to extract Sassoon from trouble by pleading shell-shock! By 1917 Stefan Zweig, writing his vaguely antiwar drama *Jeremiah*, thought that opposition to the war had actually become fashionable. The following summer he called for an end to the war at any price—"defeatism"—but by that time the exhausted powers were obviously staggering toward the end.[60] Yet opposition to the war, even on the Left, made relatively little progress. Thus in Britain the *New Statesman*, which traditionally spoke for much of the radical intelligentsia, remained prowar to the end, attacking Lord Lansdowne for his 1918 peace proposals and incurring Lytton Strachey's epithet of "Northcliffism." In Russia, the March Revolution brought in a more popular government, soon headed by the agrarian radical Kerensky, which was more nationalistic and more determined to fight the war than had been the decrepit autocracy it replaced. And before Lenin's return in April, 1917, even the Bolsheviks were accepting the defensist line: *Pravda* under Stalin and Kamenev supported the Mensheviks on this issue in March.

Turin Anarchists denounced the war in September, 1916, and there was a "peace and bread" insurrection there August 21, 1917, but this was a local rather than national situation. And in Ireland the Socialist James Connolly, who had opposed the war from the beginning, was driven to the famous but futile insurrection of Easter week, 1916, while Roger Casement made his ill-fated contacts with the Germans. Frustration likewise drove Friedrich Adler, the son of Austria's leading Socialist, to assassinate the Dual Monarchy's prime minister, Stürgkh, at his midday meal on October 21, 1916; such actions were the fruit of desperation.

As we noted earlier, most Socialists stuck to their tragic decision for war. The mood of the Franco-Belgian group was typified by Hendrik de Man's visit to Russia after the March Revolution, to speak against German "militarism and despotism" in an effort to keep Russia fighting. Stirrings of unease among a few young French Socialists affected Pierre Laval and Marx's grandson, Jean Longuet, from 1915 on. But in July, 1915, the national council of the SFIO unanimously reaffirmed the need to fight to the final defeat of German militarism, while in December the party congress passed patriotic resolutions by large majorities despite some opposition. A few French Socialists attended the landmark Zimmerwald Conference of September, 1915, which was held in Switzerland upon the initiative of Italian Socialists and which witnessed the international debut of the Leninist Left; but these did not officially represent the SFIO. Three obscure French Socialists voted against the war credits in May, 1916, after they attended the Kienthal conference. Others, as was the case in Germany and England, concentrated on criticism of their country's war aims. Longuet wrote early in the war to Rolland of "this abominable butchery," while a notable center of resistance was the Metal Workers'

Union, led by Alfred Rosmer, whose organ *L'Union des Metaux* declared in 1915 that "this war is not our war." Their delegate Merrheim was one of the few antiwar militants at the conference of Allied Socialists held in London early in 1915.[61]

A handful of German Socialists opposed the war early. Karl Liebknecht voted publicly against war funds in the Reichstag for the first time on December 2, 1914. A year later, nineteen joined him. Liebknecht together with Rosa Luxemburg, Clara Zetkin, and Franz Mehring had published a declaration on September 10, 1914, in Switzerland, expressing disagreement with the official SPD policy. SPD opponents of the war controlled some important party organs until 1916 when these were seized by the government. The Kaiser's government was by no means as repressive as legend suggests, however; British war resisters liked to point out that Professor F. W. Foerster was able to proclaim pacifism at the University of Munich while Cambridge ejected Bertrand Russell. The German government could easily afford to ignore a small component of intellectuals without a mass following.

The courage of the intrepid four was not in question. A French correspondent of Rolland's thought that theirs was the greatest.[62] They launched an organ, *Die Internationale*, of which only one issue appeared, in April, 1915, the censor confiscating it and banning future issues. Rosa was soon to enter prison, and her murder along with Liebknecht's at the war's end ensured her standing as the leading antiwar martyr. But in preaching that there can be no justifiable national war, or any defensible war at all, and in her extreme internationalism, Luxemburg was out of touch even with Lenin, who criticized her "Junius" pamphlet. She had long been regarded as an inveterate trouble-maker in the somewhat male-chauvinist SPD. It is worth noting that Rosa, at least, along with fellow left-winger Franz Mehring, had not been an unequivocal opponent of the war at first. Mehring's early articles, while expressing doubts about the war, do not forthrightly reject it.[63] Luxemburg fell ill and contemplated suicide at the beginning of the war. (Another case of this psychosomatic phenomenon was that of Houston Stewart Chamberlain, the ideologist of Aryan racism—and a great favorite of George Bernard Shaw's—who suffered a paralytic stroke at the start of the war; Chamberlain had based his intellectual career on the affinity of Germany and England.)

Meanwhile, former revolutionary Socialists such as "Parvus"

170

the war from the start and sat in both the Asquith and Lloyd George cabinets, visited post–February Revolution Russia along with other French, Belgian, and British Socialists, to prop up the collapsing war spirit there; but the experience convinced Henderson that the provisional government faced disaster and should make some concessions to the Leninist Left in the interest of survival. In 1917 Dutch Socialists attempted to convene a meeting at Stockholm bringing together Socialists from both sides of the war; the Allies, as well as Lenin, spurned it as a German trick, but on his return to England Henderson persuaded the British Labour party to support it, as the French Socialists also did in July. For this heresy he was expelled from the Cabinet, and soon joined forces with Ramsay MacDonald and Sidney Webb to write a new Labour party platform specifically embracing socialism. The result was the famous Webb-drafted *Labour and the New Social Order* (1918), a landmark in the evolution of the British Labour party. Henderson never wavered in his support of the war: he turned to the Left under the impact of his visit to Russia, but he wanted to help the Mensheviks and save bleeding Russia from the horrors of a Bolshevist seizure of power.[66] In the event, the Stockholm conference never took place, and of course Lenin's Bolsheviks did topple the Kerensky regime in November. Whether a stronger peace initiative might have saved it is doubtful, but the attempt was never made. Kerensky, Henderson, Vandervelde, Longuet—they were all caught in the net of uncertainty woven from 1914 determination mixed with growing socialist doubts as the war dragged on. Only Lenin stood unequivocally for revolution and (international) peace.

V

Despite the renewed grim determination, which was only its obverse, war idealism did of course steadily wane. "The farther into the past the first days of the war retreat, the dimmer grow the idealistic watchwords which originally lent a spiritual glory to the patriotism of the warring nations," a Russian observed in 1916.[67] Friedrich Naumann, the distinguished German publicist, noted in alarm about the same time that "today there are people who no longer rightly know why we are fighting."[68] One had to keep reminding them! The August spirit was as perishable as most mystiques.

The final irony was that virtually without exception those who had, to a greater or lesser degree, opposed the war—men such as Rolland and his friends in France, Russell and the UDC in Britain, Foerster and Einstein in Germany—were deeply disillusioned by the peace settlement. "Sad peace! Laughable interlude between the massacres of peoples! But who thinks of tomorrow?" Thus Romain Rolland ended his long wartime journal on June 23, 1919. War hatred carried over into the peace, poisoning the League of Nations too: the Woolfs, Dickinsons, Brailsfords, all expressed their disappointment that this hoped-for symbol of a new era became an instrument, as they thought, of an unjust settlement, simply a new "Holy Alliance" of victor powers to underwrite a war of conquest.

Hopes for a brave new world emerging out of the chaos had lightened the gloom of slaughter, of course. Simplest and most popular of these was the idea of a league of nations, of civilization, of peoples, something to abolish or mitigate national sovereignty—a Parliament of Man. "In the future we must fight, not alone for England, but for the welfare of the world," Shaw wrote early in the war, as H. G. Wells was coining the "war to end wars" slogan.[69] "A new order of Europe," in Einstein's phrase, a league of Europeans, a league of Western civilization (Shaw's idea of one would have included the United States but excluded Russia)—soon some expanded it to a world-wide league of nations, vaguely. "During the last weeks [of the war], in common with most other people, I based my hopes upon Wilson with his Fourteen Points and his League of Nations," Bertrand Russell recalled.[70] The American president managed to associate his name with a plan which was mainly of European provenance; but, as one outside the corrosive hatreds of war-ravaged Europe, he imparted to it a larger vision of internationalism.

"Without that vision of the better future we should have found the carnage, the embitterment and the waste of the war an unendurable nightmare of horror," Brailsford wrote.[71] Logical inconsistencies in plans which relied on sovereignty by entering into long-term pledges to refrain from war, or to go to war against a violator of the peace, created a measure of confusion when the broad idea of a "league against war" or a "league to enforce peace" came down to specific details. Here is no place to go into that. The basic contradiction was that the power of nationalism emerged from the war as strong as or even stronger than before. Allied self-interest resulted in an appeal to the emergent nationalism of the Dual Monarchies' "subject peoples," Czechs, Croatians, and others, while Germany had directed a similar propaganda against the multinational Russian Empire, and to the Irish. The war and the final peace settlement was a victory for the nationalities, or many of them, if nothing else. Faced with the obvious fact that no superstate was going to emerge from this war to subdue the sovereign nations, peace planners among the intellectuals conceived of a league of sovereign states joined by an agreement to suppress war, through pledging to submit their disputes to arbitration or mediation and to discipline any member state defying this rule. As Lord James Bryce, pioneer of the league idea, put it, "The League shall undertake to defend any one of its members who may be attacked by any other State who has refused to accept Arbitration or Conciliation."[72]

It was perhaps the most important positive idea to emerge from the troubled consciences of those intellectuals who like Bryce and Wells fully supported the war, or like Dickinson and Woolf had found no practical way to oppose it. It offered the consoling hope that by preparing the way for a complete new deal in international relations the existing slaughter justified itself.

It too was destined to fail; the sad peace led to another massacre of peoples. L. P. Jacks, writing in 1916, was one of those who correctly divined that a league based on existing international hatreds and aspirations would result only in transferring quarrels from one arena to another; "the federation of the world would be a cockpit of civil war."[73]

—*9*—

Conclusions

I

The initial source of my interest in this subject, several years ago, was simply a desire to correct what seemed to me an egregious case of historical neglect. My belated discovery of the fantastic war spirit among 1914 intellectuals brought a shock with it, and led me to think there had been deliberate suppression or at least total misunderstanding. A professional historian with a strong interest in twentieth-century Europe, I had gone years without suspecting this phenomenon; my experience was something like a tardy repetition of Bertrand Russell's at the time, when he wrote that

> I discovered to my amazement that average men and women were delighted by the prospect of war. I had fondly imagined, what most pacifists contended, that wars were forced upon a reluctant population by despotic and Machiavellian governments.[1]

Reading the literature on the origins of the First World War, a voluminous and controversial one, I had formed the impression that either greedy capitalists searching for profits, and somehow expecting to find them in selling death, or blundering diplomats playing a deadly game of power had brought on the fateful war, dragging behind them a reluctant populace. True, much was said about war propaganda, but this was a matter of an elite cynically manufacturing lies to keep the

people fighting. Hardly much of a tribute to the intelligence of Europe
(or America); and the war was generally just dropped out of intellectual histories (including my own), appearing only after it was over, as
a terrible jolt responsible for the pessimism of the 1920's. The pre-1914
Socialists had unaccountably renounced and betrayed their whole heritage; most of the other intellectuals had either gone stark raving
mad or sunk into a deep slumber for the duration. Very little was
said about them.

So it seemed to me that the glad welcoming of the war by Europe's
ranking poets, philosophers, theologians, historians, sociologists, psychologists, scientists, was grossly understated and, where grudgingly
acknowledged, quickly shoved aside without explanation. A bit of
probing was enough to reveal evidence of the ghastly truth, but few
wanted to probe; and so I could agree with my colleague Professor
Warren Wagar when he wrote a few years ago that "the spiritual
history of the first World War remains to be written."[2] The same
could perhaps not be said today; yet I think by comparison with whole
libraries dedicated to other aspects of the war origins—diplomatic,
political, economic—the intellectual dimension is still egregiously
neglected.

The reasons for this neglect are familiar ones to students of his-
toriography: a lack of historical imagination combined with the subsequent development of a framework or "paradigm" which some data
fail to fit. In the establishment of such a framework, ideology in-
truded. After 1918 a revulsion against war took place, quite as powerful as the welcoming of it in 1914. The mood in 1914 became both
shameful and incomprehensible, so it was repressed; nor did it fit the
new canons of interpretation formulated to explain the origins of the
Great War. It became standard doctrine with almost all intellectuals
—who are in fact prone to extremely rigid structures of value, held
with a quasi-religious emotionality—that the war was a crime against
humanity; therefore it could not have been approved by Europe's
intellectual and spiritual leaders, or if so, one did not wish to think
about this alarming anomaly. The mechanized slaughter into which
the great 1914 crusade turned, as well as the inordinate damage it did
to European civilization, brought a reaction against war after 1918; it
is in the light of this and later experiences that "today's public refuses
to accept any romanticization of battle fronts as intellectually bear-

able."[3] But we should not read later changes in attitudes back into the situation in 1914.

A tenable Marxist interpretation would have to blame the war on capitalism, not because the capitalists contrived it, for which there is no shred of evidence—the businessmen were appalled, the stock markets collapsed—but because capitalism had created an inhuman society that bred frantic hostility to the regime of calculation and comfort; the human spirit rebelled against Economic Man and against the division of labor, against loss of community from the cash nexus. People turned to war as relief from anomie, materialism, the corrosion of values. The restless modernisms of the intellectual avant-garde grew in the swelling cities, product of a technological order and the disintegration of traditional structures within society. It is remarkable that Marxists have so seldom developed this hypothesis, for which a persuasive case could be made, preferring the simplistic and patently erroneous paradigm of peace-loving masses somehow duped into war by profiteering munitions makers.

We should be clear about the role of the intellectual dimension: it did not cause the war to happen. If intellectuals of all hues eagerly embraced the war when it came, this is not to say, first of all, that they saw it coming. The total unexpectedness of the war is a familiar fact. "Who then in 1914 thought of the possibility of a war? Perhaps a few specialists, some diplomats and strategists." Max Brod's recollection in Prague matches George Bernard Shaw's in London ("only the professional diplomats and the very few amateurs whose hobby is foreign policy even knew the guns were loaded"), Rémy de Gourmont's in Paris, and that of countless others. "We thought of war occasionally," Stefan Zweig remembered, "but no more than we thought of death—as a possibility but probably a distant one." Political passions for the most part vented themselves on the numerous and exciting internal issues, in this era of the beginnings of the welfare state, trade unionism, strikes, feminism, etc. Herbert Read recalled that in Britain "the great issues of Free Trade and Protection, Home Rule for Ireland, the Disestablishment of the Church, and the Reform of the House of Lords were being debated with fervour and energy in every newspaper and at every street corner."[4] After France got over the terrible ordeal of the Dreyfus Affair, she proceeded to debate laicization, the income tax, socialism, tariffs. There was little thought of war. The same was true

179

all over Europe. The intellectual community in any case tended to be absorbed in art in the pre-1914 years.

This must be qualified by the occasional literary vision of total destruction, which can perhaps be found in almost any period. For example, Hilaire Belloc: "How I long for the Great War! It will sweep Europe like a broom, it will make kings jump like coffee beans on the roaster." Or Paul Valéry in 1891: "Je désire presque une guerre monstreuse où fuir parmi le choc d'une Europe folle." Flaubert had dreamed of "being at the gates of Paris with 500,000 barbarians, and burning the whole city" in 1840.[5] Edward Carpenter's popular piece of rhetoric *Towards Democracy*, first published in the 1880's, ends with an apocalyptic vision: "From this hour, War! Ever more splendid and glorious War!"

H. G. Wells, who had allowed his science-fiction imagination to play on disastrous wars in such books as *The War in the Air* and *The World Set Free*, the latter published in the very year 1914, confessed that "I was taken by surprise by the war. I saw long ahead how it could happen, and wove fantastic stories about it, but at the bottom of my heart I did not believe it would really happen."[6] As Ezra Pound wrote many years later (from St. Elizabeth's Hospital) about the motives of 1914:

> Some for adventure
> some from fear of weakness,
> some from fear of censure,
> some for love of slaughter, in imagination . . . .

Love of slaughter in the literary imagination ought not to be taken quite at full value during the years of the great peace.

The conventional wisdom, of course, held that war was impossible, making imaginative speculation about it the more apparently harmless. The American radical Randolph Bourne, in an article printed in *International Conciliation* on the eve of the conflict (June, 1914), thought that "Our modern civilization with its international bonds of financial and economic dependence is a civilization organized for peace and peace alone." In the August issue of the same peace-movement journal, George A. England was able to announce that "A world emancipated from the thrall of war, long only the speculation of philosophers, is growing real and tangible." If it be thought that this was only Anglo-American, compare the remarks of Emil Ludwig in the April, 1914, issue of the German *Neue Merkur*; central European pacifism as represented by Bertha von Suttner, though slightly comical to serious literary men, was quite as strong as any other, while the great Jaurès was a French link to international pacifism.

"Power and culture were in separate compartments," Shaw observed. More than two. The diplomatists and strategists lived in monastic isolation; what J. F. C. Fuller said about the British army applied equally well to the diplomatic set, a body apart from the nation, walled up within an archaic tradition, an aristocratic caste founded upon ancient traditions. In his study of Baron Holstein, *eminence grise* of the German Foreign Office, Norman Rich was struck by the fact that "In all his writings there is scarcely an allusion to the cultural life going on around him."[7] The Peace Movement was in another compartment, slightly cranky and American, though Tolstoy, as well as Jaurès, supplied a link to serious culture—a decidedly old-fashioned writer, of course, by the 1900's, revered as he might be.[8] The avant-garde literary, artistic, and intellectual set was remote from both practical politics and crusading pacifism. Compartmentalization, a function of the modernized urban society, was one key to the situation in 1914.

This is not to dismiss the vague premonitions of war which haunted the literary imagination on the very eve, about which we have said enough. So earthy a historian as A. J. P. Taylor writes:

Men's minds seem to have been on edge in the last two or three years before the war . . . as though they had become unconsciously weary of peace and security . . . . Men wanted violence for its own sake; they welcomed war as a relief from materialism.

"In the air there was a feeling of approaching apocalypse," another noted historian remarks, citing Hermann Hesse's Damian: "I sense the coming of conflicts . . . . The world as it is now, wants to die, wants to perish, and it will."[9] "Wants to die" was the name of the 1914 game for (one says with awareness of the paradox) vital streams of European consciousness: "So be merry, so be dead," "Come and die, it will be such fun." But at the same time this feeling was divorced from reality; there was no sense that it would actually happen, until the thunderbolt of the first four days of August, 1914. After all, this Romantic gesture was as old as Keats' immortal "half in love with easeful death." (Or Hotspur's, "die all, die merrily.") It drew too on the ingrained Western religious tradition of apocalypse, stated secularly by socialists and anarchists, and especially by Nietzsche's vision of a Europe moving toward catastrophe, "restless, violent, precipitate, like a river that wants to reach its end."

But, though in his "War Song" John Davidson (a late Victorian tormented by visions of violence who finally committed suicide) foresaw that

> Some diplomat no doubt
> Will launch a heedless word
> And lurking war break out

this was hardly a major preoccupation. The intellectual atmosphere had very little to do with the beginning of the war. In a lecture rightly calling attention to the need for more study of this atmosphere, James Joll has argued that historians need to "re-create the climate of opinion in which political leaders operated."[10] But it is doubtful that the political leaders concerned in the vital decisions of July and early August paid much attention to this factor. The game was not one of thinking about whether to go to war or not and then asking whether public opinion wanted this or would put up with it; it was rather one of responding to urgent situations abroad, beginning with the Austrian response to the assassination on June 28 and continuing with decisions in St. Petersburg, Berlin, and Paris about whether to support an ally, fearful of the consequences if they did not. Statesmen were immersed in their own world. We may suppose that had there been a powerful adverse reaction, they might have been forced to find another route. For them, obviously, war was by no means unthinkable. But in fact there *was* something of an adverse response early in the crisis, as we noted; meetings and demonstrations against the war were held in France and Germany July 27–29, and the Socialist International called a meeting of its executive council. British opinion seemed overwhelmingly antiwar down to August 4, and many a person shared Carl Zuckmayer's amazement that he had viewed war with "disgust and loathing" only three days before he was inflamed with passion for battle and rushed to enlist.[11] The screaming crowds which poured into the streets, some shouting "À Berlin!", or surrounding Buckingham Palace for days, while other crowds cheered the Kaiser through the streets of Berlin—"as though a human river had burst its banks and flooded the world"[12]—followed rather than preceded the declarations of war. They were unleashed, having been latently, more than consciously, present.

It is, then, difficult to invoke public opinion of any sort as a cause of the coming of the war. But it is quite possible to see it as by far the most important cause of the war's long continuance. If statesmen had blundered into a war no one really wanted (they "glided, or rather staggered and stumbled" into it, Lloyd George thought), if as everyone claimed they were fighting defensively or because they could not think of an honorable alternative, then it should have been possible to find a way out. What really calls for an explanation is not why the war began but why it went on for more than four awful years, consuming millions of lives. And the reason for this is clearly the incredible support public opinion gave to the war. One must explain why the desertion rate in the French army, despite the bleak conditions and terrible losses (far worse than Vietnam!), was less than 1 percent; why more than a million volunteers poured into the nonconscripted British armies during the first two years, in the greatest expression of enthusiasm for war in all history; why the Germans, outnumbered and blockaded, held their morale for four years and almost won the war the last year, extracting from Winston Churchill the tribute that this was the most gallant performance in history; why the Russians, hopelessly ill-equipped for the war and dying like flies, did not weary of the war until late 1917 though many thought it would happen in 1915; why soldiers laid down their lives loving the war.

One would perhaps have to explain also why other countries, including Italy and the United States, not in at the beginning, watched the war with growing fascination and joined in despite no very obvious reason for entry. One would have to remember that at the start rational men were all but unanimous in predicting that the war could not possibly last more than a few months or at most a year.[13] The mobilization of six million men in France, who were replaced at their jobs by women, children, and old people, impressed observers as unprecedented. The Germans performed miracles of substitution for the materials they were deprived of by the blockade. Women threw themselves into the war to an astonishing degree, serving heroically in military roles as well as behind the front. The incredible endurance of the soldiers, along with the total cooperation of the entire community—down to 1917 at least—was what prolonged the war; something so extraordinary as to confound rational predictions, and clearly a matter of fantastic morale.

It would be hard to claim that this morale was entirely due to the intellectuals, but they did staff the propaganda ministries, write the books and articles, create the war's extravagant mystique. The best brains and pens of Europe devoted themselves to the war. More, they joined it and gave their lives to it. One cannot be cynical about this "treason of the clerks," for as a class they shed more than their share of blood. Of 161 students of the famous École Normale Superieure in France from the classes of 1911, 1912, and 1913, Barrès calculated, 81 died in the war and another 64 were wounded.[14] A French *Anthology of Writers Killed in the War*, published in 1924–26, contains 500 names, among them Péguy, Alain-Fournier, Apollinaire, Psichari. Sacrificed to the war were the brilliant Austrian painters Franz Marc and Egon Schiele; August Macke, Raymond Duchamp-Villon, and Umberto Boccioni were other slain artists. Such a list might go on and on. In *The Lost Generation of 1914*, Reginald Pound gives information on the many British victims of the war from the universities, who rushed *en masse* to enlist, in the first fever of enthusiasm. Among the first-rank British poets who lost their lives—to choose just one category—were Rupert Brooke, Wilfred Owen, Isaac Rosenberg, Charles Sorley, Edward Thomas; Ivor Gurney went mad. To those who fell in battle one must add the suicides, like Georg Trakl or the sculptor Wilhelm Lehmbruck who could not "stay behind after these murders," for "my brothers are no longer here." Annoyed by a low-left innuendo, L. P. Hartley once bristled that "man for man, and woman, the aristocracy suffered more in the First World War than any other stratum of society."[15] The heaviest casualties in the murderous war were among the junior officers, where one typically found educated young men.

II

The explanation we have offered for this unusual and fateful phenomenon involves the development of the civilized European consciousness together with the impact of society on that consciousness. The years just before 1914 clearly witnessed a critical moment in that equation. The process, of course, has gone on; the individual ego, increasingly emancipated and enriched, stands over against a bureau-cratic "iron cage" society, to employ Max Weber's formulation. But there is much evidence to support the view that the first great crisis in this relationship, beginning early in the nineteenth century, ripened to reach a climax about 1910, the year in which, as Virginia Woolf put it dramatically, "human character changed." Objective social reality and subjective cultural consciousness split apart. The "intellectuals" made their appearance as a group whose sensitivity involved them in an intolerable conflict with a "bourgeois" society. The "masses" were losing their traditional folk culture in an urban environment which gradually eroded forms of community long basic to human living. Capitalism, urbanization (into megalopolis and beyond, which Lewis Mumford called necropolis), deracination, atomization, anomie, con-tract replacing status, cash nexus instead of human, an overly rational-ized or mechanized set of norms, *Gesellschaft* rather than *Gemein-schaft*—a bevy of social theorists gave different names to what was, at bottom, much the same thing.

Gustave LeBon argued then, and many sociologists have agreed, that war is an antidote to anomie or decadence, a restorer of solidarity. For the intellectuals, separated from the rest of the community in particular ways, war had the additional advantage of reuniting them with the "kindly race of men" on a plane of idealism.

There were, of course, some types of traditional and perhaps archetypal thought that were prowar. As Georges Sorel liked to remind people, war had nourished the high culture of the ancient world. The great classics of the West, whether pagan or religious, rang with the sound of battle, and in the education of Europe's intellectual elite Homer and Virgil were still as *de rigueur* as the Bible. Charles Richet, the French pacifist, complained that Latin was now read more than Greek in the schools—birth of the great language decline—and that Sallust, Caesar, Livy, as well as Virgil, constantly narrate battles and praise militarism. He might have recalled that Schiller's young noble-men had joined the robber band, in disgust at a decadent society, after reading Plutarch. Down through the Renaissance and into the eight-eenth century, a familiar line of thought pointed with alarm to the danger of peace breaking out, war being "the medicine for Common-wealths sicke of too much ease and tranquility."[16] Shakespearean images of war haunted the English, those of Corneille the French: "Life is a little enough thing, and what remains of mine is not worth

185

purchasing at a price so shameful." (Honor, that antibourgeois virtue, has come back, Rupert Brooke sang. What has a man but honor? the World War I poet Robert Nichols asked in "The Man of Honour.") "Every man thinks meanly of himself for not having been a soldier, or not having been at sea," Dr. Johnson observed. In his classic account of the Roman decline and fall, Edward Gibbon found that "the slow and secret poison" undermining Roman civilization had been "effeminate luxury," fruit of the long peace.

"Death was beautiful in those days . . . . It was the very stuff of youth." Thus Alfred de Musset recalled the Napoleonic years. Alexis de Tocqueville was hardly an arch-Romantic, but the great French student of society saw uses for war, especially in encouraging unselfishness and fostering grandeur of soul: "war almost always enlarges the mind of a people and raises their character."[17] The German philosopher Hegel accepted war's necessity, as any optimistic historical progressivist must, for it seems inextricably human; Hegel also stressed "preserving a people's moral health" in the discipline of battle. Among the Socialists, Pierre-Joseph Proudhon wrote an appreciation of war in 1861, while Marx, as we know, looked upon it as the midwife of history, the accelerator of the historic process. So equable a temperament as the poet Tennyson was aroused to martial fury during the Crimean War of the 1850's: "Hail once more to the banner of battle unroll'd!" The archetypes the British poet evoked in *Maud* include some of the same ones that arose in 1914: splendid heroism as relief from "Britain's one sole god," Gain, and from the mediocrity of "the whole weak race of venomous worms." Likewise, the exultation of unity was found in a common purpose: "I have felt with my native land, I am one with my kind."[18] In 1861 Henry David Thoreau used the phrase "moral regeneration of the nation" to describe the American Civil War, a note frequently heard among northern writers.[19] The Spanish-American War precipitated an outburst of talk in the United States in 1898 about "elevating the tone of national life," creating "a new civic spirit," and striking down a low-minded materialism—even contributing to socialism.[20] Throughout the nineteenth century, passionate idealists kept alive the mystique born in the French Revolution of "the people armed in a holy cause," a war in which, as Mazzini explained in 1848,

a *principle*, a grand idea, boldly proclaimed and faithfully applied . . . awakens to a kind of inspired life, and exalts to enthusiasm those capacities for struggle and sacrifice which are so easily kindled or extinguished in the heart of a people.

So despite the gradual growth of the Peace Movement, born in the eighteenth century, by no means all the liberals were pacifists; they were easily rallied then as now to "wars of liberation" or for some cause conceived as just. This nineteenth-century concept of the holy revolutionary war was basically not different from the Just War of the Christian and other religions.

It would be difficult to argue that this old and deeply planted rationale for war was any stronger in Germany than in France and Britain, where proud traditions of national military might and of just war flourished. The Futurist Marinetti, in his 1910 speech to the English, praised "the indomitable bellicose patriotism" of "your great muscular courageous race," an image of John Bull quite commonly held by his own subjects as well as others. The British Socialist Henry Noel Brailsford compared the "impulse which fired the British democracy in the early months of this war" (1914) to the "young levies of revolutionary France" which "marched to encounter the leagued kings of the old order at Valmy,"[21] and this comparison of 1789 and 1914 was made by a German Socialist, Johann Plenze, as well as by many in France, where the word "Valmy!" was on everyone's lips as the war began.

Those who had arisen in the nineteenth century to oppose war were heavily marked with the brand of the bourgeoisie, a poor recommendation to the intellectuals and rebellious youth of this generation. In England, the Peace Movement brought to mind John Bright, who suggested Manchester School economics more than Quakerism—people who rejected war because it wasn't profitable. Types like Andrew Carnegie and Leon Bourgeois, or Nobel, the inventor of dynamite, led the Peace Movement.

So, with all these credentials from the past, war was scarcely a stranger in 1914. Nevertheless, though it made use of some familiar materials, the war spirit of 1914 was a new concoction. The structure, if not all the components, was unique. The old rationale for war, whether as necessity, as duty, or as justice, had ceased to have much compelling power in the later nineteenth century. The new one placed more stress on the motifs we have encountered—renewal, adventure, apocalypse.

There is a unique quality about the 1914 situation which, like most things in human history, had never quite existed before and would not again; it was a moment in the growth of consciousness. We can try to recapture it by an effort of the historical imagination. To the historian, that is worth doing for its own sake—to understand, to defeat the tragedy of misunderstanding. We can then disapprove, if we like, but we do not have the right to misconstrue, to falsify, to travesty a moment of history. For as Paul Fussell writes in his recent major study *The Great War and Modern Memory*, this past cultural history is a part of our own "buried lives," and to re-enact it, rescuing it from repression, is to contribute to our collective psychic health, just as is the case with an individual suffering from a neurosis.

Among peculiar elements in the 1914 situation which require some imagination to appreciate, because they differ from present perceptions, are peace as representing the bourgeois establishment, and the war as a youth rebellion. "Ein Kampf zweien Generationen gegeneinander," a young German called the war.[22] The young German poet Ernst Lotz, killed in the first months of the war, in 1913 imagined youth "pouring out like a stormflood into the city streets and washing away the ruins of a shattered world" ("The Rise of Youth") and in 1914 thought he was doing this when he rushed to join the war. In England, Vera Brittain wrote that "Those who are old and think this war so terrible do not know what it means to us who are young."[23] Accustomed in the seventies to watching youth pouring into the streets to burn their draft cards and desecrate the flag, people today may be understandably bewildered by the scene in 1914. But the roles then were exactly reversed. That oldsters hastened to the front, or advertised their willingness to go, was the parallel to recent examples of middle-aged radicals trying to look like turned-on youths. Anatole France tried to shoulder a rifle at seventy, the German poet Richard Dehmel insisted on service in the trenches at fifty-one, Alain went to war at forty-six, Italian Socialist Bissolati joined the army at fifty-eight, and innumerable other such cases existed—all these examples only prove what a youth movement the war was. In some ways 1914 was the beginning of that practice which Kingsley Amis rather inelegantly has called "arse-creeping youth." To be with-it was to be martial, patriotic, death-seeking, in the summer of 1914. Fashions simply change.

The thirst for community may also have become incomprehen-

sible, though commune-forming and cults of mystic fellowship pro-
liferating among today's urban youth—e.g., the mass ritual of rock
concerts*—suggest its persistence. "This situation does not bother me,"
a recent writer on the theater remarks, the situation being one where
"there exists in the West no set of artistic, cultural or social standards
so sacrosanct that they are not constantly under attack nor any standards readily at hand to replace them."[24] We have become more or less
inured to pluralism and to scepticism. It no longer much bothers most
intellectuals that there are no orthodoxies and no structures, no rules
and no hierarchies, no authorities and no rituals; they know they could
not endure any of them. For some it may be hard to reconstruct the
state of mind in which being without group solidarity could cause an
inner uneasiness, leading even to mental breakdown. A quest for
identity and self-understanding marked the whole 1885–1914 Modernist movement in the arts. We ought to be able to understand the
magnitude of the psychic crisis that confronted human nature when
it was first released from primeval group solidarity to face the anomic
megalopolitan wilderness, the terrible freedom of total permissiveness.
Then in 1914, as young intellectuals repeatedly testified, the sense of
community suddenly reappeared with the shock of war, and struck
them with the force of a raw *reality* they could not resist. It is the
most significant single motif. It was *felt* deeply, perhaps most strongly
in Germany, but in fact everywhere.

One relatively neglected feature of the 1914 situation is the
similarity of the war mood in all the belligerent countries. The structure of bellicosity was the same from London (or, indeed, Dublin) to
Moscow. I have throughout this book quoted from British, French,
and German sources in parallel manner to try to make this point clear.
Less familiar with Russian sources, I received the following striking
comments in a letter from a scholar-expert in this area, who had read
an article of mine published in 1973:[25]

---

* Which, as news reports frequently bear witness, can all too easily turn violent.
A Reuters story dated August 4, 1979, reported that "A trail of wreckage was scattered
through central Brussels today after police clashes with hundreds of rioting punk-rock
fans." Hardly an unusual event. The violence accompanying football matches also has
become a scandal; see, for example, "Fans Bring Disgrace on England," *Manchester
Guardian*, June 22, 1980; the story refers to rioting at an international match in Turin,
which had to be broken up by the use of tear gas.

Just about every theme you detail can be found in Russian intellectuals in the period after 1905, but most especially what you call
"pallid timidity of middle class business values"—known in Russian as *meshchanstvo*, philistinism or mediocrity; the search for
sobornost (approximately equal to *gemeinschaft* but having a different connotation*) and the spiritual renewal . . . . All the
themes you mention in your article feed into the revolution in
Russia and are important in explaining the appeal of revolution to
essentially apolitical types such as the Symbolist artists. One theme
which is probably stronger in Russia is the exaltation of suffering—salvation through suffering, etc.[26]

Whether Socialist or Symbolist, the ideas and "movements" of Europe
were international. So were individual masters. The French made a
cult of Richard Wagner even more than did the Germans, whose
Nietzsche preferred French culture to German; the Italians were
Hegelian; the English went mad over the Russian novel and Russian
ballet on the eve of 1914. Russian painters worked in Munich, Italian
ones in Paris. The adherents of naturalism, anarchism, and psychoanalysis, the Futurists, the Theosophists, as well as the Marxists—these
and many others knew no national boundaries, had followers in every
country, and often formed close friendships across borders. That they
broke these connections in 1914 is a tribute to the power of the 1914
ideas. But the pre-1914 European intellectual community was cosmopolitan even as it was also nationalistic; nationalism was an international idea. (It is by no means clear that prewar German nationalism
was much different from that in other major countries, though some
thought that it was.)[27]

Much evidence belies the trite explanation of the war as a breaking forth of evil, whether Christian Original Sin or, more fashionably,
Freudian inner aggressions. Too many went forth joyfully to war,
cheered on by happy crowds, in a spirit of adventure but also serious
search for fulfillment in a worthy purpose, and for true companion-
ship. Doubtless they found hell, but they did not go seeking it; rather
than an itch to kill, hurt, or torture their fellow men, as Freud
claimed, they felt something much more akin to love. Odd as this

---

* Presumably closer to a religious congregation; Russian *sobor* means "synod" as
well as "assembly."

may seem, the testimony of articulate warriors bears it out. Rolland reflected that "a war in which two men such as Dehmel and Péguy can kill each other with the same fervor, for the liberty of the world, is it not monstrous and ridiculous."[28] Doubtless it was, but it happened that way—Dehmel and Péguy were spiritual companions who would have loved each other personally, but they marched happily off to fight in rival armies, and in Péguy's case, of course, to die. The war had psychic explanations, but these are not of the order of hidden springs of malevolence; they involve, rather, a powerful thirst for identity, community, purpose—positive and, in themselves, worthy goals, perverted and misdirected but not poisoned at the springs.

We would do well, then, to consider the possibility that war is something for which a moral substitute must be found (as William James memorably put it in 1898), rather than something whose roots must simply be destroyed. "The impulse to danger and adventure is deeply ingrained in human nature, and no society which ignores it can long be stable," Bertrand Russell concluded.[29] There is abundant evidence that the impulse to fight and die in some holy cause still exists, transferred now to the streets, or to the jungles of some more "backward" society where the game of war can still be played. Violence, needless to say, it still with us, in the streets and home, as murder, rape, senseless destruction, terrorism. It appeared on college campuses a few years ago as another Youth Movement very like that of 1914 in basic ways—a fuzzy but powerful idealism, communitarian and revolutionary, protesting against false education, meaningless life, accusing the older generation, this time rioting *against* war and yet doing so often violently! And equipped with ideologies of self-redemption through confronting a tangible enemy, which seem to have been borrowed from 1914. The youth of the sixties paid homage to thinkers who called for guerrilla warfare, the politics of confrontation, the psychic wholesomeness of armed resistance. Their hero, Che Guevara, called for the conversion of men into "cold-blooded killing machines." Europe's leading philosopher, Jean-Paul Sartre, declared that "violence can be a means of curing Europe." "You've got to let yourself get angry . . . and maybe violent as well—before you can find out who you are" was the cliché of the campus revolution.[30]

These gestures have now spread far beyond the small intellectual elite which responded to similar notions in 1914, becoming somewhat coarsened in the process, but recognizably similar. The same social factors which drive those capable of criticizing their society quite mad with hostility continue to operate. There are now more possible avenues of unconventional behavior—an important point, for in 1914 the weight of traditional moral tabus was just beginning to be lifted; today it is in sight of vanishing in an anarchy of permissiveness. But the regimentations of a bureaucratic society, the hyperspecialization of the ant-world, the awful philistinism of popular culture (now much worse), the commercial standardization, the loss of community in urban anomie—all these and related forces continue to assault the emancipated and educated individual consciousness, squeezing it in the "double bind" vice, Max Weber's Iron Cage. As Saul Bellow's Mr. Sammler observes drily, "This liberation into individuality has not been a great success."

In particular, life becomes ever "safer" in that one cannot any longer even shoot off fireworks, or see the bears in Yellowstone Park —the wild kingdom may be glimpsed only on television or at the zoo—or go hunting, except for gentle animals, or seek adventure on the high seas. The entire world is classified, organized, regulated, predictable. And so in retaliation the spirit breaks out now in—motorcycle clubs, youth gangs, urban terrorism, hijacking airplanes, vandalism, all manner of juvenile crime. The cult of sports, never stronger than in today's urban society, supplies one acceptable sublimation— sometimes erupting in actual violence among the fanatical "fans" who destroy property, attack referees, fight each other. (In Central America an actual war broke out between two small countries as the result of a football match.) But for all save a few, this must be a vicarious struggle. Motorists sometimes discharge their aggressions in reckless and hostile driving, waging mock war on the highways. Conflict, of course, is sublimated in the business world's "competition," once frankly put forward as the moral equivalent of war in the time of "merchant adventurers,"[31] hardly an appropriate description today of the bureaucrats who manage vast corporations. The labor movement has also entered a much less heroic age, though frustrations may still be discharged in the unauthorized local strikes which plague some industrial societies. Irrational manias such as jogging serve as outlets.

"If war did not satisfy an elementary desire—to be in a state of strain, to feel more intensely," it would not have persisted so long, wrote a leading member of the recent radical generation, hostile to all forms of indigenous patriotism or nationalism, indeed to any defense of Western civilization, which she sees as a "cancer on the human race."[32] Perhaps the practice of pacifist violence, the vicarious support of wars provided they are against the West, the writing of literature and making of plays and films marked by themes of cruelty, torture, obscenity, provocation, have provided effective "equivalents" for these intellectuals. It would seem, in any case, that the persisting and legitimate human needs which war has evidently always satisfied, and which it satisfied classically in 1914, must be met in some way. Society should pay far more attention to this problem than it does. For its tendency is to deplore all forms of conflict, rather than seek to channel it. Violence on television, for example, is seen as incitation rather than substitution, and elicits complaints. Most authorities would rather punish youth gangs than divert them to relatively constructive uses. In need of recruits, the army advertises itself as an educational institution rather than as anything soldierly. (If it depicted anything so shocking as a bayonet it would presumably be denounced in all the newspapers.)

IV

Much happened between then and now, as a result of the 1914 war mania and the reactions against it. The experience was typically a shattering one, whatever the path taken next. "Before and after 1914 differed absolutely," only nominally on the same earth, Max Brod said in his autobiography, *A Life in Combat (Streitbares Leben)*. "A limit in the history of the world," to Georges Bernanos, the war "opened the gates of chaos" for Franz Kafka—"the outer bulwarks of human existence broke apart."[33] Kafka and Brod, of course, experienced the break-up of the old Empire under which they had grown up, as was even more catastrophically the case in Russia. But in England H. G. Wells observed that "No intelligent brain that passed through the experience of the Great War emerged without being profoundly altered," and of G. Lowes Dickinson his biographer, E. M. Forster, remarked that "the shock broke something in him which was never mended." These instances stand for nearly everybody among the writers, artists, and intellectuals who went through the war and managed to survive. "The mind is in fact cruelly stricken," Paul Valéry reflected (1922).[34] The Western world never quite recovered from this shock; the mind's distrust of itself, of thought and expression and reason, was a permanent legacy, a legacy of scepticism and nihilism and cynicism found in all intellectual circles—one is tempted to say—ever since.

The shock expressed itself in all kinds of ways. "The war crushed hopes, raised fears of the futility of Western civilization, set off a revival of religious feeling, killed outright half a generation of European youth, and discredited much of the thought and many of the thinkers of the prewar generation," Warren Wagar writes in naming some of the results.[35] But he has not named them all; some obstinately or lovingly kept alive war moods, especially the comradeship of the trenches, or went back to pre-1914 teachings, while a variety of new ideas and movements, some hopeful, grew out of the war. We should not forget that, as some unrepentant Socialists pointed out, the war did at least in part fulfill its mission to revolutionize the old society, not only in Russia, but in other countries where without barricades or social collapse much had changed: social barriers disappeared, institutions were democratized, the vote extended to women, conceptions of national economic management implanted.

And the numbing casualties, which cause us to wonder what potential earth-shaking achievements were buried with the tens of thousands of brilliant youth killed (what *Ulysses* or Theory of Relativity or *Waste Land* was *not* created by some even more talented Joyce or Einstein or Eliot who happened to fall in battle?), are counteracted by the immense stimulus which the war had on those who survived—both because the war itself was a stimulant, as it obviously was, bringing forth a flow of poetry, novels, and plays based on it, and because those who survived often were driven by a sense of guilt at having been spared. Thus Arnold Toynbee tells us that this spurred him to the labors of his multivolumed *Study of History*, and Harold Laski reported a similar effect. Henri Pirenne wrote his *History of Europe*, Jacques Rivière deepened his religious speculations. Fr. Teilhard de Chardin testified to a heightening of lucidity during his time at the front, during which he conceived the philosophical point of view he later elaborated. Maurice Bowra formed the habit of reading, and said that the war experience "did me a lot of good" by "greatly extending my horizon" as well as reducing his conceit and creating a "love of the comradeship that comes from living with other people

194

and sharing their interests and work."[36] André Breton, a medical assistant, worked the war into Surrealism.

After the war, of course, came that flood of memoirs, novels, and recollections with which men flushed the war out of their systems or came to terms with it. Some could not bear to think about it and only wrote much later. "For years I could not physically stand the people who quietly conversed about their war experiences," Oskar Kokoschka said.[37] But others, like the authors Arnold Zweig and Ford Madox Ford, immediately began large literary chronicles. Roger Martin du Gard did not write his *Summer of 1914* until the 1930's, by which time the views of a new political generation retrospectively altered his vision. If the war books deflated the rhetoric and undercut the heroism, they were by no means all "antiwar," a common misconception. The camaraderie received recognition in many novels.[38] Criticism of society carried over from the war; the restless idealism remained, looking for something better, now deeply disillusioned and perhaps cynical. The thirst was not satisfied. At the war's end the Dadaist retreat into nihilism, beginning in Switzerland, reiterated the call to "Sweep, sweep clean" (Tzara).

The thirst aroused in 1914 carried on into many powerful if erratic ideological quests of the postwar years. The spirit was fragmented and shattered, but its rays shot off in all directions. Total demoralization was of course not absent; Spenglerian Decline of the West, Barthian visions of total evil filled the 1920's. Charles Richet, the prewar pacifist-psychologist, wrote now of *L'homme stupide* and *L'homme impuissant* (1919, 1927). A whole category of literature castigated decadent democracy, saw the revolt of the masses as destructive, called for a new elite leadership—H. G. Wells, Clive Bell, and Bernard Shaw joining the Spaniard Ortega y Gassett and Germanic revolutionaries here. In a celebrated polemic of the twenties Julien Benda flayed the intellectuals for their treason, which consisted of running after political causes rather than upholding eternal values—he would later reverse this to become committed to communism. The reaction of Henri Barbusse and his circle against all irrationalism, and toward an austerely geometric social science, led the *Clarté* group somehow into the camp of Stalin. One of the most curious and sad odysseys was that of the great Romain Rolland, who was eventually taken in along with so many other intellectuals by the myth of Stalin and became an apologist for the mass exterminations carried out by the bloody Soviet

Russian regime—whose victims may have exceeded in number the casualties of the entire First World War.[39] Intellectuals continued to be victims of illusions, as Ludwig Marcuse noted.[40] They deceived themselves about the Russian Revolution and its Communist dictatorship—the "great illusion of our time," Arthur Koestler called it in the 1930's—just as they had deceived themselves about the 1914 war. The two deviations were not dissimilar in basic structure. Communism became the postwar generation's moral equivalent of war. The saga of an underground spy such as Kim Philby reveals the elements of danger, adventure, and commitment to a violent cause, akin to war experience, undertaken by a sensitive and idealist intellectual, a product of Cambridge University.[41] The October Revolution itself had not been so different in spirit and structure from the 1914 event against which it was a violent protest; the same people could be found acting in the same way, ecstatic then about the defense of Russia and now about the class war at home. Both exhibited that fatal tendency for the intellectual to feel powerfully, and to articulate this feeling in powerfully aggressive ways, and yet to confuse fantasy and reality, becoming the most absurdly gullible of persons, immune to evidence—as the Western intellectuals were in the case of Stalin's USSR, heaping worshipful praise on a bloody tyranny.

A great figure of the interwar years, André Malraux, found in action, revolutionary or military, where one joined with other men, the only worthy ideal—a creed which led the fabulous writer-activist to revolutions in China, civil wars in Spain, communism, a restless quest for salvation via fighting *cum* literature, which seems a perfect inheritance from 1914–18. He ended in the camp of a war hero of World War II.

Adolf Hitler's regime of terror and extermination had its roots in the war too, of which Hitler was an admiring survivor and a bitter revanchist, dedicated to forging a nation so united and forcefully led that it could win the second round. Intellectuals such as Ernst Jünger perpetuated in literature the myth of war's excitement and heroism. The Italian Fascist Revolution of Benito Mussolini, prowar ex-Socialist, took place in an atmosphere of hectic excitement combined with *delusione* immediately after the war. The apocalyptic mood of "a new era and a new social order" was still abroad, and no one thought that after the mighy storm there could be a peaceful return to the past. The mystique of fascism and nazism, a mixture of perfervid idealism looking toward a new order cleansed by fire, the herd spirit of *völkisch* community, and a brutal "triumph of the will" activism, was a prolongation of the August ideas in a country driven mad not so much by the sufferings of defeat as by the felt injustice of it.

The defeat of 1918 was temporary; the German nation had been weakened by the forces of individualism, liberalism, and Marxism, but this humiliation could be overcome if the Germans renounced alien, materialistic philosophies and returned to the roots of their true nature. Freed from "un-German" ideologies, this nation of heroes and poets, artists and philosophers, would come to dominate the Continent as Greece had once dominated the ancient world.[42]

Nazism and fascism were desperate prolongations, or caricatures, of the August ideas, but in fact the war signalled the failure of nationalism as a form of community for modernized humanity. For the intellectuals, much more typical and significant a reaction was the passionate pacifism which vowed never again, "nie wieder krieg," not a man and not a sou for defense, and thus left the road wide open for Hitler. This offshoot of World War I was led by those whose disillusionment was so deep because it fell from such a height. Thus Georges Duhamel, who demanded "disavowal of the war, of every war, without distinction, without pious sophism."[43] Such unreasoning hatred of war prepared the way for another war by encouraging the aggressions of Nazi Germany until finally men turned again, repudiated their pacifism, and went to war again, this time without illusions. Another of the many ironies is that Charles Maurras, pre-1914 prophet of a French war against Germany, ended World War II as a collaborator with the German conqueror, a path also followed by former left-wing Socialist Hendrik de Man, among others.

These are all questions of enormous size lying well beyond the limits of this work. To trace the influences of the August ideas as, refracted and distorted but still strong, they spread into later years and affected the turbulent, tragic history of the years between the world wars would make another sizable book.[44]

How, in the end, are we to explain this so fateful explosion of warlike ideas and sentiments among all manner of European intellectuals in 1914? Of the ingredients we have found to be pervasive, all are important: hatred of the existing society; the apocalyptic "sense of an ending"; need for some kind of worthy cause to give meaning to one's life; sheer thirst for adventure against the background of a dreary materialism, for honor and courage against bourgeois pettiness of spirit; the belief that somehow burning away the old would prepare for a clean new order of things; a historicist respect for whatever mighty events came forth—and above all a desire to rejoin the national community in order to repair the divisions of a fragmented, sundered society. All of these—and one might add others, especially the obscure psychic association between war and the erotic revolution—had been prepared for by the intellectual ferment of the years preceding the war, by the ideas of Nietzsche, Bergson, Croce, Weber, by the imaginative writings of Barrès, D'Annunzio, Conrad, Dostoyevsky, by the art of the Futurists, Expressionists, Symbolists, Vorticists, to name only some of the greater people and movements. And all of these exciting expressions in an age of unparalleled expansion of individual consciousness reduced to the same thing: the effort of this individual consciousness to come to terms with the collective mentality from which it was being separated. The most basic factor was the resurrection of community. The 1914 spirit was an antidote to anomie, which had resulted from the sweep of powerful forces of the recent past—urban, capitalistic, and technological forces tearing up primeval bonds and forcing people into a crisis of social relationships. The primitive instinct to do battle against a common foe was a remedy for this crisis, unfortunately at too high a price. We are still searching for a viable alternative. So the failed attempt of 1914, overlooked and misunderstood as it has been, should engage our interest.

Illusion is pointed out by Philip D. Supina in an article in *Journal of Peace Research*, Spring, 1972. The work was translated into a score of languages and sold two million copies.

16. See Walter Laqueur, *Young Germany* (New York, 1962); Werner Kindt, ed., *Grundschriften der Deutschen Jugendbewegung* (Dusseldorf, 1963); Robert Wohl, *The Generation of 1914* (Cambridge, Mass., 1979), chap. 2.

17. Thomas Mann, "Gedanken im Kriege" (1914), in *Schriften zur Politik* (Berlin, 1970).

18. Gundolf, the Goethe scholar, was a notable disciple of Stefan George; his "Tat und Wort im Krieg" appeared in *Frankfurter Zeitung*, October 11, 1914. See also his *Briefe* (Amsterdam, 1950), pp. 139, 143; and *Stefan George, 1868–1968: Der Dichter und Sein Kreis* (Marbach, 1968).

19. J. C. Powys, *Autobiography* (1934; reprint ed., Hamilton, N. Y., 1968), pp. 582–83.

20. Percy Lubbock, ed., *Letters of Henry James* (New York, 1920); H. Montgomery Hyde, *Henry James at Home* (London, 1969), pp. 255–68; *Letters of Arnold Bennett*, ed. James Hepburn (London, 1968), 2: 352; George Painter, *Proust: The Later Years* (London, 1965), pp. 223–29.

21. On war and Eros see among other sources Ernst Jünger, *Der Kampf als inneres Erlebnis* (Baden, 1922), vol. 5 of *Werke* (Stuttgart, 1960); Leroy Bruenig, *Guillaume Apollinaire* (New York and London, 1969), pp. 37–39; and a chapter in Paul Fussell's *The Great War and Modern Memory* (New York and London, 1975), on homosexuality among British soldiers. Francis Bacon had long ago observed, "I know not why, but martial men are given to love."

22. Claudel, letter of September 24, 1914, in *Correspondance, 1897–1938. Paul Claudel, Francis Jammes, Gabriel Frizeau* (Paris, 1952), pp. 274–75: "pour le salut et la regeneration de notre pauvre pays." Maurice Barrès's influential articles in *Echo de Paris* are reprinted in his *Chronique de la Grand Guerre, 1914–1920* (Paris, 1968).

23. D'Annunzio's *Prose*, vol. I (Verona, 1947), contains many examples of his war rhetoric. His war pieces were translated into English as *The Rally* (Milan, 1919).

24. See J. M. Cohen, "The Earth is Hungry," *The Listener*, November 11, 1965.

25. Rudolf Eucken, *Knowledge and Life* (trans. ed., London, 1913).

26. See, for example, Charles R. Richet, *Le passé de la guerre et l'avenir de la paix* (Paris, 1907), translated into German by the celebrated pacifist Bertha von Suttner (Leipzig, 1909).

27. "The historian should compare the pictures of August 1, 1914, and September 1, 1939 carefully; war-beginning and war-beginning are not the same." Ludwig Marcuse, *Mein Zwanzigstes Jahrhundert* (Munich, 1960), p. 37. "It is strange that in 1914 we did not expect war and were not confused when it came. Now [1939] we have been expecting it for some time but are confused when it has come." T. S. Eliot, quoted in Roger Kojecky, *T. S. Eliot's Social Criticism* (New York, 1971), p. 172.

CHAPTER 2

1. Eucken, *Erinnerungen*, p. 65.
2. See among other discussions Lewis S. Feuer, "The Political Linguistics of 'Intellectual' 1898–1918," *Survey* 16, no. 1 (1971); William I. Gleberzon, "The Historical Evolution of American Intellectuals" (Ph.D. diss., University of Toronto, 1972), who finds the term coming into the United States during the Dreyfus affair; Roberto Michels, "Intellectuals," *Encyclopedia of the Social Sciences* (New York, 1935); Alexander Gella, ed., *The Intelligentsia and the Intellectuals* (Beverly Hills, Calif., 1976), on differences between the Russian term and the Western. Maurice Barrès, especially, used the term to denigrate pure thinkers who do not understand practical affairs yet meddle in politics. During the war Rudyard Kipling referred to "brittle intellectuals who crack beneath a strain" ("The Holy War").

In this book I have used a broad definition of "intellectuals" to include all "workers of the mind," not excluding academic philosophers, historians, scientists—anyone who seriously committed significant thoughts to paper. To an exceptional degree World War I brought them together: novelists became officers of information, academics gave their talents to war work, etc. It might be noted that some antiintellectuals of the period, such as Sorel and Péguy, counted university professors among the *parti intellectuel*, as clearly they were.

3. D. A. Prater, *Stefan Zweig: European of Yesterday* (Oxford, 1972). Lady Ottoline Morrell in her *Memoirs, 1897–1915*, 2 vols. (London, 1963), 1: 237, reports the old sea captain Joseph Conrad as saying he liked simple young men, "not the learned or intellectuals." Sorel equated intellectuals either with pedantic professors or dogmatic socialists like Jules Guesde—both marked by the *esprit de système*. For a discussion of Sorel and intellectuals, see Georges Guy-Grand, *La philosophie syndicaliste* (Paris, 1911).

4. Ludwig Klages' *Prinzipien der Characterologie* was published in 1910 (Leipzig); his *Der Geist als Widersacher der Seele* was first published in book form in 1929.

5. George Watson notes this in his discussion of George Orwell, in his *Politics and Literature in Modern Britain* (London, 1977). On Barrès's antiintellectualism, see Robert Soucy, *Fascism in France: The Case of Maurice Barrès* (Berkeley, 1972), pp. 158–63.

6. Leonard Woolf, *Sowing: An Autobiography of the Years 1880–1901* (New York, 1960), p. 72.

7. L. Marcuse, *Zwanzigstes Jahrhundert*, pp. 41–42.

8. On this theme, see Raymond Williams, *The Country and the City* (New York, 1973); chap. 4, "The City," in Alex de Jonge, *Dosto-yevsky and the Age of Intensity* (London, 1975); Malcolm Bradbury, "The Cities of Modernism," and some other essays in Bradbury and James McFarlane, ed., *Modernism, 1890–1930* (New York, 1976); Andrew Lees, "Critics of Urban Society in Germany," *Journal of the History of Ideas*, January–March, 1979; Roy Pascal, "Culture and the Metropolis," in his *From Naturalism to Expressionism: German Literature and Society, 1880–1918* (New York, 1973).

9. Percy Schramm, *Neun Generationen*, vol. 2 (Göttingen, 1964). But compare the Wittgenstein family of Vienna, which combined technological-industrial leadership with patronage of art and music, contributing at least two outstanding figures to European thought and culture in this generation. Yet several of the Wittgensteins were suicides. See Stephen Toulmin and Allan Janik, *Wittgenstein's Vienna* (New York, 1973).

10. George L. Mosse, "The Influence of the *Völkisch* Idea on German Jewry," in *Studies of the Leo Baeck Institute*, ed. Max Kreutzberger (New York, 1967), pp. 84–85.

11. Benedetto Croce, in *La Critica* 2 (1904): 5.

12. Graham Wallas, *The Great Society* (London, 1914), p. 14.

13. See J. P. Hodin, *Modern Art and the Modern Mind* (Cleveland and London, 1972), p. 18. To Virginia Woolf's celebrated dictum that "human character changed in 1910," one can add others such as Gottfried Benn's recollection of 1955 that "1910 was the year the timbers began to creak" and José Ortega y Gasset's identification of that year as marking the end of the age of reason. See R. N. Stromberg, "1910: An Essay in Psychohistory," *The Psychoanalytic Review*, Summer, 1976.

14. See Lyndall Gordon, *Eliot's Early Years* (London, 1977). Gordon notes Eliot's deliberate courting of squalor, "the contemplation of the horrible or squalid or disgusting" as escape from the boredom of gentility. Other Americans rebelled against "the genteel tradition"; faced with

Beacon Hill's smug worldliness Henry Adams yearned "for St. Simeon Stylites and sin" (*Letters* (1906), 2: 466).

15. See, among other discussion of Kafka, A. P. Foulkes, *The Reluctant Pessimist: A Study of Franz Kafka* (The Hague, 1967); he refers to Kafka's death wish of 1912–1914, p. 109.

16. Housman, Additional Poems, XVII, in *The Collected Poems of A. E. Housman* (New York, 1965). Housman, so many of whose haunting rhymes are about fallen soldiers, was a special favorite of British soldiers during the war, as Paul Fussell notes. Already in *A Shropshire Lad* (1896) is the prophecy of war: "Far and near and low and louder/On the roads of earth go by,/Dear to friends and food for powder,/Soldiers, marching, all to die."

17. Anatole France, "Homage to Zola," in *Oeuvres complètes: Trente ans de vie sociale* (Geneva, 1969), 1: 153.

18. Among books tracing the spread of Nietzscheanism, Patrick Bridgwater's *Nietzsche in Anglosaxony* (Leicester, 1972) finds the Nietzsche vogue beginning in England about 1903; by 1906 Arthur Symons could write that "No man can think, and escape Nietzsche."

19. L. Stepelevich, "The Revival of Max Stirner," *Journal of the History of Ideas*, April–June 1974; R. W. K. Paterson, *The Nihilistic Egoist* (London, 1971). Willett, *Expressionism*, pp. 13–14, points out the closeness of anarchists and avant-garde artists. Walter Hasenclever called Expressionism "the revolt of the spirit against reality"—see W. Rasch, "In Pursuit of Pathos," *Times Literary Supplement* (1972), pp. 1107–9; much pre-1914 Expressionist rhetoric is bitterly anti-Establishment.

20. D. H. Lawrence, "Georgian Poets 1911–1912," reprinted in his *Phoenix* (New York, 1936), p. 304.

21. See Bernhard C. Meyer, *Joseph Conrad, a Psychological Biography* (Princeton, 1967); Thomas Moser, *Joseph Conrad, Achievement and Decline* (Cambridge, Mass., 1957); Frederick R. Karl, *Joseph Conrad: The Three Lives* (New York, 1979), pp. 680–86. On p. 626 Karl notes Conrad's vision of impending social breakdown. For Mahler, see Anna Mahler, *Gustav Mahler: Memories and Letters*, trans. and ed. D. Mitchell (New York, 1969); also Donald Mitchell's *Gustav Mahler: The Wunderhorn Years* (Boulder, Colo., 1975), pp. 70–74.

22. According to J. P. Nettl's *Rosa Luxemburg* (London, 1966, p. 706), the "irreparable break" between the two main wings of Marxism in Germany took place in 1910. Lenin's secession from Social Democracy in Russia and, in France, the attacks of Georges Sorel and Charles Péguy on orthodox Marxism also occurred in this decade. See also Werner T. Angress, "Between Baden and Luxemburg: Jewish Socialists on the

Eve of World War I," *Leo Baeck Institute Yearbook*, vol. 22 (1977). Italian sources include Ivanoe Bonomi, *Leonida Bissolati e il movimento socialista in Italia* (Rome, 1945); Fernando Manzotti, *Il socialismo riformista in Italia* (Turin, 1965); P. C. Masini, "Gli anarchi italiani tra 'interventismo' e 'disfattismo rivoluzionario,'" *Rivista Storica del Socialismo* (1952), pp. 208–11.

23. Among comments on the spiritual anarchy of the age, see J. N. Figgis, *Civilization at the Crossroads* (London, 1911); Vernon Lee (Viola Paget), *Gospels of Anarchy* (London, 1908); Efraim Frisch's articles in *Neue Merkur*, 1914; Walther Rathenau, *Zur Kritik der Zeit* (Berlin, 1912).

24. Vera Brittain, *Testament of Youth* (New York, 1933), p. 125.

25. L. Marcuse, *Zwanzigstes Jahrhundert*. Marcuse wrote his doctoral dissertation on Nietzsche in 1917.

26. Vasily Kandinsky, *Über die Geistige in der Kunst* (Munich, 1912); Graefe, *Wohin treiben Wir? Zwei Reden über Kultur und Kunst* (Berlin, 1913). Ludwig Meidner's *Dichter, Maler und Cafés* (Zurich, 1973) contains Meidner's recollections of 1912–1914 life in Dresden and Berlin. A good source book is H. B. Chipp, ed., *Theories of Modern Art* (Berkeley, 1968). Edmund Wilson's *Axel's Castle* was first printed in 1936.

27. See Martin Green, *The Von Richtofen Sisters* (New York, 1974), pp. 167–73; Max Weber, *Sociology of Religion* (Boston, 1963), chap. 2. Georg Simmel's 1911 essay "The Adventure" is printed in Kurt H. Wolff, ed., *Georg Simmel, 1858–1918* (Columbus, 1959). Hans von Flesch's "Die Revolution der Erotik" is discussed in Armin Arnold, *Prosa des Expressionismus* (Stuttgart, 1972). On Schnitzler, see Carl E. Schorske, in his *Fin de Siècle Vienna: Politics and Culture* (New York, 1980). Schorske notes Schnitzler's sense of impending doom.

28. Wilfred Mellers, *Caliban Reborn: Renewal in Twentieth Century Music* (New York, 1967), p. 161. In 1910 Schoenberg began his work in the serialist, twelve-tone mode, a drastic break with musical tradition *and* the proposal of a deliberately subjective, arbitrary set of rules for composition.

29. Henri Lefebvre, *Everyday Life in the Modern World*, trans. Sacha Rabinovich (London, 1971).

30. See the celebrated study of the German Social Democratic party by Max Weber's friend Robert Michels, translated as *Political Parties* (New York, 1915), announcing the "iron law of oligarchy."

31. Delius, Wilfred Mellers writes, retreats in his marvelous music into "the eternal non-humanity of sea and hills," the Paradise Gardens of a lost Eden. *Caliban Reborn*, pp. 39–41.

32. Franz Marc, *Briefe, Aufzeichungen und Aphorismen* (Berlin, 1920), 1: 39. Marc's "Im Fegefeuer des Krieges," an article printed in *Kunstgewerbeblatt* 26 (1915): 128–30, is reprinted in Victor H. Meisel, ed., *Voices of German Expressionism* (Englewood Cliffs, N.J., 1970). "The great war came with such terrible suddenness, pushing words aside, sweeping dirt and decay away to give us the future society."

33. See Hanna Hafkesbrink, *Unknown Germany* (New Haven, 1948), especially p. 21, for mention of a number of Expressionist yearnings for war. For some recollections of Ernst Wilhelm Lotz, see Meidner, *Dichter, Maler*, pp. 61–68.

34. Richard Ellman, *Yeats, the Man and the Mask* (New York, 1958), pp. 97, 112; Malcolm Brown, *The Politics of Irish Literature* (Seattle, 1972), p. 365.

35. Faubion Bowers, *The New Scriabin* (New York, 1973), p. 123.

36. See Bernice G. Rosenthal, *D. S. Merezhkovsky and the Silver Age* (The Hague, 1975); C. Harold Bedford, *The Seeker: D. S. Merezhkovskiy* (Lawrence, 1975).

37. Martin Cooper, "Ecstasy for Ecstasy's Sake," *The Listener* (October 10, 1957), p. 563. Cf. Donald Fanger, "The City of Russian Modernist Fiction," in Malcolm Bradbury and James McFarlane, eds., *Modernism, 1890–1930,* who remarks that "a fascination with death was a key feature of the period," accompanying an apocalyptic mood expressed, for example, in Andrey Bely's 1913 novel *St. Petersburg.* On the "God-builders," see George L. Kline, *Religious and Anti-Religious Thought in Russia* (Chicago, 1968). James West, *Russian Symbolism* (London, 1970), discusses Ivanov. On the Symbolist cult of death see also Oleg Maslenikov, *The Frenzied Poets: The Russian Symbolists* (Berkeley, 1952), p. 25.

38. Ivanov, "The Heritage of Symbolism" (an essay written in 1910; it appeared in his book *Borozdi i Mezhi* published in Moscow, 1916). On the Acmeists, Sam Driver, "Acmeism," *Slavic and East European Journal* 2 (1968): 141–56. On Vorticism see Hugh Kenner, *The Pound Era* (Berkeley, 1971), pp. 232–47. For some material on the artist's importance in the thinking of the time, see John A. Lester, Jr., *Journey through Despair, 1880–1914* (Princeton, 1968), pp. 174–76.

39. The journal *Leonardo* (1904–1907) was an organ of Italian Pragmatism, in which Hegelian idealism, as well as "vulgar positivism," was attacked, and a message preached of will, action, and *praxis* through the means of art.

40. Giovanni Papini, *L'Esperanza futurista, 1913–1914* (Florence, 1927), p. 46.

41. F. T. Marinetti, *Selected Writings*, ed. R. W. Flint (New York, 1971),

p. 92. See also Umbro Apollonio, ed., *Futurist Manifestoes* (London, 1973).

42. Giovanni Gullace, *Gabriele D'Annunzio in France* (Syracuse, N.Y., 1966), p. 158.
43. Eugen Weber, *The Nationalist Revival in France, 1905–1914* (Berkeley, 1959); there is a good discussion of Psichari in Claude Digeon, *La crise allemande de la pensée francaise, 1870–1914* (Paris, 1959), pp. 514–18.
44. Similarly popular was a literature of German spies and of invasion scare; see Samuel Hynes, *The Edwardian Turn of Mind* (Princeton, 1968), pp. 34–53; David French, "Spy Fever in Britain 1900–1915," *Historical Journal* 21, no. 2 (1978).
45. Charles Péguy, *Oeuvres en prose*, ed. Marcel Péguy, vol. 2 (Paris, 1961), pp. 1251–56.
46. Papini, *L'Esperanza futurista*, p. 99; Rupert Brooke, *Letters from America* (New York, 1916).
47. Quentin Bell, *Bloomsbury* (London, 1974), p. 67.
48. Wilfred Owen, *Collected Letters*, ed. Harold Owen and John Bell (London, 1967), pp. 296, 300 (November–December, 1914).
49. This point is made by William J. McGrath in his *Dionysian Art and Populist Politics in Austria* (New Haven, 1974).
50. Julien Benda, *Un régulier dans le siècle* (Paris, 1938), pp. 136–37. For Sorel's shift, see his letter to Croce, printed in *La Critica* 25 (1928): 33–48.
51. Gustav Janouch, *Conversations with Kafka* (trans. ed., New York, 1971), p. 103.
52. That "the rise of revolutionary movements in the first half of the nineteenth century was directly related to the development of a new class of intellectuals in continental Europe" (p. 208) is the theme of James H. Billington's *Fire in the Minds of Men: Origins of the Revolutionary Faith* (New York, 1980).
53. Ruth Muggeridge and Kitty Adam, *Beatrice Webb* (New York, 1968), p. 204. In his memoirs Herbert Read comments on the rising interest in syndicalism in Britain during the prewar years; see also Bob Holton, *British Syndicalism, 1900–1914* (London, 1977). Rupert Brooke felt that Fabianism was going out of fashion among university youth in favor of something more drastic: Michael Hastings, *The Handsomest Young Man in England* (London, 1967), pp. 75–77.
54. Max Scheler, *Der Genius des Krieges und der Deutsch Krieg* (Leipzig, 1915), p. 74.
55. Christopher Hassall, *Rupert Brooke* (London, 1964), p. 244.
56. Jean Guehenno, *Journal d'un homme de quarante ans* (Paris, 1937), p.

220. On André Breton, see Anna Balakian, *André Breton, Magus of Surrealism* (New York, 1971).

CHAPTER 3

1. Friedrich Meinecke, *Die Deutsche Catastrophe* (Wiesbaden, 1946).
2. *Briefwechsel Benedetto Croce–Karl Vossler* (Berlin and Frankfurt, 1955), pp. 198–99; letter of September 24, 1914.
3. H. N. Brailsford, *A League of Nations* (New York, 1917), p. 4.
4. *Lettres d'Alain-Fournier à sa famille* (Paris, 1948), p. 386.
5. Paul Claudel, *Journal* (Paris, 1968), 1: 294–97.
6. Hans Rogger, "Russia in 1914," *Journal of Contemporary History* 1, no. 4 (1962), 112. See also Daniel Balmuth, "Russian Intellectuals and the First World War," paper presented at American Historical Association meeting, New York City, December 30, 1979.
7. Harry Graf Kessler to Hugo Hofmannsthal, *Hofmannsthal–Kessler Briefwechsel* (Frankfurt, 1968), p. 384.
8. See Waugh's memoir, *The Early Years of Alec Waugh* (London, 1962), p. 110.
9. Painter, *Proust: The Later Years*, 1: 223–29; Hyde, *Henry James at Home*, pp. 255–68.
10. André Gide, *Journal, 1889–1939* (Paris, 1948), entries for August and September, 1914.
11. M. Barrès, "L'Aurore," *Echo de Paris*, August 9, 1914.
12. Leon Edel, ed., *Selected Letters of Henry James* (New York, 1955), p. 217.
13. Thomas Mann, *Briefe, 1889–1936* (Frankfurt, 1962), pp. 113 ff.; "Gedanken im Kriege," 1914; *Stefan George, 1868–1968*, p. 262.
14. Joachim Fest, *Hitler* (New York, 1974), p. 64.
15. George Santayana, *Soliloquies* (New York, 1922), pp. 104–5. Bertrand Russell remarked that Santayana "had not enough respect for the human race to care whether it destroyed itself or not." Lady Ottoline Morrell, *Memoirs*, 1897–1915 (London, 1963), 1: 266–70.
16. Santayana, *Letters*, ed. Daniel Cory (New York, 1945), p. 145.
17. E. L. Woodward, *Short Journey* (London, 1946), pp. 73–74; Robert Blatchford, *My Eighty Years* (1931), p. 235.
18. One compilation of the numerous manifestoes, open letters, etc., issued during the first months of the war is Herman Kellermann, *Der Krieg der Geister* (Weimar, 1915).
19. *Correspondence of André Gide and Edmund Gosse* (New York, 1959),

p. 115, letter of November, 1914. Gilbert Murray, "Herd Instinct and the War," *Atlantic Monthly*, June, 1915.

20. Sidney Low, ed., *The Spirit of the Allied Nations* (London, 1915), p. 22, also p. 68.

21. Compton Mackenzie, *My Life and Times* (London, 1965), 4: 224. Cf. Vera Brittain, *Testament of Youth*, p. 97: "The great fear is that our bungling government will declare England's neutrality"; Alec Waugh, *Early Years*, pp. 55–57: "How soon could I get to France" was the only question on his mind.

22. Ernst Jünger, *Aus dem Tagebuch eines Stosstruppführer*, 10th ed. (Berlin, 1929), p. 6.

23. Robert Gilson, *The Quest of Alain-Fournier* (London, 1953), p. 255.

24. Herbert Read, *The Contrary Experience* (New York, 1963), p. 90.

25. "An Irish Airman Foresees His Death," in W. B. Yeats, *The Wild Swans at Coole* (1919).

26. Herbert Read, *Annals of Innocence and Experience* (London, 1940), p. 138.

27. Malcolm Muggeridge, *Jesus Reconsidered* (London, 1969), p. 40.

28. Margaret Drabble, *Arnold Bennett* (New York, 1974), pp. 199–200; Kinley E. Roby, *A Writer at War: Arnold Bennett* (Baton Rouge, 1973). In this respect at least, World War II for many was not dissimilar; in Patrick Hamilton's novel *Hangover Square* (London, 1941, reprinted 1972), the war "is an event for which all the characters appear to have been waiting . . . to make sense of their lives . . . which would put an end to their meaningless existences . . . ." (Review in *Times Literary Supplement*, July 14, 1972, p. 795.)

29. See Jane Lidderdale and Mary Nicholson, *Dear Miss Weaver* (New York, 1970), pp. 95 ff. The founder of *Der Sturm*, Alfred Döblin, a literary medical doctor, was a staunch patriot; he defended the German shelling of Reims in *Neue Rundschau* 2: 1717–22. Like Georg Lukacs he turned suddenly to the Left after the Russian Revolution, and was later an exile from Hitler. During World War I he worked as a physician in the army, as did the French writer Henry de Montherlant.

30. See Guy Stern, *War, Weimar and Literature: The Story of the Neue Merkur, 1914–1925* (University Park, Pa., 1971), pp. 15 ff.

31. Published in *Neue Zürcher Zeitung*, November 3, 1914; reprinted in Hesse's *If the War Goes on . . .*, trans. Ralph Manheim (New York, 1971). See Ralph Freedman, *Herman Hesse: Pilgrim of Crisis* (New York, 1978), pp. 166–69, also Robert Galbreath, "Herman Hesse and the Politics of Detachment," *Political Theory* 2, no. 1 (February, 1974). On Karl Kraus, Frank Field, *The Last Days of Mankind: Karl Kraus and His Vienna* (London, 1967), chaps. 3, 4.

32. Harold Poor, *Kurt Tucholvsky* (New York, 1968), p. 30.
33. Carter Jefferson, *Anatole France: The Politics of Scepticism* (New Brunswick, N.J., 1965), pp. 189–93. Also on France, Jean Levaillant, *Essai sur l'evolution intellectuelle d'Anatole France* (Paris, 1965).
34. Klaus Schwabe, *Wissenschaft und Kriegsmoral: Die Deutsche Hochschullehrer und die politischen Grundfragen des Erstes Weltkrieges* (Göttingen, 1969), p. 24.
35. *L. T. Hobhouse: His Life and Work*, ed. J. A. Hobson and Morris Ginsberg (London, 1931), p. 49; Hobhouse, *Mind in Evolution*, 2nd ed. (London, 1915), p. 382. See also Harold L. Smith's article on Hobhouse and the war in *Albion*, 1974.
36. Kenneth O. Morgan, *Keir Hardie* (London, 1975), pp. 265–67.
37. "Why the Workers Must Fight in This War," *John Bull*, October 10, 1914. Generally on trade unions and the war, see Peter Stansky, ed., *The Left and War: The British Labour Party and World War I* (Oxford, 1969); John L. Snell, "Socialist Unions and Socialist Patriotism in Germany, 1914–1918," *American Historical Review* 59 (1953): 66–76; J. O. Stubbs, "Lord Milner and Patriotic Labour, 1914–1918," *English Historical Review* 87 (October, 1972); Jacques Julliard, "La CGT devant la guerre," *Mouvement Social* 49 (1964): 47–62; Becker, *1914*, part II, chap. 2.
38. Prater, *Stefan Zweig*, p. 70; Stefan Zweig, *Welt von Gestern*, translated as *The World of Yesterday* (New York, 1943), p. 197.
39. Jünger, *Der Kampf als inneres Erlebnis*, p. 31; Bruenig, *Apollinaire*, pp. 37–39; Mosley, *Grenfell*. Other examples of the cult of death are Gustav Roethe, *Vom Tode fürs Vaterland* (Berlin, 1915); Mario T. Rossi, *Lettere* (Turin, 1919), the letters of a young Italian who died in 1917; Bowers, *The New Scriabin*, pp. 124–25.
40. *Stefan George: Der Dichter und Sein Kreis*, p. 262.
41. Stravinsky, letter to Romain Rolland in Rolland's *Journal des années de guerre*, pp. 59–61. For a Stravinsky wartime anti-German piece of music, see the catalogue in Robert Craft, *Stravinsky, Chronicle of a Friendship, 1948–1971* (London, 1972). On David Burlyuk, see Vladimir Markov, *Russian Futurism* (London, 1969). Edward Lockspeiser, *Debussy* (London, 1965), 2: 206-9. But by the time of his death in 1916, Debussy had soured on the war, which he thought "with each passing day loses some of its nobility."
42. See Ted Morgan, *Somerset Maugham* (London, 1980).
43. Stanley Weintraub, *Reggie* (New York, 1965).
44. Ronald W. Clark, *Einstein: The Life and Times* (New York, 1971), p. 185.
45. Karl Lamprecht, *Deutsche Zukunft* (Gotha, 1916), p. 23. See also Fritz

Klein, "Gli Storici Tedeschi di fronte alla Prima Guerra Mondiale," *Studi Storici* 3 (1962): 730–56; Ivo Shöffer, "Friedrich Meinecke in de eerste Wereldoorlog," *Tijdschrift voor Geschiednis* 70 (1957).

46. Marianne Weber, *Max Weber: Ein Lebensbild* (Tübingen, 1926), p. 530 (trans. New York, 1975, as *Max Weber: A Biography*); H. Stuart Hughes, *Consciousness and Society: The Reconstruction of European Social Thought, 1890–1930* (New York, 1958), p. 325; Ilse Dronberger, *The Political Thought of Max Weber* (New York, 1971), p. 153; Wolfgang J. Mommsen, *Max Weber und die Deutsche Politik, 1890–1920* (Tübingen, 1959); R. N. Stromberg, "Max Weber and World War I: Culture and Politics," *Dalhousie Review* 59, no. 2 (Summer, 1979).

47. See Arthur Mitzman, *Sociology and Estrangement: Three Sociologists of Imperial Germany* (New York, 1973), pp. 129–31. In addition to Tönnies, Mitzman discusses Werner Sombart and Robert Michels.

48. Ross Terrill, *R. H. Tawney and His Times* (Cambridge, Mass., 1973), p. 49; see also Tawney's *Commonplace Book, 1912–1914* (London, 1972, supplement to *Economic History Review*). *Democracy or Defeat* was the title of one of his wartime tracts. Tawney's fellow socialist historian, G. D. H. Cole, seems to have tried to ignore the war; see L. P. Carpenter, *G. D. H. Cole: An Intellectual Biography* (Cambridge, 1973). Carol S. Gruber, *Mars and Minerva: World War I and the Use of the Higher Learning in America* (Baton Rouge, 1975), documents the belligerence of American historians and social scientists, also philosophers such as Royce, Lovejoy, and Dewey. An illuminating American document is the *War Encyclopedia*, ed. Edward S. Corwin, Frederic L. Paxson, and Samuel B. Harding (Washington, 1918). Among other major historians, Lewis Namier tried to enlist, and when kept out of service by poor eyesight worked in Political Intelligence in the Foreign Office.

49. See Friguglietti, in *French Historical Studies* 7, no. 4 (1972).

50. Among Durkheim's war writings were *Deutschland über Alles* and *Who Wanted War?* (1915) in the series "Studies and Documents on the War" by various French scholars, translated into English.

51. Marrin, *The Last Crusade*, pp. 77–79 passim.

52. Hensley Henson, "The Paradox of Christianity," *Challenge*, February 12, 1915; among many others, Edward Lee Hicks, *The Church and the War* (1914); Charles Gore, *The War and the Church* (1914); and F. J. Foakes-Jackson, ed., *The Faith and the War* (1915).

53. Rae, *Conscience and Politics*; Maurice Bowra, *Memories, 1898–1939* (London, 1966); Arthur Marwick, *The Deluge: British Society and the First World War* (Boston, 1965), pp. 32–33, 48; Stanley Cooperman,

World War I and the American Novel (Baltimore, 1967), pp. 19–20.

54. Claudel, *Journal* 1: 299; cf. his 1915 poem, "Aux morts des armées de la Republique."

55. Ernst Troeltsch, *Deutsche Glaube und Deutsche Sitte in unseren grossen Krieges*, Heft 9 of Kaiser-Wilhelm-Dank Kriegesschriften (Berlin, 1915). Troeltsch interrupted his long friendship with his fellow "modernist" theologian Friedrich von Hügel, who though of Austrian birth had long resided in England; see Troeltsch, *Briefe an Friedrich von Hügel, 1901–1923* (Paderborn, 1974).

56. See Charles E. Bailey, "Gott Mit Uns: Germany's Protestant Theologians in the First World War (Ph.D. diss., University of Virginia, 1978). Also articles on German churches and the war by Karl Hammer and Richard von Dülmen in *Francia* 1 (1974).

57. See Ludwig Volk, "Pater Rupert Mayer vor der NS-Justiz," *Stimmen der Zeit*, January, 1976.

58. Werner E. Mosse and Arnold Paucker, ed., *Deutsches Judentum in Krieg und Revolution, 1916–1923* (Tübingen, 1971), pp. 30, 409–10. On French Jews, see André Spire, *Les juifs et la guerre* (1917), and Bernhard Blumenkranz, ed., *Histoire des juifs en France* (Toulouse, 1972), pp. 365–73. Hervé, the popular French syndicalist editor, turned away from an earlier anti-Semitism in adopting his national defense, prowar posture.

59. Martin Buber, *Briefwechsel* (Heidelberg, 1972), 1: 364–65, 370–71. Buber wrote in *Zeit-Echo*, no. 3 (1914).

60. Arthur Koestler, *The Case of the Midwife Toad* (New York, 1971), p. 151. This statement was made in 1919! Rolland, *Journal*, p. 917. *Echo de Paris*, January 6, 1915. Max Scheler discussed the breakdown of scientific objectivity in *Der Genius des Krieges*, pp. 318 ff. See also works cited in note 9, chap. 1; Pierre Duhem and Émile Picard, *Les allemands et la science* (Paris, 1916).

61. Albert Mathiez, "La mobilisation des savants en l'an II," *Revue de Paris*, December 1, 1917, pp. 542–65.

62. J. L. Heilbron, *H. G. J. Moseley: The Life and Letters of an English Physicist, 1887–1915* (Berkeley, 1974). The quotation is from the review of the book in *Times Literary Supplement*. William Osler, *Science at War* (Oxford, 1915), saw the war as meaning the death of international science.

63. Daniel J. Kevles, "Into Hostile Political Camps: The Reorganization of International Science in World War I," *Isis* (Spring, 1971).

64. See Prater, *European of Yesterday*, and Zweig, *World of Yesterday*. Dostoyevsky had strongly influenced Mahler.

65. Henri Pirenne, *Journal de Guerre*, ed. Bryce and Mary Lyon (Amsterdam, 1976).

66. Stanley Weintraub, *Journey to Heartbreak: The Crucible Years of Bernard Shaw, 1914–1916* (New York, 1971), p. 27.

CHAPTER 4

1. See A. E. Pilkington, *Bergson and His Influence* (London, 1976). A similar tribute to Bergson as liberator appears in Étienne Gilson, *The Philosopher and Theology* (New York, 1962).

2. Péguy, *Note conjointe sur M. Descartes et la philosophie cartésienne* (1913), pp. 246–47.

3. Georges Guy-Grand, *La philosophie syndicaliste* (Paris, 1911), pp. 144–51.

4. See William D. Williams, *Nietzsche and the French* (Oxford, 1952). Émile Faguet, *On Reading Nietzsche* (1904, trans. 1918) was a characteristic French appreciation, by a notable popularizer of ideas.

5. Patrick Bridgwater, *Kafka and Nietzsche* (Bonn, 1974), notes that Kafka was a Nietzsche reader around 1900. Karl Barth, Carl Jung, and Martin Buber were among others whom Nietzsche deeply influenced. On Nietzsche in England, in addition to Bridgwater's *Nietzsche in Anglosaxony*, see David S. Thatcher, *Nietzsche in England, 1890–1914* (Toronto, 1970).

6. A. R. Orage, *Friedrich Nietzsche: The Dionysian Spirit of the Age* (London, 1906), p. 12. Cf. Paula Modersohn-Becker (1899): "It was a strange experience for me to find latent feelings of my own, still unclear and undeveloped within me, now being clearly formulated." *Briefe und Tagebuchblätter* (Berlin, 1949), pp. 109–10. Gide's remarks are in his *Pretextes* (Paris, 1903).

7. Erich Ruprecht and Dieter Bänsch, ed., *Literarische Manifeste der Jahrhundertwende, 1890–1910* (Stuttgart, 1970), p. 543.

8. Georg Brandes, *An Essay on the Aristocratic Radicalism of Friedrich Nietzsche* (trans. 1909).

9. Siegfried Lipiner, in *Deutsche Zeitung*, March 9, 1881. For light on this Austrian Wagner-Nietzsche circle, which touched such diverse people as Viktor Adler and Gustav Mahler, see William J. McGrath, *Dionysian Art and Populist Politics in Austria*.

10. *Freud-Jung Letters* (Princeton, 1974), pp. 298–99 (1910 letter). Cf. Nicholas Berdyaev, who wrote his first book, *The Meaning of the Creative Act*, in 1914: the "myth-creating" process is a better route to

truth than the conceptual one; objective reason, product of man's fallen nature, reifies and obscures.

11. William Butler Yeats, *Letters*, ed. Allan Wade (New York, 1955), pp. 209–10.

12. Christian von Krockow, *Die Entscheidung* (Stuttgart, 1958), pp. 29–38.

13. An American book on *Six Major Prophets* (1917) included Eucken in the company of Shaw, Wells, Chesterton, John Dewey, and the British Pragmatist F. C. S. Schiller as masters of modern thought.

14. See especially Dilthey's *Introduction to the Human Studies*, 1883. H. P. Rickman has edited a selection of Dilthey writings in translation under the title *Pattern and Meaning in History* (New York). Recent major studies of Dilthey are Rudolf A. Makreel, *Dilthey: Philosopher of the Human Studies* (Princeton, 1975), and Michael Ermarth, *Wilhelm Dilthey: The Critique of Historical Reason* (Chicago, 1978). A good guide to the *Methodenstreit* may be found in Carlo Antoni, *From History to Sociology* (Detroit, 1959).

15. On Scheler, see Ernest W. Ranly, *Scheler's Phenomenology of Community* (The Hague, 1967), and John R. Staude, *Max Scheler: An Intellectual Portrait* (New York, 1967).

16. J. P. Hodin, *Oskar Kokoschka* (New York, 1966), p. 85.

17. Ernst Troeltsch, "Ideen von 1914," in *Deutscher Geist und Westeüropa* (Tübingen, 1966), pp. 42–43—essay written in 1916.

18. Émile Durkheim, *The Elementary Forms of Religious Life* (1912).

19. Cf. Hugo Hofmannsthal's "Letter of Lord Chandos," 1902: "The abstract terms of which the tongue must avail itself as a matter of course in order to voice a judgment . . . crumbled in my mouth like moldy fungi." In his despair he imagines "a language none of whose words is known to me, a language in which inanimate things speak to me." Hofmannsthal, *Selected Prose*, ed. M. Hottinger and T. J. Stern (London, 1952), pp. 129–41.

20. Antonio Gramsci, *Scritti giovanile, 1914–1918* (Turin, 1958), pp. 84–85.

21. A good discussion is Edmund E. Jacobitti, "Labriola, Croce, and Italian Marxism," *Journal of the History of Ideas*, April–June, 1975.

22. Edouard Berth, *Les mefaits des intellectuels* (1914). Cf. Gabriel Terrail, *Le syndicalisme contre le socialisme* (1907). Peter Avrich, *The Russian Anarchists* (Princeton, 1967), discusses the antirationalism of the anarchists. Lewis D. Wurgaft, *The "Activists": Kurt Hiller and the Politics of Action on the German Left, 1914–1933* (Philadelphia, 1977), describes a group of independent leftists influenced by Sorel, Futurism, and Expressionism, who sought to be more *geistig* than the materialistic Marxists.

23. Marcel Péguy, *La rupture de Charles Péguy et de Georges Sorel* (Paris, 1930), p. 7.
24. Romain Rolland, *Péguy* (Paris, 1944), 1: 245.
25. David D. Roberts, "Croce and Beyond: Italian Intellectuals and World War I," *International History Review*, April, 1981.
26. Croce, "Address to Neapolitans," May 3, 1915, in his *Pagine sulla guerra* (Bari, 1928), p. 47.
27. See Marcuse's autobiography, *Mein Zwanzigstes Jahrhundert.*
28. Georg Kaiser, 1922 essay "Formung von Drama," in *Werke*, vol. 4 (1972), pp. 572–74.
29. Sigmund Freud, *Group Psychology and the Analysis of the Ego* (1921). On LeBon, see Robert A. Nye, *The Origins of Crowd Psychology: Gustave LeBon and the Crisis of Mass Democracy in the Third Republic* (Beverly Hills, 1975). Nye notes the conjuncture of LeBon and Georges Sorel, from opposite political directions, sharing "a profound belief that non-rational emotional components underlay the overwhelming majority of individual and social actions" (p. 109).
30. Gustave LeBon, *Première consequences de la guerre* (1916).
31. LeBon, *La vie des verités* (Paris, 1914).
32. In this connection it may be significant that in 1896 Hardy forswore novel-writing, the medium of his bitterly agnostic philosophy (*Tess, Jude*), to express himself thereafter in poetry.
33. See Bernard Semmel, *Imperialism and Social Reform* (London, 1960), especially chap. 2.
34. L. T. Hobhouse, *Development and Social Purpose* (London, 1913), p. 9.
35. Bowra, *Memories*, p. 57. See, generally, Leon Poliakov, *The Aryan Myth: A History of Racist and Nationalist Ideas in Europe* (trans. ed., New York, 1974); Christine Bolt, *Victorian Attitudes toward Race* (Toronto, 1971); George L. Mosse, *Toward the Final Solution: A History of European Racism* (New York, 1978).
36. G. B. Shaw, *Collected Letters, 1898–1910*, ed. Dan H. Laurence (New York, 1972), p. 558.
37. In addition to Scheler's *Genius des Krieges*, see Friedrich Naumann, on the "power struggle" of world politics as a "principle of progress," in *Die Hilfe*, no. 15 (1898) and elsewhere in Naumann's writings. Also see Max Weber's statement on "the fundamental fact of the eternal struggle of men with one another," and especially his 1895 address, "The National State and Economic Policy."
38. LeBon, *The Psychology of Revolutions* (1913).
39. Cited in L. Pearce Williams, ed., *Relativity Theory: Its Origins and Impact on Modern Thought* (New York, 1968), pp. 111 ff.
40. *Freud-Jung Letters*, pp. 343–46.

41. Thomas Mann, *Freud, Goethe, Wagner* (New York, 1937).
42. R. K. Gupta, "Freud and Schopenhauer," *Journal of the History of Ideas*, October–December, 1975. Eduard von Hartmann, author of the popular *Philosophy of the Unconscious*, was a Schopenhauer disciple.
43. See especially Freud's letters to Einstein, "Why War?" in Freud, *Collected Papers*, vol. 5 (New York and London, 1950), pp. 273–87. Also passages in *Civilization and Its Discontents* (1930). His writings *On War, Sex, and Neurosis* were edited by Sander Katz (New York, 1947).
44. Donald Fanger, "The City in Russian Modernist Fiction," in Bradbury and McFarlane, *Modernism*, p. 474.
45. Foulkes, *The Reluctant Pessimist*, p. 109.
46. But Moore's *Principia Ethica* was in some ways a retreat from rationalism, in affirming the ultimate indefinability of the "good": our perception of values is intuitive, common-sensical, a brute fact not capable of explanation. Bertrand Russell substantially shared this belief.
47. On Dewey and the war, see Charles E. Howlett, *Troubled Philosopher: John Dewey and the Struggle for World Peace* (Port Washington, N.Y., 1977); John C. Farrell, "John Dewey and World War I," *Perspectives in American History* 9 (1975); Alan Cywar, "John Dewey in World War I," *American Quarterly* 21 (1969): 579–94.

CHAPTER 5

1. Troeltsch, "Ideen von 1914," *Deutsche Geist und Westeuropa*, p. 43.
2. Scheler, *Genius des Krieges*, p. 2. Marianne Weber uses exactly the same words in her *Max Weber*, p. 526.
3. Ludwig Binswanger, *Die seelische Wirkungen des Krieges* (Stuttgart and Berlin, 1914); also Rudolf Binding, *Erlebtes Leben* (Frankfurt, 1928), p. 237.
4. Georg Simmel, *Der Krieg und die geistigen Entscheidungen* (Munich, 1917), p. 10; Gaudier-Brzeska, in *Blast*, reprinted in Bernard Bergonzi, *Heroes' Twilight* (London, 1965), p. 30.
5. Croce, *Pagine sulla guerra*, p. 47.
6. Hans Rogger, "Russia in 1914," *Journal of Contemporary Hist.* 1: 4, 112.
7. S. Zweig, *World of Yesterday*. Arthur Schnitzler wrote to Georg Brandes, "Every private selfish interest merged into the common interest." *Georg Brandes-Arthur Schnitzler Briefwechsel* (1956), pp. 11–12.
8. Arnold Zweig, *The Time Is Ripe* (London, 1962), p. 283.

9. Steven Lukes, *Émile Durkheim: His Life and Work* (London, 1973), p. 514.

10. *Stefan George, 1868–1968*, pp. 265–66. On 1914 as a "thunderstorm," cf. Carl Zuckmayer, *Als war's ein Stück von Mir* (Vienna, 1966), p. 185 (translated as *A Part of Myself*, New York, 1970).

11. Cited by Krockow, *Die Entscheidung*, p. 47. Further on Jünger, see Karl Heinz Bohrer, *Die Asthetik des Schreckens: Die pessimistische Romantik und Ernst Jüngers Frühwerk* (Munich and Vienna, 1978). Robert Wohl also discusses him in *The Generation of 1914*.

12. Herbert Read, *Annals of Innocence*, p. 146.

13. Herbert Read, introduction to George Panichas, ed., *Promise of Greatness* (New York, 1968), p. vi.

14. Guy Chapman, *A Passionate Prodigality* (New York, 1966), p. 6.

15. Anthony Eden, *Another World*, p. 148.

16. Judith Shklar, *Men and Citizens: A Study of Rousseau's Social Theory* (Cambridge, 1969), p. 15.

17.   Keep away from dirtiness,—keep away from mess,
    Don't get into doin' things rather-more-or-less!

    . . . .
    Mind you keep your rifle and yourself jus' so!

18. Jünger, *Das Wäldchen 125: Eine Chronik aus den Grabenkämpfen 1918* (Berlin, 1925), p. 6. (In vol. 1 of Jünger's *Werke*, Stuttgart, 1960.)

19. See, for example, Walther Rathenau, *Zur Kritik der Zeit* (1912).

20. Carl Schmitt, *Der Begriff des Politischen* (Hamburg, 1927), p. 33.

21. A good World War I identity-crisis novel is Henry Montherlant's *Le Songe*. See Eric J. Leed, *No Man's Land: Combat and Identity in World War I* (London, 1979).

22. Buber, *Briefwechsel*, 1: 364–65, 370; also letter to him from Christian Rang, 1: 367–68.

23. Guy Chapman ed., *Vain Glory* (London, 1968).

24. Bowra, *Memories*, p. 90. Chapman in *Vain Glory* reprints material on the famous Christmas truce of 1914 when opposing troops met, partied, and exchanged gifts (p. 101).

25. Eugen Weber in *Peasants into Frenchmen: The Modernization of Rural France, 1870–1914* (Stanford, 1976), a major work of scholarship, has shown how persistent traditional, local peasant cultures were; "French culture became truly national only in the last years of the [nineteenth] century" (p. 470). Sanford Elwitt, *The Making of the Third Republic* (Baton Rouge, 1975), records the urge to national solidarity found in bourgeois circles.

26. See Nisbet's *The Quest for Community* (1953).

27. Isaac Deutscher, *Lenin's Childhood* (London, 1970), p. 14.
28. Robert Gittings, *Young Thomas Hardy* (London, 1975), p. 4. Shaw declared, "From the village street into the railway station is a leap across five centuries from the brutalizing torpor of Nature's tyranny over Man into the order and alertness of Man's organized dominion over Nature." (*The Wit and Wisdom of Bernard Shaw*, ed. Stephen Winsten, p. 166.)
29. Edward J. Brown, *Mayakovsky, a Poet in the Revolution* (Princeton, 1973), p. 148. On Esenin, see Gordon McVay's biography (Ann Arbor, 1976).
30. See again Donald Fanger's essay on "The City in Russian Modernist Fiction," in Bradbury and McFarlane, *Modernism*. Bely's novel *St. Petersburg* was translated by John Cournos (New York, 1959).
31. H. H. Gerth and C. Wright Mills, ed., *The Sociology of Georg Simmel* (Glencoe, Ill., 1950), p. 409.
32. Walther Rathenau, cited in Donald C. Sanford, "Walther Rathenau: Critic and Prophet of Imperial Germany" (Ph.D. diss., University of Michigan, 1971), p. 74. See also James Joll, *Three Intellectuals in Politics* (New York, 1961).
33. Durkheim, *The Division of Labor in Society* (transl. George Simpson, Glencoe, Ill., 1947), p. 408.
34. Friedrich Tönnies, *Community and Society*, (transl. Charles P. Loomis, New York, 1963).
35. See Robert W. Lougee, *Paul de Lagarde, 1827–1891: A Study of Radical Conservatism in Germany* (Cambridge, Mass., 1962); Fritz Stern, *The Politics of Cultural Despair* (Berkeley, 1961).
36. Michael Duggett, "Marx on Peasants," *Journal of Peasant Studies* 2 (March, 1975); cf. A. Walicki, *The Controversy over Capitalism among Russian Populists* (1969).
37. Arthur Mitzman, *Sociology and Estrangement*, part 4.
38. See Eugene Lunn, *Prophet of Community: The Romantic Socialism of Gustav Landauer* (Berkeley, 1974); also Charles B. Maurer, *Call to Revolution: The Mystic Anarchism of Gustav Landauer* (Detroit, 1971), and Wurgaft, *The "Activists,"* pp. 32–35.
39. In addition to McGrath, *Dionysian Art and Populist Politics in Austria*, see Andrew G. Whiteside, *The Socialism of Fools: Georg Ritter von Schönerer and Austrian Pan-Germanism* (Berkeley, 1976), who notes the popularity of Schönerer's nationalist and anti-Semitic party among students. Also a chapter in Carl E. Schorske, *Fin de Siècle Vienna*, and A. J. P. Taylor's introduction to Heinrich Friedjung, *The Struggle for Supremacy in Germany* (trans. ed., New York, 1966).
40. George Mosse, "Influence of the *Völkisch* Idea on German Jewry," re-

printed in his *Germans and Jews* (New York, 1970). Also Gary B. Cohen, "Jews in German Society: Prague, 1860–1914," *Central European History* 10, no. 1 (March 1977); Richard B. Levy, *The Downfall of the Anti-Semitic Parties in Imperial Germany* (New Haven, 1975); Peter Gay, "Encounter with Modernism: German Jews in German Culture," *Midstream* 21 (1975).

41. Gustav Landauer, *Vom Judentum: Ein Sammelbuch* (Leipzig, 1913), p. 254. See also Grete Schoeder, *The Hebraic Humanism of Martin Buber* (Detroit, 1973), pp. 228–32. On the assimilation of French Jews, Michael R. Marrus, *The Politics of Assimilation* (Oxford, 1971).

42. L. T. Hobhouse, *Morals in Evolution* (London, 1906), p. 334.

43. Sanford, "Rathenau," p. 329.

44. See Wolfgang Mommsen, *Max Weber und die Deutsche Politik*, also his "Max Weber's Political Sociology and His Philosophy of World History," *International Social Science Journal* 17, no. 1 (1965): 23–45. Weber's political writings, including his wartime writings, are contained in his *Gesammelte Politische Schriften*, ed. J. Winckelmann (3 vols., Tübingen, 1971).

45. Klaus Schwabe, *Wissenschaft und Kriegsmoral*, chap. 6. Hugo Preuss, *Die Deutsche Volk und die Politik* (Jena, 1915), urged that the *Obrigkeitstaat* was not adequate for the German national spirit.

46. Fritz K. Ringer, *The Decline of the German Mandarins*, pp. 2–3.

47. On Wilhelmine Germany lacking "a true sense of citizenship, a loyalty to Germany as a community," see Lysbeth W. Muncy in *Central European History* 11, no. 1 (March, 1978): 113–15. On the pan-Germanists, Alfred Kruck, *Geschichte des Alldeutsches Verbandes 1890–1939* (Wiesbaden, 1954). Also see Jeffrey A. Bader, "The Nationalist Leagues in France after Dreyfus" (Ph.D. diss., Columbia University, 1972).

48. Stephen Wilson, "History and Traditionalism: Maurras and the *Action Française*," *Journal of the History of Ideas* 29 (1968): 365–80, thinks that Maurras was less rational than he believed himself to be, a view reminiscent of Jules Romains' "mystics of reason," or of John Davidson: "No mind is as much given to delusion as the logical one." Paul Mazgaj, *The Action Française and Revolutionary Syndicalism* (Chapel Hill, 1978), stresses the inroads made by Maurras' movement into the working class Left in the years just before the war.

49. Barrès had many rivals in the literature of Alsatianism, among them André Lichtenberger, Jean-Jacques Waltz (*Mon Village,* 1913), and Georges Ducrocq, author of a Barresian novel, *Adrienne*, in 1914. On Barrès himself, in addition to Robert Soucy, *Fascism in France* (Berkeley, 1973), see C. Stewart Doty, *From Cultural Rebellion to Counter-*

revolution: The Politics of Maurice Barrès (Athens, Ohio, 1976). Randolph Bourne's "Maurice Barrès and the Youth of France" in *Atlantic Monthly*, September, 1914, was a timely tribute to Barrès's dominance. "Barrès remains the enchanter and master of our youth": quoted in Phyllis Stock, "Students versus the University in Pre-World War Paris," *French Historical Studies* 71: 96.

50. See P. J. Keating, *The Working Classes in Victorian Fiction* (London, 1970). Other examples of demophilia are provided by Walt Whitman in the United States and Arno Holz in Germany.

51. West, *Russian Symbolism*, pp. 142 ff.; Rosenthal, *Merezhkovsky*.

52. It also perhaps suggests why Russian music was so great in this era of Mussorgsky, Tchaikovsky, Rimsky-Korsakov, Scriabin, Rachmaninoff, for the language of music is able best to communicate wholes. Gustav Mahler sought to convey the entirety of experience in his symphonies. It is also notably true that writers and artists were accorded a peculiarly exalted prestige in Russia—"nowhere is literature so vital as it is in Russia, nowhere else does the word pass into life and become bread or stone as it does in our country." Alexander Blok, in Pyman, *Life of Blok*, vol. 2, pp. 358.

53. For some attempts at description, see Karl Polanyi, *The Great Transformation* (New York, 1944); Robert Nisbet, *The Quest for Community* (New York and London, 1953); S. N. Eisenstadt, "Studies of Modernization and Sociological Theory," *History and Theory* 13 (1974).

54. Sebastian de Grazia, *The Political Community: A Study of Anomie* (Chicago, 1948), p. 161.

55. See David Mitchell, *Monstrous Regiment* (New York, 1965); Arthur Marwick, *Women at War, 1914–1918* (London, 1977). Jo V. Newberry, "Anti-war Suffragists," *History* 62, no. 4 (October, 1977), finds some exceptions.

56. Kurt Wolff, ed., *Emile Durkheim, 1858–1917: A Collection of Essays* (Columbus, 1960), p. 266. Maurice Halbwachs' *Les causes de suicide* first appeared in 1930; reprinted New York, 1975. See also Elwin H. Powell, *The Design of Discord: Studies in Anomie* (New York, 1970), including a study on war. For a critique of Durkheim's theory of suicide, see Jack D. Douglas, *The Social Meanings of Suicide* (Princeton, 1967); Anthony Giddens, "A Theory of Suicide" in *Studies in Social and Political Theory* (London, 1977).

57. Bertrand Russell, *Principles of Social Reconstruction* (London, 1915), p. 131.

58. But Brian Harrison, *Separate Spheres: The Opposition to Women's Suffrage in Britain* (London, 1978), finds much feminine resistance to "liberation."

CHAPTER 6

1. Peter Dodge, *Beyond Marxism: The Faith and Works of Hendrik de Man* (The Hague, 1966), p. 29. Ford Madox Ford (as he called himself after changing his Germanic surname) recalled, "I said to myself, 'oh, the Socialists and Labour will stop the war.'" *Return to Yesterday* (London, 1931), p. 435.

2. *Die Neue Zeit* 2: 133 ff.

3. Scholars have pointed out that the *Manifesto*, written by Marx and Engels for the Communist League, represents something of a compromise with the outlook of that artisan group, with which the two theorists did not entirely agree. See, for example, Richard N. Hunt, *The Political Ideas of Marx and Engels*, vol. 1 (Pittsburgh, 1974), pp. 187–91.

4. Jaurès criticized the methods of military occupation but approved of "peaceful penetration," holding that no people has a right to remain out of the path of progress. His statement that "the law of expansion and progress is a law of nature" may be found in *Les alliances européennes* (1896), pp. 99–103. August Bebel said in the Reichstag, December 1, 1906, that "colonial politics is itself no crime" if humanely pursued, which seems to have been standard Social Democratic doctrine. Abraham Ascher, "Radical Imperialists within German Social Democracy 1912–1918," *Political Science Quarterly* 76, no. 4 (1961), calls attention to a more extreme group.

5. Conceding the autonomy of the "superstructure" has been a major revision of twentieth-century "critical Marxism," of which Gramsci was one prophet, along with Georg Lukacs and Karl Korsch. But Engels was annoyed at excessively simplistic versions of the materialist interpretation; see the letters on historical materialism, 1890-1893, reprinted in Robert C. Tucker, *The Marx-Engels Reader* (New York, 1972), pp. 640–50. For an elucidation of the issues, James P. Scanlan, "A Critique of the Engels-Soviet Version of Marxian Economic Determinism," *Studies in Soviet Thought*, vol. 13 (June, 1973).

6. Eduard David, *Die Sozialdemokratie im Weltkrieg* (Berlin, 1915), pp. 178–87. I. Bonomi, *Bissolati e il movimento socialists in Italia*.

7. See *Marx-Engels Werke*, vol. 22 (Berlin, 1972), pp. 245–60. A useful secondary work is Horace B. Davis, *Nationalism and Socialism: Marxist and Labour Theories of Nationalism to 1917* (New York and London, 1967). See also Martin Berger, "War and Revolution in Classical Marxism," presented at Bloomsburg State College History Conference, May 3, 1974, and Frederic C. Burin, "The Communist Doctrine of the Inevitability of War," *American Political Science Review* 57 (June,

1963): 334–54. Diane Paul, "Marxist Views of Race and Culture in the Nineteenth Century," *Journal of the History of Ideas* 42 (January–March, 1981): 115–38, notes Eurocentered biases of Marx and Engels.

8. Fernand Pelloutier, quoted by Robert Wohl, *French Communism in the Making*, pp. 24–25.
9. Milorad M. Drachkovitch, *Les socialismes français et allemand et la problème de la guerre, 1870–1914* (Geneva, 1953), pp. 101–14.
10. See the section "Nation" in Louis Levy, ed., *Anthologie de Jean Jaurès* (London, 1947), pp. 1–49. Jaurès' writings on war and peace were edited by Max Bonnafous in 5 volumes (Paris, 1931–1939), under the general title *Pour la paix*. The standard biography is by Harvey Goldberg (Madison, 1962).
11. Claude Willard, *Les Guesdistes* (Paris, 1965).
12. Marx's son-in-law Paul Lafargue is the subject of a doctoral dissertation by William E. Cohn (University of Wisconsin, 1972).
13. McGrath, *Dionysian Art and Populist Politics*; Julius Braunthal, *Viktor und Friedrich Adler* (Vienna, 1965).
14. Franz Mehring, *Gesammelte Schriften* (Berlin, 1966), vol. 15, p. 121. A helpful article is William H. Maehl, "The Tradition of Nationalism in the German Socialist Party on the Eve of the First World War," *Journal of Modern History* 24 (March, 1952); Maehl has also written "August Bebel and the Development of a Responsible Socialist Foreign Policy, 1878–1896," *Journal of European Studies* 6 (1976): 17–46. See also B. K. Buse, "Ebert and the Coming of World War I," *International Review of Social History* 13, no. 3 (1968).
15. David, *Die Sozialdemokratie im Weltkrieg*, p. 20.
16. In his *Krieg und Kapitalismus*, published in 1913, Werner Sombart sought to show that in capitalism's early stage (seventeenth and eighteenth centuries) war was its essential stimulus, whether by seizing wealth, enlarging the market area, or supplying profitable military orders. War was thus seen as an organic part of historical growth.
17. Karl Kautsky, *The Social Revolution* (Chicago, 1908).
18. On the debate over imperialism, see D. K. Fieldhouse, ed., *The Theory of Capitalist Imperialism* (London, 1967); Daniel H. Kruger, "Hobson, Lenin, and Schumpeter on Imperialism," *Journal of the History of Ideas*, 1955; K. E. Boulding and T. Murkerjee, ed., *Economic Imperialism* (Ann Arbor, 1972); Trevor Lloyd, "Africa and Hobson's Imperialism," *Past and Present*, May, 1972.
19. In addition to David, *Sozialdemokratie*, and Drachkovitch, *Socialismes français et allemand*, other good accounts of the socialists and the coming of the war are Jack D. Ellis, *The French Socialists and the Problem of War* (Chicago, 1966); Georges Haupt, *Socialism and the*

Great War: The Collapse of the Second International (Oxford, 1972); William E. Walling, ed., *The Socialists and the War* (New York, 1972).

20. See Maurice Dommanget, *Edouard Vaillant, un grande socialiste, 1840–1915* (Paris, 1956).

21. Hervé's articles in *La guerre sociale*, from July 1 to November 1, 1914, were published in book form as *La patrie en danger* (Paris, 1915).

22. See Renner's *Oesterreicher Erneurung* (Vienna, 1916); also Jacques Hannak, *Kurt Renner und Seine Zeit* (Vienna, 1965), pp. 215–47.

23. Edward Crankshaw, *The Fall of the House of Hapsburg* (New York, 1963), p. 303.

24. Max Brod, *Strietbares Leben* (Munich, 1960), pp. 136–44.

25. Peter Avrich, *The Russian Anarchists*, p. 116; Balmuth, "Russian Intellectuals and the First World War."

26. Bertram Wolfe, "War Comes to Russia in Exile," *Russian Review* 20, no. 4 (1960); Alfred E. Senn, *The Russian Revolution in Switzerland, 1914–1917* (Madison, 1971); O. Gankin and H. H. Fisher, ed., *The Bolsheviks and the World War* (Stanford, 1940).

27. See Trotsky's *The War and the International*, November, 1914; Irving H. Smith, "Lenin's Views on the First World War," *Europa* 3, no. 1 (1979).

28. Henriette Roland-Holst, quoted by Georges Haupt in *Der Kongress fand nicht statt* (Vienna, Frankfurt, and Zurich, 1967), p. 172. Carl Schorske in *German Social Democracy, 1905–1917*, p. 290, quotes a former left-wing socialist on the conflict he felt and how it was resolved in favor of nationalism.

29. Konrad Haenisch, *Die Deutsch Sozialdemokratie in und nach dem Weltkrieg*; Guenther Roth, *The Social Democrats in Imperial Germany* (Totowa, 1963), pp. 122, 289.

30. G. Arfe, *Storia del socialismo italiano* (Turin, 1965); John M. Cammett, *Antonio Gramsci and the Origins of Italian Communism* (Stanford, 1967); Gramsci, *Scritti, 1915–1921* (Milan, 1968); A. Lepre, "Bordiga i Gramsci di fronte alla guerra," *Critica Marxista*, no. 3 (1967), 134–74; R. Paris, "La première expérience politique de Gramsci, 1914–1915," *Le mouvement sociale*, no. 42 (1963), 31–57. Also Renzo de Felice, *Mussolini*, vol. 1, chap. 9.

31. James Joll, *The Second International* (New York, 1956), p. 157. In 1913 the unusually anti-German Andler, a distinguished socialist pedagogue, charged that the German comrades were "social imperialists," but the Party disavowed him.

32. David, *Sozialdemokratie im Weltkrieg*, p. 42.

33. In *Wiener Arbeitzeitung*, February 14, 1915.

34. By October 31, 1914, Hervé was writing that "There is too much blood between us for us to be able, for a long time, to shake hands within the International"; Karl Liebknecht was "one of the few German socialists to whom I can write without nausea" (*La guerre sociale*).

35. In 1910, Hendrik de Man commented on Hyndman's anti-German "jingoism." Dodge, *Beyond Marxism*, p. 29. On H. G. Wells, see Bruno Schultze, *H. G. Wells und der Erste Weltkrieg* (Berlin, 1971).

36. See David Marquand, *Ramsay MacDonald* (London, 1977), pp. 167–85. MacDonald was not a pure pacifist, and did not want a German victory; Marquand notes the "tortured" quality of his statements about the war. With other Union of Democratic Control members he felt most strongly that British foreign policy had been deceitfully wrong, convincing himself of something like the German thesis of an encirclement plot masterminded by perfidious Albion. See also Stansky, *The Left and War*, p. 60.

37. Morgan, *Keir Hardie,* pp. 265–67.

38. Blatchford's *Germany and England: The War That Was Foretold* (1914) reprinted his writings of 1909 in *The Clarion*, when the popular socialist editor began issuing warnings about the German menace.

39. Kitty Muggeridge and Ruth Adam, *Beatrice Webb*, pp. 206–7. Margaret Cole, *Beatrice Webb* (New York, 1946) p. 144: "The Webbs followed the crowd, at least the Labour crowd, on the war." Graham Wallas lamented in 1916 that socialism "had no more influence than Christianity on either the war's origin or its cause." *Men and Ideas* (London, 1940), p. 107.

40. Croce in *La Critica* 14 (1916): 243.

CHAPTER 7

1. R. W. Seton-Watson et al., *The War and Democracy* (London, 1914), p. 348; Werner Sombart, *Händler und Helden* (Munich and Leipzig, 1915).

2. Eucken, *Lebenserinnerungen*, p. 99.

3. Walter Raleigh, *England and the War* (1918). Cf. James Bryce, *Essays and Addresses in War Time* (1918); Gilbert Murray, *Faith, War, and Policy: Addresses and Essays on the European War* (Boston and New York, 1917); John C. Powys, *The Menace of German Culture* (London, 1915).

4. Ford Madox Ford, *When Blood Is Their Argument* and *Between St. Denis and St. George*, both London, 1915. See Peter Buitenhaus,

"Writers at War: Propaganda and Fiction in the Great War," *University of Toronto Quarterly*, Summer, 1976.

5. Georges Bernanos, *La grande peur des bien-pensants* (Paris, 1931, 1969), p. 371. Bernanos cites a number of examples of such exaggerations from the French press, pp. 371–74.

6. See, for example, H. F. Winnik, Rafael Moses, and Mortimer Ostow, ed., *Psychological Bases of War* (New York and Jerusalem, 1973), p. 91.

7. Raleigh, *England and the War*, pp. 9–10, 26, 40, 50–51.

8. Gore, *The War and the Church* (1914).

9. Seton-Watson, in Seton-Watson et al., *War and Democracy*, p. 239.

10. Ernest Lavisse and Charles Andler, *German Theory and Practice of War* (Studies and Documents on the War, No. 6; transl. from the French, Paris, 1915), p. 48.

11. Herman Oncken, *Unsere Abrechnung mit England* (Kriegsschriften des Kaiser-Wilhelm-Dank, no. 8; Berlin, 1915).

12. Ernst Troeltsch, *Deutscher Glaube und Deutsche Sitte in unserem grossen Kriege* (Berlin, 1915), pp. 5–7; "Die Ideen von 1914," in Troeltsch's *Deutscher Geist und Westeuropa*, p. 47. Dr. Paul Herre, *Unsere Feinde* (Leipzig, 1915), similarly lamented the false picture created by hatred, which he tried to counter by reprinting some pro-German neutral and deviant Allied opinion, including E. D. Morel, Georg Brandes, and some Dutch and Swedish socialists.

13. Eucken, *Lebenserinnerungen*, pp. 97–98. See also F. W. von Bissing, *Die Kriegziele unserer Feinde* (Dresden and Leipzig, 1916), p. 97, in the series Bibliothek für Volks- und Weltwirtschaft, ed. Franz von Mammen; Gustav Roethe, *Vom Tode fürs Vaterland*, p. 29.

14. Croce, *Germany and Europe* (1944); "Philosophy and War," *La Critica* 13 (1915): 398–99.

15. Jules Romains, *Problèmes européens* (Paris, 1933), pp. 21–22; essay written in December, 1915.

16. Bergson's address to the Paris Academy of Moral and Political Sciences on December 12, 1914, was translated as *The Meaning of the War* (London, 1915). Cf. Robert Michels: "the capacity for herd organization, the ability to obey, the quality of subordination." Cited by Arthur Mitzman, *Sociology and Estrangement*, p. 309.

17. Bennett, *Liberty: A Statement of the British Case* (1914).

18. John Dewey, *German Philosophy and Politics* (1915); "On Understanding the Mind of Germany," *Atlantic Monthly*, February, 1916. Cf. George Santayana, *Egotism in German Philosophy* (1916), and "German Freedom" in *Soliloquies* (1922), indicting the Germans for dogmatism, "metaphysical conceit."

19. Bridgwater, *Nietzsche in Anglosaxony*, p. 133. For a French claim that the German philosopher was really on their side, see Remy de Gourmont, *Pendant la guerre* (Paris, 1917), pp. 33–35.

20. *Manchester Guardian*, October 7, 1914; cf. Hardy also in *Daily Mail*, September 27.

21. Croce, "Germanofilia," in *Pagine della guerra*, p. 73, reprinted from *Roma*, October, 1915: "If the Germans need to learn something about Western European democracy, we in our turn ought to learn from that severe concept which the Germans cultivate of the state and of the fatherland." Treitschke's *Politik* (1899) was his work most often cited. See C. McClelland, *The German Historians and England* (Cambridge, 1971).

22. "German Culture and the British Commonwealth," in Seton-Watson et al., *War and Democracy*. This symposium went through six editions in 1915.

23. See, e.g., Gustave LeBon, *Premières consequences de la guerre*, pp. 140 ff., and Raleigh, *England and the War*, who thought that German students were pedants unable to think for themselves.

24. Robert Horn, *Volkscharacter und Kriegspolitik in Frankreich, Russland, England* (Berlin, 1916), pp. 11–16.

25. Georg Brandes, *The World at War* (transl. New York, 1917), p. 87.

26. Klaus Schwabe, *Wissenschaft und Kriegsmoral*, p. 290; *Erklarung der Hochschullehrer des Deutschen Reiches auf die Angriffe unserer Feinde, bei Beginn des Grossen Krieges* (Berlin, 1914).

27. F. W. von Bissing, *Die Kriegziele unserer Feinde*, p. 37.

28. Thomas Mann, *Briefe, 1889–1936*, p. 114. On the other hand, there was much popular abhorrence of "the hordes of the bloody tsar," but a strong tendency in the press to declare "no quarrel with France if she gives up her support of Russia." See Haenisch, *Die Deutsche Sozialdemokratie in und nach dem Weltkrieg*, pp. 22–30.

29. V. H. Rothwell, *British War Aims and Peace Diplomacy, 1914–1918* (Oxford, 1971), p. 288.

30. Scheler, *Genius des Krieges*, pp. 442–43. See also Oswald Spengler, "Engländer und Preussen," in *Preussentum und Sozialismus* (Munich, 1920).

31. From "Notes on the English Character," reprinted in Forster's *Abinger Harvest* (London, 1936): "We have produced no series of prophets, as has Judaism or Islam. We have not even produced a Joan of Arc, or a Savonorola. We have produced few saints. In Germany, the Reformation was due to the passionate conviction of a Luther. In England, it was due to a palace intrigue. . . . The Englishman is an incomplete person . . . undeveloped, incomplete."

32. Werner Sombart, *Händler und Helden*, pp. 84–88. Caught in a conflict of loyalties, the Austrian-born British theologian Friedrich von Hügel tried to distinguish between German culture and the ruling militarism; see his *The German Soul and Its Attitudes* (London, 1916).
33. Mann, "Gedanken im Kriege," in *Schriften zur Politik.* See also Thomas Mann–Heinrich Mann, *Briefwechsel*, ed. Hans Wysling (Frankfurt, 1969); Hermann Hesse-Thomas Mann, *Briefwechsel*, ed. Anni Carlson (Frankfurt, 1969).
34. See Schwabe, *Wissenschaft und Kriegsmoral*, for the best account of this controversy.
35. Dover Wilson, in Seton-Watson et al., *War and Democracy*; also see Members of the Oxford Faculty of Modern History, *Why We Are at War* (Oxford, 1914), p. 115. Hervé's editorial of September 12, in *La guerre sociale.*
36. H. N. Brailsford, *The Origins of the Great War* (London, 1915).
37. Paul Valéry, *Collected Works*, transl. Denise Folliot and Jackson Mathews, vol. 10 (New York, 1962), pp. 230–31.
38. Barbara Tuchman, in *Stilwell and the American Experience in China* (New York, 1972), p. 557, comments that "No nation has ever produced a military history of such verbal nobility as the British."

CHAPTER 8

1. Read, *Annals of Innocence*, p. 142.
2. Panichas, ed., *Promise of Greatness*, p. 487.
3. Georges Bernanos, *Correspondance,* ed. Albert Béguin and Jean Murray (Paris, 1971), pp. 102, 104–6, 117. George's line is from his poem "Der Krieg," which was begun in 1914 but finished in 1917.
4. Shaw, in London *Daily Chronicle*, March 5–8, 1917, reprinted in Winsten, ed., *Wit and Wisdom of GBS*, pp. 311–12. Cf. Karl Kraus, "Mit der Uhr in der Hand," *Die Fackel*, May, 1917, pp. 457–61.
5. See Wiktor Woroszylski, *Life of Mayakovsky* (transl. New York, 1971), pp. 128–29; Brown, *Mayakovsky*, pp. 109–11, 145. Avril Pyman, *Life of Aleksandr Blok*, vol. 2 (London and New York, 1980), 213, notes that Blok's enthusiasm for the war waned, though he did not condemn it.
6. Rolland, *Journal des années de guerre*, pp. 125–26.
7. Rolland printed Wells' letter in his *Journal*, pp. 717–22, together with the reply to it in *Labour Leader* by C. J. Bundock, March 23, 1916. An English edition of *Au-dessus de la melée* first appeared in Great Britain at this time (George Allen & Unwin, March, 1916). Rolland

NOTES TO PAGES 154–159

mentions favorable reviews of it by Bundock, Clutton Brock, and Lady Margaret Sackville.

8. Rolland said that the petition was mutilated by Heinemann in London and, replying to Shaw, observed that he probably would not have signed it himself. It proved to be a vehicle for anti-German propaganda, which Rolland seems not to have intended. See *Journal*, p. 99, for Henri Bergson's refusal to sign.

9. See Edward Lockspeiser, "Roman Rolland: New Perspectives," *The Listener*, January 5, 1967. Also on Rolland, Stefan Zweig, *Romain Rolland: The Man and His Work* (New York, 1921); William T. Starr, *Romain Rolland and a World at War* (New York, 1956), who notes that Rolland "never ceased to believe in the need for Allied victory" (p. 67).

10. *Parthenon*, February 29, 1913, discussed the opposition between Jean-Christophe and "Agathon" (Henri Massis and Alfred de Tarde), mouthpieces for the prewar youth spirit.

11. Rolland, *Journal*, p. 209.

12. Ibid., pp. 117, 156, 159.

13. Ibid., p. 211; Saint-Saens, in *Echo de Paris*, January 12, 1915.

14. Rolland, *Journal*, p. 1130. However, Rolland was later pro-Bolshevik; cf. pp. 1577, 1595.

15. Pierre Teilhard de Chardin, *Writings in Time of War*, transl. René Hague (London, 1968); Jacques Rivière, *Carnets, 1914–1917*, ed. Isabelle and Alain Rivière (Paris, 1974).

16. Ronald W. Clark, *Life of Bertrand Russell* (New York, 1975), p. 251. Pyman, *Blok*, vol. 2, 212.

17. Paul Klee, *Diaries, 1898–1918* (Berkeley, 1964), nos. 352, 356.

18. E. M. Forster, *Goldsworthy Lowes Dickinson* (London, 1934), p. 162.

19. James H. Meisel, *The Genesis of Georges Sorel* (Ann Arbor, 1951), p. 120; Rolland, *Journal*, p. 136.

20. Rolland discussed Nicolai in an article included in his *Les Precurseurs* (Paris, 1919); see also *Journal*, pp. 1607–1610. In this context see the studies of Gustav Landauer cited in note 38, chap. 5. Karl Korsch also refused to carry a weapon, yet served with distinction in the army. See generally James D. Shand, "Doves among the Eagles: German Pacifists and Their Government during World War I," *Journal of Contemporary History*, January, 1975.

21. Richard Aldington, *Life for Life's Sake* (New York, 1941), p. 177. For Romains, see his *Problèmes européens*.

22. Brod, *Streitbares Leben*, p. 147. Kurt Wolff, the famous German publisher, agreed with Heinrich Mann that the latter's *Der Untertan*

would have to wait for publication until after the war: Wolff, *Brief-wechsel, 1911–1963* (Frankfurt, 1966), pp. xxx–xxxi.

23. Quentin Bell, *Bloomsbury*, p. 68.
24. Among other recollections of this circle, see Julian Huxley, ed., *Aldous Huxley 1884–1963* (London, 1965); Clive Bell, *Old Friends* (New York, 1957); *Ottoline at Garsington: Memoirs of Lady Ottoline Morrell, 1915–1918*, ed. Robert Gathorne-Hardy (London, 1974); S. P. Rosebaum, ed., *The Bloomsbury Group: A Collection of Memoirs, Commentary, and Criticism* (London, 1975); David Gadd, *The Loving Friends: A Portrait of Bloomsbury* (London, 1974); Leon Edel, *Bloomsbury* (London, 1979).
25. David Garnett, *The Golden Echo* (New York, 1954), vol. 1, p. 268, recalled that he was alone in rejecting the war when news of it reached a camp-out with Cambridge friends.
26. Leonard Woolf, *Beginning Again: An Autobiography of the Years 1911–1918* (New York, 1964), p. 177. On Keynes, Elizabeth Johnson, "Keynes' Attitude to Compulsory Military Service," *Economic Journal* 70 (March, 1960). G. L. Dickinson says in his *Autobiography* (London, 1973), p. 190, that he probably would have enlisted had he been younger (he was fifty-two).
27. *Letters of Virginia Woolf*, ed. Nigel Nicolson and Jeanne Trautmann (New York, 1976), vol. 2, pp. 57, 76.
28. Clark, *Life of Russell*, pp. 259–65; James L. Jarrett, "D. H. Lawrence and Bertrand Russell," in Harry T. Moore, ed., *A D. H. Lawrence Miscellany* (Carbondale, Ill., 1959); Lawrence, *Collected Letters*, ed. Harry T. Moore (New York, 1962), vol. 1, pp. 329–30, 350–53, 356, 360, 364, 369, 433.
29. Lawrence, *Complete Poems* (London, 1964), p. 677.
30. Harry T. Moore, *The Intelligent Heart* (New York, 1954), p. 169; *The Priest of Love* (New York, 1974), pp. 206–7. Further on Lawrence and the war, Paul Delany, *D. H. Lawrence's Nightmare: The Writer and His Circle during the Years of the Great War* (London, 1979); Stephen Spender, "D. H. Lawrence, England, and the War," in Spender, ed., *D. H. Lawrence: Novelist, Poet, Prophet* (New York, 1973).
31. Edward Nehls, ed., *D. H. Lawrence: A Composite Biography* (Madison, 1957), vol. 1, pp. 358–59.
32. Lawrence, *Complete Poems*, p. 715.
33. Nehls, *Lawrence*, vol. 1, pp. 280, 282, 302, and generally 260–360. Cynthia Asquith, *Diaries 1915–1918* (London, 1968), p. 89, reports Lawrence "quite mad with rage" because the war is "just pure senseless destruction" without any "constructive ideal," yet on the other hand

feeling that the war had to come "because of the nullity of life . . . the result of a vacuum."

34. Stanley Weintraub, ed., *Shaw: An Autobiography, 1898–1950* (New York, 1970), pp. 81 ff.

35. Colin Wilson, *Bernard Shaw: A Reassessment* (London, 1969), pp. 225–27.

36. See Weintraub, *Journey to Heartbreak*, p. 110.

37. Shaw drew together his war pieces in *What I Really Wrote about the War* (London, 1931).

38. Bertrand Russell, *Portraits from Memory* (New York, 1956), pp. 6–7; *Autobiography*, vol. 2 (New York, 1968), p. 7; Feinberg and Kasrils, eds., *Bertrand Russell's America* (New York, 1974), pp. 49–76.

39. Clark, *Life of Russell*, pp. 248 ff. In 1960, Russell wrote that "I have never been a complete pacifist at any time. During the First World War, which I opposed, I explained that there have been wars I would have supported." *The Listener* 64 (October 6, 1960): 543. See also Jo Newberry, "Russell and the Pacifists in World War I," in Kenneth Blackwell and John Thomas, ed., *Russell in Review* (Toronto, 1974).

40. Russell, letter to R. B. Perry, February 21, 1915. See Marvin R. Pollack, "British Pacifism during the First World War" (Ph.D. diss., Columbia University, 1971), p. 117. Further on Russell and the war, G. H. Hardy, *Bertrand Russell and Trinity* (Cambridge, 1970).

41. Russell, "The Ethics of War," *International Journal of Ethics*, January, 1915, reprinted in Russell's *Justice in Wartime* (London, 1916).

42. Russell, *Justice in Wartime*, p. 75. Cf. his statement on p. 107: "There is a wild beast slumbering in almost every man, but civilized men know that it must not be allowed to awake."

43. Russell, *Portraits from Memory*, p. 27.

44. *Principles of Social Reconstruction* (London, 1916), p. 64. In *Portraits from Memory*, Russell observes that he was at that time "completely ignorant of psychoanalysis," but was led to conclusions resembling Freud's by his observations of war hysteria.

45. *Justice in Wartime*, pp. 197–98.

46. *Principles of Social Reconstruction*, pp. 57–58.

47. Ibid., pp. 68, 163.

48. *Justice in Wartime*, pp. 53, 105–6, 108.

49. Clark, *Life of Russell*, p. 255.

50. Michael Holroyd, *Lytton Strachey*, a Critical Biography (London, 1968), vol. 2, p. 176.

51. See A. J. Anthony Morris, *Radicalism against War, 1906–1914* (Totowa, N.J., 1972).

52. See Klaus Schwabe, *Wissenschaft und Kriegsmoral*; Mommsen, *Max Weber*; Clark, *Einstein*, pp. 181–83; Pierre Grappin, *Le Bund "Neues*

Vaterland," 1914–1916: Ses rapports avec Romain Rolland (Paris and Lyon, 1952).

53. Marvin Swartz, *The Union of Democratic Control in British Politics during the First World War* (Oxford, 1971); also A. J. P. Taylor, *The Troublemakers* (Bloomington, 1958), chap. 5, and H. Hanak, "The Union of Democratic Control in World War I," *Bulletin of the Institute of Historical Research* 36 (1963): 168–80.

54. For a specimen, see Walter Raleigh, *England and the War*, containing essays and addresses from 1914–1918.

55. G. L. Dickinson, *The Choice before Us* (New York, 1917), p. 236. The Blue Books published by the belligerent governments had revealed the German offer to respect Belgian neutrality and even guarantee French territorial integrity in exchange for a promise of British neutrality. See Rolland, *Journal*, pp. 200–3; Marquand, *Ramsay MacDonald*, pp. 167–85.

56. Cf. Dickinson, *The Choice before Us* and *Problems of International Settlement* (1918); H. N. Brailsford, *A League of Nations* (1917); Leonard Woolf, ed., *The Framework of a Lasting Peace* (1917). Also Keith Robbins, *The Abolition of War: The "Peace Movement" in Britain, 1914–1919* (Cardiff, 1976); Henry R. Winkler, *The League of Nations Movement in Great Britain, 1914–1919* (New Brunswick, N.J., 1952); Roland N. Stromberg, "Uncertainties and Obscurities about the League of Nations," *Journal of the History of Ideas* 33 (January–March, 1972); George W. Egerton, *Great Britain and the Creation of the League of Nations* (Chapel Hill, 1978).

57. See Laurence W. Martin, *Peace without Victory: Woodrow Wilson and the British Liberals* (New Haven, 1958).

58. Miss Paget, "Vernon Lee," exhibited her "Neutral Heart" in *Atlantic Monthly*, November, 1915.

59. Rolland, *Journal*, p. 1793. Rolland hailed *Le Feu's* success as "a ray of sunlight" in an otherwise black sky. Later, it seems, he was seduced by its author's rabid Stalin-worship. See David J. Fisher, in *Peace and Change*, Winter, 1981.

60. The Sassoon-Graves episode is mentioned in Jon Stallworthy, *Wilfred Owen* (London, 1974), pp. 206 ff, also Wohl, *Generation of 1914*, pp. 98–100. On Zweig, see L. B. Steiman, "The Agony of Humanism in World War I: The Case of Stefan Zweig," *Journal of European Studies*, June, 1976, in addition to D. A. Prater's magnificent study.

61. It has been noted that the metal workers were unusually militant in all countries. Rosmer subsequently wrote a multivolume history of *Le mouvement ouvrier pendant la guerre* (7 vols., 1936–1954). A founder of the French Communist party, Rosmer was expelled from it in 1924 as a Trotskyist, evidence of his nonconformist nature. On his life, see

Christian Gras, *Alfred Rosmer et le mouvement révolutionaire international* (Paris, 1971). Margaret L. Silsby, "Marcel Cachin, French Marxist" (Ph.D. diss., Georgetown University, 1972), studies a *Humanité* editor who supported the war early but moved toward opposition in 1916, ending as a founder of the French Communist party. See also Wohl, *French Communism in the Making*, pp. 61–68, and Wurgaft, *"Activists,"* who finds this group of independent German left-wingers enthusiastic about the war at first but becoming restless by 1916. Also Marvin H. Kabakoff, "The Anti-War Movement in France in World War I" (Ph.D. diss., Washington University, 1975).

62. Rolland, *Journal*, p. 1241. Karl Liebknecht's statement of December, 1914, when he alone voted against the war credits in the Reichstag, is reprinted in Jules Humbert-Droz, *Der Krieg und die International* (Vienna, 1964), pp. 59–60.

63. Reprinted in Franz Mehring's *Gesammelte Schriften*, Band 15, 642–67.

64. See Z. A. B. Zeman and W. B. Scharlau, *The Merchant of Revolution* (London, 1965).

65. Senn, *The Russian Revolution in Switzerland*, p. 213. Lenin's theses on the war are printed in Gannin and Fisher, ed., *The Bolsheviks and the World War*, pp. 140 ff. See also Samuel Baron, *Plekhanov* (Stanford, 1963); Rex Wade, *The Russian Search for Peace* (Stanford, 1969).

66 J. M. Winter, *Socialism and the Challenge of War: Ideas and Politics in Britain, 1912–1918* (London, 1974), pp. 244–59. On the aftermath of wartime socialist conflicts, see also Albert S. Lindemann, *The Red Years: European Socialism versus Bolshevism, 1919–1921* (Berkeley, 1975).

67. V. Kershentsëv, in *Severnia Zapiski* (Petrograd), reprinted in *Current History* 5 (October, 1916): 112–13.

68. *Die Hilfe*, August 17, 1916.

69. Shaw, "The Last Spring of the Old Lion," *New Statesman*, December 12, 1914.

70. Russell, *Portraits from Memory*, p. 30.

71. Brailsford, *A League of Nations*, p. 5.

72. James Bryce, "Concerning a Peace League," in his *Essays and Addresses in War Time*.

73. Jacks, "Human Nature and the War," reprinted in *Current History* 5 (October, 1916): 113–15.

CHAPTER 9

1. Bertrand Russell, *Portraits from Memory*, p. 27.

2. W. Wagar, *H. G. Wells and the World State*, p. 30.
3. Robert B. Johnson, *Henry Montherlant* (New York, 1968), p. 39.
4. Herbert Read, *Annals of Innocence and Experience*, p. 73.
5. Robert Speaight, *Life of Hilaire Belloc* (New York, 1957), p. 41; *André Gide–Paul Valéry Correspondance, 1890–1942* (Paris, 1955), p. 83; Gustave Flaubert, *Intimate Notebook, 1840–1841*, transl. Frances Steegmuller (New York, 1967), p. 19. Cf. *The Letters of Gustave Flaubert 1830–1857*, ed. Steegmuller (Cambridge, Mass., 1980), pp. 13–14: "I hate Europe, France . . . ."
6. Wagar, *Wells*, p. 31 n.
7. Norman Rich, *Holstein* (London, 1965), p. 839. J. F. C. Fuller, *War and Western Civilisation* (London, 1932).
8. Peter Brock, *Pacifism in Europe to 1914* (Princeton, 1972), finds Anabaptists, Mennonites, and Quakers the main source of pacifism, along with Tolstoyans. Tolstoy's disciple Gandhi supported the war, as apparently did other Tolstoyans. The count himself, who died in 1910, had had serious difficulty in 1904–1905, during the Russo-Japanese war, in holding back his "feeling of grief when I hear that the Russians are getting beaten." A man of imperious will, about whom Maxim Gorky said that there was no room in the same universe for God and Tolstoy, the latter was perhaps an unusual pacifist. Roger Chickering, *Imperial Germany and a World without War, 1892–1914* (Princeton, 1975), indicates the weakness of the German peace movement. Chap. 4 of Martin Ceadel, *Pacifism in Britain 1914–1945* (London, 1980) deals with the war.
9. Robert Wohl, *French Communism in the Making*, p. 449; A. J. P. Taylor, *The First World War* (London, 1963).
10. James Joll, *1914: The Unspoken Assumptions* (London, 1968).
11. Zuckmayer, *Als Wär's ein Stück von Mir,* pp. 185–213; also his *Pro Domo* (Stockholm, 1938), pp. 33–34. On the brief antiwar mood of July 27–30 in France, see Becker, *1914.*
12. Ilya Ehrenburg, *People and Life, 1891–1921* (transl. New York, 1962), pp. 162–63, describing Paris scenes. Joachim C. Fest, *Hitler* (New York, 1974), p. 64: "Photographs taken during those days of August, 1914, have preserved the hectic air of festivity, the gay expectancy, with which Europe entered the phase of its decline: mobilizing soldiers pelted with flowers, cheering crowds on the sidewalks, ladies in bright summer dresses on the balconies." Sergei Kournakoff described how a howling mob in St. Petersburg pulled German statues off the roof of the German Embassy and made a bonfire of the embassy's furnishings, including a large portrait of the Kaiser, while women tore off their dresses and offered themselves to soldiers in the middle of St. Isaac

Square—an interesting case of Mars and Eros. See Guy Chapman, ed., *Vain Glory*, pp. 12–13.

13. The brilliant economist John Maynard Keynes explained to his friends that "the war could not last much more than a year" because most of the world's capital could not be converted to warmaking and the rest would soon be exhausted. David Garnett, *The Golden Echo*, vol. 1, p. 27; Clive Bell, *Old Friends*, p. 45. "It was a great relief to have Maynard's assurances on this point," Garnett adds.

14. Barrès, *Pour la haute intelligence française* (Paris, 1925), p. 80. By another calculation, 104 of a total of 304 Normalians were killed in the war.

15. L. P. Hartley, "In Defence of Lady Cynthia," replying to Leonard Woolf's review of Lady Cynthia Asquith's *Diaries,* in *The Listener* 79 (1968): 703–4. On Lehmbruck, see Paul Westheim, *Wilhelm Lehmbruck* (Potsdam, 1919), p. 198.

16. See Paul A. Jorgensen, "Elizabethan Ideas of War," *Clio* 3, no. 2 (1974).

17. See Marvin Zetterbaum, *Tocqueville and the Problem of Democracy* (Stanford, 1967), p. 136.

18. Michael C. C. Adams, "Tennyson's Crimean War Poetry," *Journal of the History of Ideas*, July–September, 1979, notes that some commentators try to explain away "Maud's" belligerence, evidently refusing to believe that a poet could be warlike.

19. Henry Seidel Canby, *Thoreau* (Boston, 1939), p. 436. Liberal theology accepted war as a fact of history, evidently providential.

20. David A. Healy, *U.S. Expansionism: The Imperial Urge in the 1890s* (Madison, 1970), pp. 99–109.

21. Brailsford, *A League of Nations,* p. 1.

22. Kindt, ed., *Grundschriften der Deutschen Jugendbewegung*, p. 58. The most ambitious examination of the 1914 spirit as a generation phenomenon is Robert Wohl's recent *The Generation of 1914.* As he notes on p. 65, the word generation is used to identify something that is not really a matter of age. In 1914 the old were often as eager as the young to go to war.

23. Brittain, *Testament of Youth*, p. 42.

24. John Elsom, *Erotic Theatre* (New York, 1973), p. 193.

25. "The Intellectuals and the Coming of War in 1914," *Journal of European Studies* 3 (1973): 109–22.

26. Letter from Bernice Rosenthal to author, December 22, 1975. Professor Rosenthal, the author of a book on Dmitri Merezhkovsky, has also written "Eschatology and the Appeal of Revolution," *California Slavic Studies*, XI (1980).

27. A relatively unbiased witness, the Dane Georg Brandes, wrote in 1913 that "If patriotism is vibrant in France, it is fanatic in Germany." "German patriotism," in his *The World at War.*

28. Rolland, *Journal*, p. 55.

29. Russell, *The Impact of Science on Society* (London, 1952), pp. 86–87; also pp. 134–35: "War . . . offers an escape" from the suppression of "individual impulses" in the regimented industrial society. "I think it would be found that a very considerable percentage are less happy now than during the war."

30. "Letter on Confrontation," *Change,* January–February, 1969. On "Psychic Motives for War," see Erich Gumbel in H. Z. Winnik et al., *Psychological Bases of War:* "War is an ecstasy of instinctual drive satisfaction, both of Eros and Thanatos," p. 177; also pp. 91 ff, 190–91, 245–46. Cf. Franco Fornari, *The Psychology of War* (transl. Bloomington, 1975).

31. See Albert O. Hirschman, *The Passions and the Interests: Political Arguments for Capitalism before Its Triumph* (Princeton, 1977). Professor Hirschman quotes a latter-day repetition of once-familiar arguments, by John Maynard Keynes: "Dangerous human proclivities can be canalized into comparatively harmless channels by the existence of opportunity for money-making and private wealth . . . . It is better that a man should tyrannize over his bank account than over his fellow citizens."

32. Susan Sontag, *The Benefactor* (New York, 1963). On the transference of war energies to movements of protest, see Erik H. Erikson, *Life History and the Historical Moment* (New York, 1975), pp. 198, 203.

33. *Das Kafka Buch*, ed. Heinz Politzer (Hamburg, 1965), p. 165. Statement made in 1920. Frank Field, *Three French Writers and the Great War* (London, 1975), includes a discussion of Bernanos.

34. Paul Valéry, *Collected Works*, vol. 10, pp. 307–8; also p. 117, "Nothing was more completely ruined by the war than the pretension to foresight."

35. Wagar, *H. G. Wells*, pp. 30–31.

36. Bowra, *Memories*, pp. 88, 91. Teilhard de Chardin, *Writings in Time of War.*

37. Edith Hoffmann, *Kokoschka: Life and Work* (London, 1947), p. 144. The hero in Ernest Hemingway's *A Farewell to Arms* (1929) says that "I was always embarrassed by the words sacred, glorious and sacrifice . . . . There were many words that you could not stand to hear and finally only the names of places had dignity."

38. Bernard Bergonzi looks at war fiction in his *Heroes' Twilight.* Jean M.

Cru's *Temoins* (Paris, 1929) was a study of all the books by French soldiers of World War I.

39. Robert Conquest, *The Great Terror* (London, 1971), pp. 500–12. But Friedrich Adler, the assassin of 1916, lived to expose Stalin's tyranny.

40. Ludwig Marcuse, *Mein Zwanzigstes Jahrhundert*, pp. 41–42.

41. See Patrick Seale and Maureen McConville, *Philby: The Long Road to Moscow* (London, 1973).

42. John Haag, paraphrasing Othmar Spann, influential Austrian reactionary thinker of the 1920s—"Knights of the Spirit: The *Kameradschaftsbund*," *Journal of Contemporary History* 8 (1973): 134. Robert Soucy, *Fascism in France: The Case of Maurice Barrès*, pursues the theme of French fascism as rooted in the 1914 ideas. A study that stresses the war as a decisive moment in the emergence of a proto-Nazi "radical right" is Abraham Peck's *Radicals and Reactionaries: The Crisis of Conservatism in Wilhelmine Germany* (New York, 1978).

43. See Georges Duhamel, *Anniversaire* (1925). On the extreme pacifism of the French socialists in the early 1930s, see John T. Marcus, *French Socialism in the Crisis Years, 1933–1936* (New York, 1963).

44. A major work of scholarship which essays something like this task, though almost exclusively in terms of British literature, is Paul Fussell's *The Great War and Modern Memory*, published in 1975. Cf. Robert Wohl, *The Generation of 1914*, chap. 6. on the post-1919 "Wanderers between Two Worlds." Frank Field, *Three French Writers and the War*, traces lines from the war to both Fascism and Communism.

Notes on Sources

The primary sources for this study were the words—in a few cases the works of art and music—of about three hundred European intellectuals of all sorts from the belligerent countries on the eve of 1914 and during the first stages of the Great War: their memoirs, letters, journals, diaries as well as their more formal publications, i.e., poems, novels, essays, etc. The leading secondary sources were biographies and other studies of these men and women of 1914. The purpose was to secure a representative cross-section of "the European mind," including the most famous and important leaders of thought in all fields, along with a few of the less renowned. Most of these sources have been cited in the footnotes or text and will not be repeated here. A breakdown by types discloses that the largest number were the novelists and poets, but with significant numbers of historians, philosophers, theologians, sociologists, psychologists, artists, musicians, a few hard scientists, essayists, journalists, quite a few socialists and other political ideologists, and many "men of letters" difficult to classify (was Chesterton a poet, essayist, novelist, journalist, or social critic?). For my purposes, the last category was often the most interesting. In terms of nationality, about 30 percent were British (including a few Irish), 25 percent German, 22 percent French, 7 percent Austro-Hungarian, 5 percent Russian, 5 percent Italian, and 6 percent other, including Belgians, Danes, and Dutch as well as a few Americans, mostly those attached to Europe, like Ezra Pound, T. S. Eliot, George Santayana, Henry James (who became a British citizen during the war), Isadora Duncan. There was no doubt some skewing because of personal factors: I enjoy the novelists and poets most, I do not read much Russian, I am inevitably better acquainted

237

with the English-speaking tradition. But these factors were conceivably counteracted by others, such as the fact that I find the Russians incredibly interesting and am much attracted to French intellectual life (like many others). Obviously, the sources differ quantitatively; some wrote material of larger quantity and/or greater interest than others. When all is said, I feel confident that the sources used were numerous and diversified enough to sustain the interpretations presented. It is, after all, not a matter of generalizing from discrete "facts" in a positivistic manner, but of reading a mood or spirit, an exercise in interpretation.

Among important scholarly books that have explored this terrain, in ways that differ more or less from mine, the following deserve to be mentioned: Reginald Pound, *The Lost Generation of 1914* (New York, 1964); Hanna Hafkesbrink, *Unknown Germany, an Inner Chronicle of the First World War* (New Haven, 1948); Robert Wohl, *The Generation of 1914* (Cambridge, Mass., 1979); Jean Jacques Becker, *1914: Comment les français sont entrés dans la guerre* (Paris, 1977); Paul Fussell, *The Great War and Modern Memory* (New York and London, 1975); Mario Isnenghi, *Il mito della grande guerra* (Bari, 1973); Hans Rogger, "Russia in 1914," *Journal of Contemporary History* 1, no. 4 (1962). On the Socialists, M. M. Drachkovitch, *Les socialismes français et allemand et la problème de la guerre, 1870–1914* (Geneva, 1953); Georges Haupt, *Socialism and the Great War: The Collapse of the Second International* (Oxford, 1972); Jack D. Ellis, *The French Socialists and the Problem of War* (Chicago, 1966). I am equally indebted to special studies of intellectual communities, such as Albert Marrin's of the Church of England in the First World War, *The Last Crusade* (Durham, N.C., 1974), and Charles E. Bailey's doctoral dissertation on the German Protestant theologians in the War (University of Virginia, 1978); likewise works on the poets, such as are cited in note 3, chap. 1; on women and the war (note 5, chap. 5); and of course biographical and critical studies of particular intellectuals, too numerous to list here, such as are cited in the footnotes. James Joll, *Three Intellectuals in Politics* (New York, 1961), and Frank Field, *Three French Writers and the Great War* (London, 1975), as well as Eric J. Leed, *No Man's Land: Combat and Identity in World War I* (London, 1979), and Bernard Bergonzi, *Heroes' Twilight* (London, 1965) are examples of works which creatively compare a number of individuals. Peter Stansky, ed., *The Left and War: The British Labour Party and World War I* (Stanford, 1969); George Panichas, ed., *Promise of Greatness: The War of 1914–1918* (New York, 1968); and Guy Chapman, ed., *Vain Glory* (London, 1968) are collections of source materials valuable to all students of the war's intellectual and literary side.

On the important matter of the pre-1914 climate of opinion, especially valuable to me were the following: H. Stuart Hughes, *Consciousness and Society: The Reconstruction of European Social Thought, 1890–1930* (New York, 1958; Gerhard Masur, *Prophets of Yesterday: Studies in European Culture, 1890–1914* (New York, 1961); Barbara Tuchman, *The Proud Tower: A Portrait of the World before the War, 1890–1914* (New York, 1966); Eugen Weber, *The Nationalist Revival in France, 1905–1914* (Berkeley, 1959); Carl E. Schorske, *Fin de Siècle Vienna* (New York, 1980); William J. McGrath, *Dionysian Art and Populist Politics in Austria* (New Haven, 1974); Fritz Stern, *The Politics of Cultural Despair* (Berkeley, 1961); George L. Mosse, *Germans and Jews* (New York, 1970); Roy Pascal, *From Naturalism to Expressionism: German Literature and Society, 1880–1918* (New York, 1973); Fritz K. Ringer, *The Decline of the German Mandarins* (Cambridge, Mass., 1969); John A. Lester, Jr., *Journey through Despair: Transformations in British Literary Culture, 1880–1914* (Princeton, 1968); Samuel Hynes, *The Edwardian Turn of Mind* (Princeton, 1968); Malcolm Bradbury and James McFarlane, ed., *Modernism, 1890–1930* (New York, 1976); and Walter Laqueur, *Young Germany* (New York, 1962).

Among other important works which have only recently been published, especially worthy of note is Jo Vellacott's *Bertrand Russell and the Pacifists in the First World War* (New York, 1980), based on research in the valuable Bertrand Russell Archives at McMaster University in Hamilton, Ontario.

Index